THE LOST VOICES OF POMPEII

THE LOST VOICES OF POMPEII

The Final Day in Seven Lives

JESS VENNER

Mudlark
HarperCollins*Publishers*
1 London Bridge Street
London SE1 9GF

www.harpercollins.co.uk

HarperCollins*Publishers*
Macken House, 39/40 Mayor Street Upper
Dublin 1, D01 C9W8, Ireland

First published by Mudlark 2026

1 3 5 7 9 10 8 6 4 2

© Dr Jess Venner 2026

Dr Jess Venner asserts the moral right to
be identified as the author of this work

A catalogue record of this book is
available from the British Library

HB ISBN 978-0-00-875680-2
PB ISBN 978-0-00-875681-9

Printed and bound in the UK using 100%
renewable electricity at CPI Group (UK) Ltd

All rights reserved. No part of this publication may be
reproduced, stored in a retrieval system, or transmitted,
in any form or by any means, electronic, mechanical,
photocopying, recording or otherwise, without the
prior written permission of the publishers.

Without limiting the exclusive rights of any author, contributor
or the publisher of this publication, any unauthorised use of
this publication to train generative artificial intelligence (AI)
technologies is expressly prohibited. HarperCollins also exercise
their rights under Article 4(3) of the Digital Single Market
Directive 2019/790 and expressly reserve this publication
from the text and data mining exception.

For Mr Oz, *in aeternum*.

CONTENTS

Map of Pompeii in 79 CE		ix
Preface		xi
INTRODUCTION:	Beneath the Sleeping Mountain	1
CHAPTER ONE:	The Invisible Slave	21
CHAPTER TWO:	The Wealthy Businesswoman	67
CHAPTER THREE:	The Everyman	105
CHAPTER FOUR:	The Working Poor Family	157
CHAPTER FIVE:	The Innkeeper	193
CHAPTER SIX:	The Priest of Isis	225
CHAPTER SEVEN:	The Politician	255
CHAPTER EIGHT:	The Final Hours	293
	The Aftermath	317
	Author's Note	327
	Sources	335
	Picture Credits	339
	Acknowledgements	341

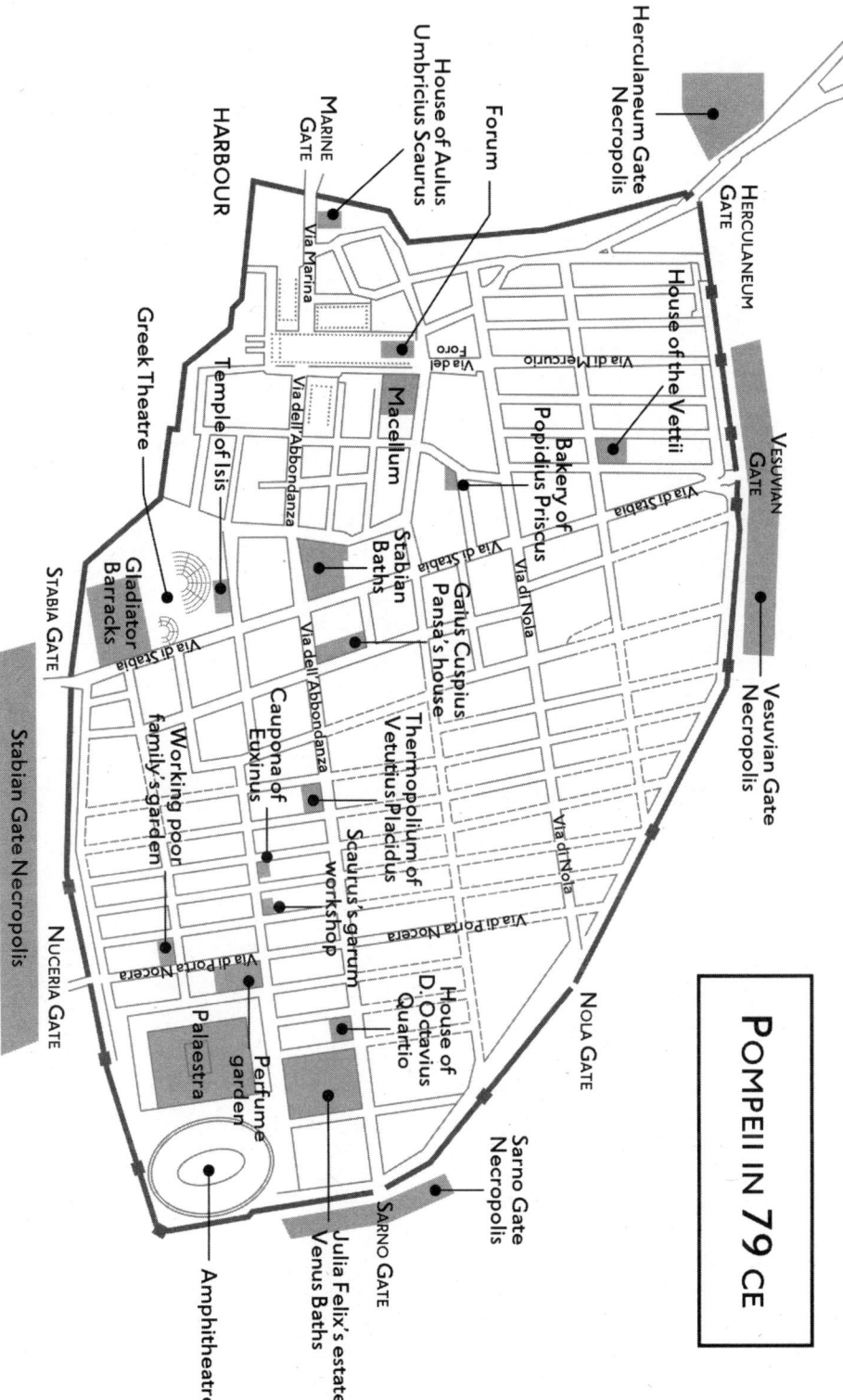

PREFACE

In the same week that I found out this book was going to be published, I travelled to the Bay of Naples for the Herculaneum Congress. Naturally, I had to take a trip to Pompeii, by now my second home, while I was there. Walking down the streets one early morning, before the groups and crowds arrived, I paused in front of a small inn I knew well and felt a wave of emotion wash over me. There was the counter where the innkeeper and his workers once served food and drink. There was the painted shrine, asking for protection over the household. Through that door lay the small 'pub garden' vineyard he'd planted, possibly with his own hands, which I had studied in depth for my doctoral thesis. I knew the owner, Euxinus, so well, and yet 2,000 years separated us. Finally, I would get to bring him and his inner thoughts to life.

My journey here began in 2014, when I was 22 and working as a marketing executive at a leading media agency, placing adverts on TV for huge clients who spent multi-millions. I made friends for life, went out far too much, and turned up to work hungover more days than I probably should have. But – something was missing. While I was busy chasing deadlines, I was also quietly feeding a growing passion: ancient Roman history. It had started when I picked up a book on the first empresses of Rome during my degree in publishing. Reading the stories of these bright, brave and, at times, devious women working behind the curtains of one of the most powerful empires history had seen, I was hooked. From that point on, I devoured anything and everything I could find on the Romans, and despite asking my parents if I could change my degree, they insisted I finish. I did well and passed with a first, but publishing no longer felt like the end goal.

One morning, on a whim, I decided to email Professor Mary Beard. I'd never met her and didn't expect a reply, but she wrote back. Her response was generous and encouraging, and when she suggested I apply for an MA at Birkbeck, University of London, something clicked. Her support came at just the right time and gave me the confidence to take that next step.

I can still picture myself sitting out on my parents' deck in East London, the sun shining, prospectuses spread around me. It felt both exciting and impossible. I didn't know Latin; my school had failed routine Ofsted inspections during my time there and didn't offer the kinds of subjects that opened classical doors. Instead, I'd been held at knifepoint by a fellow pupil, survived riots, watched teachers get sprayed with fire extinguishers and been physically attacked by bullies. So, the prospectuses told me, Classics wasn't for someone like me. Classical Civilisation was the only route, and I'm so grateful it was.

I started taking evening classes at Birkbeck and wrote my essays whenever I could, during lunch breaks, after work, always with my darling dog, Mr Oz, curled up at my feet. It was my escape. It was during this time that I discovered my passion for Pompeii. Finally, I could study the ordinary people of the early Roman Empire – how they lived, the trades they worked in, even the small details of their diet and health. I soon became fascinated by the depictions of

PREFACE

gardens in wall art, which led to me specialising in the urban vineyards, orchards, vegetable plots and flower gardens inside the city walls. Within this one city was the Roman Empire in miniature – but ordinary. I thought it was better than anything I'd ever studied.

I graduated from my MA with a distinction at Senate House in London, my now-husband beaming with pride in the audience. I didn't know that I would later return to the building as a research associate, a position which would help lead me to even greater things. It was upon receiving my master's that I realised this wasn't just a side interest; it was something I was actually quite good at. A doctorate had always seemed like something other people went on to do, a distant, unattainable goal, but why not me?

Still, I knew I had a lot to catch up on if I were to apply for a PhD. Without any financial help, I saved what I could and signed up for every course and opportunity I could afford. Then, in the spring of 2015, I took the plunge and quit my job.

For the next 5 months, I threw myself into a new world. I took a course in ancient epigraphy at Oxford, archaeobotany at UCL and zooarchaeology at a Saxon dig. I attended conferences in Rome and took Latin in the summer. I also joined archaeological digs at Oplontis near Pompeii and at a Saxon site in the UK, camping out under the stars. It felt like a dream come to life. By September I had landed a 1-year contract at The British School at Rome, an interdisciplinary community producing world-class research and practice in the heart of Rome, and over time, my confidence in my abilities built slowly. The following year I was offered two scholarships to study Classics, Ancient History and Archaeology for my PhD. I accepted the one at the University of Birmingham and, despite a blip called COVID in between, I had the time of my life, completing it in 2022. My research subject was, of course, Pompeii.

I often think back to the start of that self-funded sabbatical summer in 2015, when my bravery led me down a new path. Just days after leaving my old life behind at my work leaving do, I had stood in the forum of Pompeii, alone, my headphones in my ears. I'd never travelled solo before, especially not for an entire summer, and I had no job to return to. For someone from a working/lower-middle-class background, with no safety net, taking a risk like this was unheard of in my family. I was breaking generational patterns and taking a huge gamble on myself. I pressed play on my phone and the familiar sound of Bastille filled my ears. The lyrics spoke of what I had been feeling all those years: 'I was left to my own devices, many days fell away with nothing to show.' Cheesy, but the words hit me in the heart. Looking up at the looming shape of Mount Vesuvius, connecting with people who stood in this very spot 2,000 years ago, a now-familiar feeling settled in my chest. This was it. This was where I was supposed to be.

It was around this time that I made a promise to myself: to not only approach ancient history from the bottom up, and share it with people like me, but also to help make the path into understanding it less difficult, and less delayed, than mine had been. To this day, I listen to that song when I need a boost and picture myself standing in the forum of Pompeii, feeling overwhelmed by hope and fear, and the sense that I was finally heading in the right direction. If you're reading this with that same feeling, that a career you have long admired 'isn't for people like you', or that it's taking time to get started, please believe me when I say: it can happen. It's never too late to change course. And turning a passion into your work is something you won't regret.

Now, as this book goes to press, I am writing from the sunny library garden of The British School at Rome, where I am undertaking a 3-month Rome Award. It is here that I am preparing for a

PREFACE

3-year Leverhulme Early Career Fellowship at the University of Oxford, which I will begin in early 2026. At 17, having just dropped A Level history after my head of sixth form (and history teacher) told me I'd never amount to anything because I was too 'ditsy', I could never have imagined myself here. To be writing the preface to this book at The British School at Rome feels both like a homecoming and a new beginning, and the promise I made back then continues to shape everything I do. This book is a part of keeping that promise.

THE LOST VOICES OF POMPEII

INTRODUCTION

BENEATH THE SLEEPING MOUNTAIN

Today, Pompeii is known for how it ended rather than how it lived. When we think of Pompeii, we picture the crumbling walls, the worn stone streets and the plaster casts of bodies frozen mid-motion. The circumstance of its destruction and preservation has caused this ancient Roman city to become a monument to disaster.

In 79 CE, Pompeii was a city full of life, a sun-baked, chaotic home to around 20,000 people. Children chased one another down alleyways, bakers shouted orders, dogs barked at passers-by, dice rattled on inn tables, and the smell of bread and vines hung in the air. Families and lovers, traders and tavern-keepers, slaves and politicians filled its streets, sharing meals, falling in and out of love, arguing with neighbours, grieving, working and celebrating.

And yet, beneath the commonplace rhythms of everyday life, the population of Pompeii shared something with the greatest heroes of myth and empire: a desire to be remembered. The Greeks called it *kleos*, glory earned through actions, while the Romans called it *fama*, a name that lived on after death in the memories of those left behind. From the lowest slave to the most powerful politician, the fear of oblivion after death was widespread, and people everywhere sought to leave their mark, whether in stone, plaster, paint or architecture, as a bold and lasting declaration of, 'I was here. I was part of this city's history.'

It makes perfect sense because, in the ancient world, the only certainty was uncertainty. A harvest could fail, a mother could die in childbirth, the gods might turn their backs, or the ground beneath your feet could split open without warning. As is still the case, the poorest and most marginalised people in society often suffered first and worst, but disaster did not discriminate. It had the power to terrify both the rich and the poor and the ability to level privilege with poverty, exposing the fragility that bound them all. Seventeen years before the eruption that sealed Pompeii's fate, one specific event made this plainly clear.

On 5 February 62 (or 63) CE, a powerful earthquake shook Campania, causing widespread destruction and marking the beginning of nearly two decades of tremors that would continue right up to the eruption.* Hearing of the chaos in Campania, Seneca the Younger, the Roman philosopher and statesman, wrote to his friend Lucilius, telling him of the news:

> We have just had news, my esteemed Lucilius, that Pompeii, the famous city in Campania, had been laid low by an earthquake, which shook all the surrounding districts as well. The city lies on a beautiful bay, running far back from the open sea, and is surrounded by two converging shores, on the one side that of Surrentum and Stabiae, on the other that of Herculaneum ... It caused great destruction in Campania, which had never been safe from this danger but which had time and again got off with a fright ... They also say that a flock of six hundred sheep was killed

---

* I take the date of the earthquake to be 62 CE.

and statues were split open, and some people were deranged and afterwards wandered about unable to help themselves.

Today, we understand this quake as the start of Mount Vesuvius awakening from a long slumber. But to the people of Pompeii, the danger was not at all obvious. A handful of writers had voiced their concerns, but, to a largely illiterate population, these warnings went unheard. Strabo, the Greek geographer of the late Republic who travelled widely across the Mediterranean and recorded its landscapes, remarked on Vesuvius' summit, describing it as barren and fire-scorched. Vitruvius, the Roman architect of the first century BCE whose treatise *On Architecture* remains our most important source on Roman building, noted the local pumice and compared it to that found near Mount Etna, which they knew to be a volcano. But these were isolated observations, and for most residents the tremors were an unsettling, but ultimately familiar, part of life in Campania.

Food shortages and civic unrest only added to the pressure, meaning that by 79 CE, Pompeii was a city under strain.* Nevertheless, the hardy Pompeians refused to fold in the face of failure. In the 17 years that followed the earthquake, homes were extended, further commercial gardens took root, specialised trades flourished and new workshops popped up across the city. It was a time of extraordinary energy, when fear and hope seemed to coexist and prosperity was in the air.

As the city evolved and the Empire stretched far and wide, the people of Pompeii clung tightly to the values of honour and legacy.

---

* A famine appears to have occurred post-41 CE, while in 59 CE, a huge riot broke out between Pompeian fans and visiting Nucerian fans at the amphitheatre in Pompeii, resulting in the town being punished by the Senate with a 10-year ban on holding gladiatorial games and the dispersal of all unofficial occupational groups.

THE LOST VOICES OF POMPEII

Figure 1: Frieze from the House of Caecilius Iucundus (VI.1.26) commemorating the Great Quake of 62 CE

For the elite, power and public memory were defences against the unknowable void of the afterlife. By inscribing their names on statues, temples and dedicatory plaques, and anchoring their presence and their legacy in the physical world, they hoped their lineage – and with it, the broader Roman identity – might endure.

Even those excluded from formal political power found ways to leave their mark. People from all social strata built thriving businesses, and freedmen, former slaves who had been granted their freedom, raised children who would go on to enjoy the political rights denied to their fathers. Freedmen also joined religious organisations such as the *Augustales*, a priestly college devoted to the cult of Augustus, which offered a rare avenue towards visibility and honour. More still left their mark in subtler ways.

Graffiti, sometimes carefully painted in red by hired hands, at other times hastily scratched into plaster with a stylus pen, blanketed Pompeii's shops, houses, temples, brothels and bathhouses. Around 10,000 examples have been recorded to date, capturing everything from names and boasts to insults, advertisements, rumours and shopping lists. However trivial they may have seemed at the time, each one offers a rare and intimate glimpse into lives that might otherwise have vanished.

The eruption of Vesuvius, one of the deadliest in history, consumed the city in less than 24 hours, silencing its streets and sealing its hopes, fears and ambitions beneath 6 metres of volcanic material. On that day, the people of Pompeii achieved the immortality they had long sought, but not in a way they could ever have imagined. Though it may feel unsettling to peer so closely into lives that ended so abruptly, their longing for remembrance is a thought I try to hold onto, whether I'm standing before a plaster cast or reading a name scratched into a wall.

However, there's a difference between remembering a city and truly *knowing* its people. While visitors admire the brothels, giggle at phallic carvings and wander through grand atrium houses, they often struggle to connect with the lives behind them. It is easy to forget that Pompeii was a living, breathing place, full of people with families, dreams and anxieties who, just like us, experienced sickness, heartache, joy, wonder, jealousy and everything in between. Their lives were every bit as complex as ours, though their stories are too often eclipsed by the drama of their death, or by the better-known names of Roman history. If we are to truly under-

Figure 2: Electoral graffiti on the Via dell'Abbondanza, Pompeii's busiest shopping street

stand these people, to know them as more than footnotes to tragedy, we must return to their beginning and trace how Pompeii came to be in order to discover how its people shaped, and were shaped by, the city they left behind.

'ANCIENT' POMPEII

Pompeii lies at the heart of the fertile region the Romans once called *Campania Felix*, or 'Lucky Campania'. In fact, Strabo tells us that the land was so fruitful it could yield up to four harvests per year. For centuries, Mount Vesuvius had watched silently over this landscape, its forested slopes and rich volcanic soil nourishing orchards, vineyards and olive groves. To those who lived in its shadow, the mountain was a giver of life: a steady, unshakable presence that shaped the land and sustained the economy.

In a fresco from the House of the Centenary, we see Vesuvius depicted as a lush green giant, its slopes heavy with trellised vines and fruit trees. Beside it stands Bacchus, the Roman god of wine, lavishly robed in grapes and crowned in vines, the personification of the mountain's bounty and the blessings it bestowed. Painted some time before the eruption, this is the earliest known painting of Vesuvius, and it offers a wonderfully vivid glimpse into how the people of Pompeii viewed their landscape: not as a looming threat, but as a source of life.

By the time this fresco was painted some time after 55 CE, Pompeii was already an ancient city, its identity shaped by centuries of change. Its streets and structures had been shaped by successive waves of settlement, each one layering new customs, languages and beliefs onto the last. Greeks, Oscans, Etruscans, Samnites and finally Romans all left their mark, not only on the city's architecture and layout, but on its daily routines, rituals, religions, social structures and tongues spoken in its streets. Their legacies were not always visible on the surface, but they ran deep into the bones of the city, the population of 79 CE undoubtedly aware of the cultural tapestry that made up their home.

The Oscans, an Italic people of southern Italy, were among the first to settle in the area of Pompeii. In the eighth or seventh century BCE they founded five hamlets along the River Sarno. It is thought that Pompeii took its name from the Oscan word for 'five', though some prefer the later legend that gave the credit to Hercules. It was said that as he returned from a victory in Spain, he drove his

Figure 3: Fresco from the House of the Centenary (IX.8.6)

cattle in triumph through Campania in a *pompē*, a procession that supposedly gave Pompeii its name (and nearby Herculaneum his own). The Greeks had arrived in Campania around the same time, having been drawn by the sweep of the Bay of Naples and its fertile soil.* While they never established Pompeii as a Greek city in the way they did Cumae or Neapolis, their imprint on the region was unmistakable, and their influence in art, religion and culture would ripple through Campania for centuries.

The Etruscans also leant their influence to Pompeii. Expanding south from their homeland of Etruria (modern-day Tuscany), they too were drawn to Campania by its rich land and trade routes from as early as the ninth century BCE. By the seventh and sixth centuries BCE, the Etruscans had established cities and a connected trade network, bringing with them technologies, long-distance commerce and cultural sophistication, which helped to reshape the early settlement of Pompeii into something larger and better connected. Their dominance in Campania, however, was short-lived. After their naval defeat by the Greeks at Cumae in 474 BCE, Etruscan power in the region became almost invisible by the late fifth century, though their influence lingered in Pompeii in its fortifications, religion and trade practices.

It is almost directly after the expulsion of the Etruscans that we see changes in settlement patterns, the titles of magistrates and the language in Pompeii because, by the late fifth century, new forces were pressing into the fertile plains of Campania. The Oscan-speaking Samnites, a people from the rugged central Apennines,

---

* The earliest settlement was Cumae, founded around 750–730 BCE by settlers from Euboea (probably from the cities of Chalcis and Eretria). This became the first Greek colony on the Italian mainland. Oscan is one of the three main dialects that form the Italian branch of the Indo-European family of languages (along with Umbrian and Latin).

descended into the region and gradually took control of Pompeii and other Campanian cities. Drawing inspiration from their close contact with the Greek cities of the Bay, they adopted Hellenistic styles and ideas to express their new power.

Across Italy, the Samnites had fought bitterly against Rome in the three major Samnite Wars (343–290 BCE), but Pompeii itself stayed largely outside these conflicts. Instead, after Rome's victory over the Samnites, the city asserted its dominance over Campania, and Pompeii was forced to become a *socius*, or subordinate ally of Rome. This meant that Pompeii was bound to provide troops and resources to Rome despite being denied the rights of citizenship. Despite that unequal status, the city prospered. Agriculture flourished in the volcanic soils, and trade in oil and wine flowed through its port, bringing wealth and new connections. Between 300 and 180 BCE, the number of people living inside the city walls grew, as *insulae* (city blocks) were laid out in previously undeveloped areas likely used for agriculture.

By the second century BCE, Pompeii under Samnite control was thriving and beginning to take on a distinctly Hellenistic character in its infrastructure. Its transformation was accelerated with the construction of major public buildings such as the Temple of Jupiter, the Large Theatre and the Basilica, while the Stabian Baths were expanded and remodelled.

But this prosperity existed alongside constant threat. Pirates prowled the Mediterranean, attacking coastal towns like Pompeii and disrupting sea trade, while, closer to home, unrest among Italic peoples pushed tensions across the peninsula to breaking point. Around 216 BCE, refugees displaced by Hannibal from the nearby city of Nuceria are thought to have settled in Pompeii, expanding the area east of the Via Stabiana, one of the city's major thoroughfares, and adding further to the city's population and diversity. By this time, Rome's power was spreading quickly across the Mediterranean. Yet Pompeii, fiercely independent, held fast to its own identity, even as Roman ways crept ever deeper into daily life.

THE ROMANS

A major turning point for Pompeii came in the first century BCE, beginning with the outbreak of the Social War (91–87 BCE). In 91, the Roman politician Marcus Livius Drusus proposed a bill that would grant Roman citizenship to all Italic peoples, turning them from subjects into partners. The landed upper classes and the Senate, fearful of losing their power, rejected the proposal and, as was often the fate of reformers in the late Republic, Drusus was assassinated. His death triggered a widespread uprising among Rome's Italian allies, who had long endured the burdens of military service and taxation without the rights of citizenship.

Pompeii had served as one of these allies for centuries, and yet, like many Italic settlements, it had grown weary of supporting an increasingly autocratic and repressive power without political rights. In response to Drusus' violent death, the Italic allies of Rome took up arms and marched against Rome, with Pompeii eagerly joining the rebellion. By 90 BCE, Rome had defeated many of the northern rebels and reclaimed much of Campania, but Pompeii remained undefeated. Growing tired of the costly war, the senator Lucius Julius Caesar, cousin of the future dictator Gaius Julius Caesar, passed a law granting Roman citizenship to all Italians who had not rebelled or who were willing to surrender. Satisfied with achieving their aim, many towns laid down their weapons. Pompeii, however, refused.

In 89, Gnaeus Pompeius Strabo (the father of Pompey the Great, the brilliant general who would later dominate Roman politics alongside Julius Caesar and Crassus) was sent to crush the remaining rebels in the north, while Lucius Cornelius Sulla, one of Julius Caesar's most formidable political foes, led Roman forces against the Samnites and insurgents in Campania. Sulla's decisive victory at the Battle of Nola cemented his military reputation and paved the way for his rise to power. From there, his forces turned their attention to rebel strongholds along the Bay of Naples. Herculaneum, some 16 kilometres from Pompeii in the direction of Naples, fell after a short but fierce siege, while Stabiae, only 6 kilometres from the city, was razed entirely, a brutal display meant to deter further resistance.

Pompeii continued to resist. Surrounded by Sulla's forces, it endured a prolonged siege before finally surrendering in late 89. Traces of the battle are visible today: holes left by Sulla's *ballistae* (stone-throwing artillery) can be seen in the city walls near the Herculaneum Gate. But Pompeii wasn't punished – yet. In that same year, Rome passed the *Lex Plautia Papiria*, which extended Roman citizenship (*civitas*) to Italians who were registered in allied communities and who applied to a Roman *praetor* (magistrate) within 60 days. This law effectively incorporated most of Italy south of the River Po, including Pompeii, into the Roman state. While this formally ended the Social War and made Pompeii a citizen town, the reality was more complex.

A ROMAN COLONY

Rome did not forget Pompeii's defiance during the Social War. In 80 BCE, during the dictatorship of Sulla, Pompeii was officially declared a Roman colony. While this might seem like a reward, it was very much the opposite; instead it was punishment for resisting the Roman might during the Social War. Pompeii was renamed *Colonia Cornelia Veneria Pompeianorum*: *Cornelia* after Sulla's family name, and *Veneria* in honour of Venus, the family's patron deity. Sulla appointed his nephew, Publius Cornelius Sulla, to oversee the colonisation, settling thousands of Roman military veterans in the city, many of whom were loyalists of their former commander. These new colonists quickly took over Pompeii's political and economic life, while much of the existing Oscan and Samnite population was displaced or subordinated. Estimates suggest that between 4,000 and 5,000 settlers were added to the city's population.

Colonisation permanently altered Pompeii's urban landscape. Public buildings were Romanised, Latin replaced Oscan as the dominant language, and the city became firmly embedded within the Roman state as a conquered territory under Rome's control. Some local families managed to retain their status, but many were dispossessed, their land confiscated and redistributed to the veterans of Sulla's army. With the arrival of Roman defenders in Pompeii, the walls were no longer needed, and houses were built on top of the ramparts to take advantage of the beautiful coastal view to the west. To the south-east, former Samnite-owned homes were demolished to make way for a new amphitheatre, built around 70 BCE. Its construction was a calculated act of generosity by two leading colonists, Marcus Porcius and Quinctus Valgus, a move which aligned them with Roman traditions of public benefaction and helped reshape Pompeii's identity.

Trade, construction and commerce continued to thrive up to the mid-first century CE, but against a backdrop of uncertainty. The earthquake of 62 CE, which I generally refer to as the 'great quake' in this book, had caused widespread damage, and aftershocks continued to rattle the region. Properties were being repurposed, neighbourhoods reshaped, and the population was adjusting to new realities. It was a period of both adaptation and advancement, where opportunity and instability coexisted at every level of society. It is during this transformation that this book begins, on the day before the eruption that would seal Pompeii's place in history.

THE DATE OF THE ERUPTION

Our earliest reference for the date of the Vesuvian eruption comes from Pliny the Younger's letter to the historian Tacitus, written some two decades after the event. In it, he describes how his uncle, Pliny the Elder, observed an unusual cloud rising above Mount Vesuvius on 24 August 79 CE. Pliny's observation has gone on to shape centuries of scholarship, and in December 2024, the Director of the Archaeological Park of Pompeii, Gabriel Zuchtriegel, confirmed that the official date of the eruption would remain the one first recorded by Pliny the Younger. There are, however, several reasons why I remain unconvinced by this date.

It is worth keeping in mind that this was a private letter, written years after the event, and passed down to us only as a result of manuscript copies preserved by monastic scribes during the Middle Ages. The earliest surviving copy of Pliny's letters dates back to the sixth century. Medieval scribes copied out full texts in gruelling copying sessions, and as such were exhausted and overworked, and therefore prone to human error. Marginal notes from the time sometimes reveal their frustrations. One simply reads: 'Now I've written the whole thing. For Christ's sake, give me a drink.' Given this, it's easy to understand how skipped lines, incorrect readings, or misinterpretations of Roman calendrical terms, which were notoriously complex, could slip into manuscripts from time to time.

In ancient Rome, dates were not numbered in a simple sequence like ours. Instead, they were counted backwards from three fixed points each month: the *kalends* (the first day, traditionally the new moon), the *nones* (either the fifth day in a short month, or the seventh day in a long month, and traditionally the first quarter of a moon cycle) and the *ides* (the thirteenth or the fifteenth day, and traditionally the full moon).* The Romans also counted inclusively, meaning that they included both the day they were counting from and the day they were counting to. So, *ante diem nonum Kalendas Septembris* (a.d. IX Kal. Sept. for short) means 'the ninth day (*nonum*) before the first day (*Kalends*) of September', which works out as 24 August. You would be forgiven for thinking this is an incredibly complicated way to record the date, and it's not hard to imagine how easily a scribe might have made a mistake.†

The margin for error is not insignificant, and there is material evidence for a different date: a charcoal *graffito* found in a house

---

* I am referring here to the calendar established by Julius Caesar during his reforms in 46 BCE, the calendar system we still use today. This is when two more months, July and August, were added to the calendar which, following his assassination, were then renamed from Quintilis and Sextilis to Iulius and Augustus, after the two key political figures.

† We actually have four recorded dates for the eruption in manuscripts: 24 August, 30 October, 1 November and 23 November.

undergoing renovation in Pompeii in Region V in 2018. It reads *XVI (ante) K(alendas) Nov(embres)* – that is, 17 October – and is followed by a line which has been translated as 'he indulged in food in an immoderate manner' or 'they took the oil to the pantry'. Given the context of the house, the charcoal note was likely left by a builder or decorator. Charcoal is a temporary medium, and it seems improbable that such a note would remain untouched on a blank wall for an entire year, in view of the number of properties undergoing rapid change post-62. It is therefore far more plausible that this was written shortly before the eruption.

As an archaeobotanist, I work with ancient plant remains, and the seasonal indicators preserved in Pompeii also point to an eruption in the autumn. Pomegranates, which ripen between late September and November, were found carbonised in large quantities at Villa B, Oplontis, a working villa just outside Pompeii where I have excavated myself. Archaeologists have also found evidence of other fruits and nuts typically harvested from September or October onwards, such as figs, fresh chestnuts, walnuts and wine grapes. While some argue that climate change might have altered harvest times, and these items could be preserved (which they often were), the ancient texts and ongoing agricultural practices in the region today suggest consistency in seasonal rhythms.

Then there are the coins. In the 1970s, a hoard discovered in the House of the Golden Bracelet included two coins bearing *IMP XV* and the image of the Emperor Titus. We know from inscriptions elsewhere that the Emperor Titus had already received his fourteenth acclamation on 7 or 8 September 79 CE, meaning that his fifteenth acclamation (*IMP* XV) would have come at a later date. However, it was later found that the coin actually read IMP XIIII COS VII, marking his fourteenth acclamation, which equates to a minting date of between July and August 79 CE. While this neither proves nor disproves either an August or October date, it is unlikely that these two coins would have gone into circulation in Pompeii within this short space of time.*

Another small but curious detail lies in clothing and furniture. Several victims were found wearing cloaks and heavier garments, and braziers had been left in use in rooms and corridors. If you've been to southern Italy in August, you'll understand why this stands out as unusual. It is possible the victims were wearing heavy clothing to protect themselves from the falling dust and pumice, and while people might have grabbed what they could in haste, the use of heating equipment, such as braziers, at the time of the eruption suggests cooler weather.

Taking into account the manuscript transmission, the agricultural evidence, the coin hoard, the clothing and domestic heating, as well as the charcoal graffito, I find the case for a later eruption date more persuasive than the traditional one. While no single piece of evidence is definitive, taken together they suggest the eruption likely occurred after 24 August 79 CE. For that reason, I have adopted the date of 24 October 79 CE throughout this book.

RECONSTRUCTING LIVES

Drawing on archaeological evidence, inscriptions and material culture, this book follows six individuals and one family through their final 24 hours in the city. In their homes and workplaces,

---

* Richard Abdy (2013). The Last Coin in Pompeii: A Re-evaluation of the Coin Hoard from the House of the Golden Bracelet, *The Numismatic Chronicle* 173, pp. 79–83; Doronzo et al. (2022). The 79 CE Eruption of Vesuvius: A Lesson from the Past and the Need of a Multidisciplinary Approach for Developments in Volcanology, *Earth-Science Reviews* 231.

through their routines, beliefs and relationships, we glimpse a place not frozen in time, but caught in the midst of change, its people adjusting and enduring, unaware of what lay ahead.

After years researching Pompeii's architecture, gardens and the ways in which Roman identity and memory were woven into the fabric of daily life, the same characters emerged repeatedly. Others surfaced unexpectedly, often in moments of serendipity, when a story I had begun to piece together was suddenly reinforced by evidence or, just as often, when the evidence itself suggested a narrative I had not yet considered. Because of this, writing this book felt freeing, releasing these characters' stories from my head like Minerva from Jupiter's.

Each person featured in this book was chosen with care, choices that I describe in more detail in the Author's Note section at the back. An abundance of evidence alone was not the only criterion for their selection. In fact, it was often quite the opposite, for my aim is to illuminate the lives of people history tends to forget. Together, they represent a cross section of Pompeian society: from the enslaved and the freed to artisans, minor officials, religious leaders, women and members of the political elite. Some of them are well documented, often as a result of elite bias, while others, deliberately ignored in their own time, can be found only in the graffiti scrawls, humble cooking pots and ledgers left behind. But all represent those often overlooked in favour of more famous names or dramatic discoveries. Their stories might be quieter, but I believe they offer a deeper, more textured understanding of the city and the people who once called it home.

What follows, therefore, is evidence-based storytelling, now sometimes referred to as critical fabulation.* This is a methodology

---

* As I was finishing this book, I discovered that the method I had intuitively that uses what survives in records to expand and challenge how history is told, and in doing so, refuses to accept silence as absence. Instead, it allows the historian to restore complexity, agency and emotional depth to those who were historically marginalised or flattened by dominant narratives.

The strength of this approach lies in its refusal to treat gaps in the evidence as dead ends. Instead, it regards absence as productive space, one in which we can explore historically grounded possibilities, and reconstruct plausible scenarios using our common sense as fellow human beings, rather than simply acknowledge the loss. It allows us to move beyond the limitations of what survives in the archaeological or textual record and to imagine the interior lives, relationships and choices of those who would otherwise remain voiceless.

However, critical fabulation also presents risks and limitations. It requires careful methodological restraint to avoid projecting modern sensibilities or overstepping the limits of what the evidence can reasonably support. There is a fine line between imaginative reconstruction and unwarranted speculation, and while this method can open new perspectives, it also demands transparency about where the evidence ends and interpretation begins. These reconstructions, then, are not intended as fully formed historical certainties. Rather, they are possibilities and narratives grounded in archaeological and literary evidence that aim to shine a light on the

followed aligns with what Saidiya Hartman, in her 2008 essay 'Venus in Two Acts', defined as 'critical fabulation', a methodology which allowed her to reimagine the lives of enslaved people in the Atlantic slave trade. Like myself, Hartman was unaware that she had been practising 'critical fabulation' for 2 years prior to her coining of the term. Around the same time, other writers, such as Carole Boston Weatherford in *Moses: When Harriet Tubman Led Her People to Freedom* (2006), were also blending archival research with imaginative storytelling to recover lost voices from the past.

complexity, diversity and humanity of life in Pompeii. Through them, I hope not only to bring to life the final day of the city, but also the people that made it a living place before it became a ruin.

In the case of the people chosen for this book, some are known by name, their identities and addresses preserved, while others, unnamed but no less real, have been reconstructed from the traces they left behind. If a person, occupation or activity could not reasonably have existed, they do not appear here. Where lives survive only in fragments, I've drawn these together to create composites, grounded in material evidence, spatial logic and broader historical patterns.

Although we know the names of many individuals who lived in Pompeii before the eruption, we cannot be sure of what happened to them. Not a single confirmed survivor has ever been identified with certainty and, because of this, the fates I have given to the people in this book are imagined. Some died in their homes, surrounded by familiar objects, others collapsed in the streets or sought shelter in public buildings, while many more attempted (and managed) to flee. Together, their stories speak to the range of human responses, and fates, in the face of sudden disaster.

Population estimates for Pompeii vary, but the most accepted range is between 15,000 and 20,000, leaning towards the upper end with enslaved people included. As of a few years ago, around 1,050 bodies had been recovered from the two-thirds of the city that have so far been excavated, and more are still being found. Extrapolating this for the whole town gives an estimated death toll of around 1,600 to 1,700, suggesting a mortality rate of somewhere between 9 and 11 per cent.

While these numbers remind us of the scale of the tragedy, they do not capture the lives behind them. And so, as you turn the pages of this book, I invite you to immerse yourself in the living world of

THE LOST VOICES OF POMPEII

Pompeii. Not the silent, grey ruins of today, but the bustling, vibrant city that once teemed with life. Walk its streets, hear the chatter of its markets, smell the scent of industry and feel the pulse of a community holding a growing Empire on its shoulders, all the while unaware of the tragedy that would soon unfold. I hope the stories you find here connect you with the humanity behind the artefacts, the aspirations beyond the inscriptions and the resilience of those who lived, loved and dreamed in this altogether ordinary city. It is my privilege to bring their lost voices back into the light, to be heard and remembered once more.

CHAPTER ONE

THE INVISIBLE SLAVE

THE EIGHTH HOUR (1 P.M.), 23 OCTOBER 79 CE

The sun was high overhead in the sky, casting short shadows across the bustling streets as a young man navigated the throngs of people.* A small tattoo, GCP VI, on his sun-kissed upper arm identified him as the slave of a well-known, and much loved, political figure in the city, Gaius Cuspius Pansa, one of four *aediles* voted into office by the people in the July just passed.† The marketplace teemed with shoppers and merchants eager to make a sale, the air thick with the heady scent of exotic spices from far-flung lands, freshly baked bread and the smell of roasted meats on the

---

* The Roman day was divided into 12 variable-length hours, beginning at sunrise and ending at sunset. These hours weren't fixed like modern ones and their length stretched or shrank with the seasons. In late October, with sunrise (first hour) around 7.30 a.m., each Roman hour lasted roughly 55 minutes. The sixth hour, *hora sexta*, fell around 11.15 a.m. by modern standards, making *hora octava*, the eighth hour, about 1 p.m. Roman sundials often featured only 11 lines, marking 12 segments, and may have reflected inclusive counting, a common Roman habit.
† Roman magistrates responsible for overseeing public buildings, organising public games and managing the city's grain supply.

warm breeze. A gaggle of women clustered around a fountain, as they filled jugs with water and exchanged the latest gossip, ignoring the auction scene going on behind them. The young man stopped and let his eyes rove across the auction. His name was Petrinus.

A line of fair-skinned men and women stood shoulder to shoulder on a raised wooden podium. Their eyes, puffy from crying, were fixed on the ground, and long strands of unkempt blonde and auburn hair fell across their dirt-streaked faces. A child no older than 5 peered out from the line, his small voice breaking into sobs for his mother who stood beside the slave dealer as he haggled with the auctioneer over the lowest acceptable price for her. A sharp pang gripped Petrinus' chest. The boy's tear-streaked face was too familiar, a memory of the time he had stood in that very child's place, more than once.

Petrinus felt the scratch of his rough tunic as he readjusted the basket on his back, moving on before anyone caught his lingering glance. Hopping over the stepping stones leading from one side of the street to the other – one, two, three – over the flow of bodily fluids, horse manure and the previous night's rainwater, Petrinus mentally checked off the items he needed to buy for the evening's feast. Their household cook, a large, jovial Gaul named Lavinia, would not thank him for leaving anything out.

First were exotic fruits from the East, prized for their rarity and vibrant flavours. They were a common commodity for a man as wealthy as his master. He made his way through the town's busiest street, the Via dell'Abbondanza, to reach the forum before the traders shut up shop. Normally, they would close up shop around the tenth hour, but you never could know for sure how long they'd stay open on games day. Petrinus wove through groups chatting about tonight's games, mothers corralling their children, dogs yapping at passing carts, and a hawker shouting his wares: 'Apples! Apples!' He passed a slave stooping to retrieve urine from a public commode on a street corner, a valuable product his master would sell to the fullers for washing the town's clothes.

He made a quick stop at a *thermopolium*, one of the many hot food shops where meals were ladled from terracotta *dolia* set into the counter. Their contents had never passed his own lips.* Each morning at dawn, the shop merchants would fold back the shutters, opening their counters to the street. Poultry, garlic and herbs hung from hooks set into the ceilings, while fresh seasonal goods were laid out on little tiered steps on the counter tops. The huge terracotta *dolia* jars set into the marble counters brimmed with dried fruits, beans and nuts bought wholesale from local gardeners and farmers in the city and surrounding countryside. Calling out to the young girl behind the counter, Petrinus asked for equal measures of hazelnuts and almonds. Though he saw her every day, the slave didn't raise her eyes from the counter as she passed over the small sacks of nuts, her bright-red plait falling over her shoulder.

She turned to place the coins he had given her behind the counter, exposing a tattoo emblazoned on her right cheek: *F* for *fugitivus*, a permanent mark branding her as someone who had once tried to escape. She must have been desperate, he thought. Most slaves would never risk running away. Branding was one of the lesser punishments, public crucifixion the worst. Slaves who worked in a household or were skilled in a trade could, in theory, buy their freedom with money from their *peculium*, an 'allowance' built from tips or gifts from a generous master. In reality, so few ever managed it that the prospect seemed closer to legend than lived experience.

---

* *Thermopolium* comes from the Greek for 'hot shop' and are easily identified by their big stone or marble counters with large terracotta jars embedded in the top.

Petrinus' quiet contempt for the system that chained human beings motivated his dream to be free of it. To become a *libertus*, a freedman, a citizen. Long ago, his master had permitted him to begin his own *peculium*, though by default it was still the property of Pansa. With enough saved, he might one day buy his freedom, run a shop, start again. If Pansa allowed it. But this girl, with her rough, badly dyed tunic and the dull cast to her eyes, wore no sign of hope. Petrinus knew the owner, and he had no intention of letting her go. At least she wasn't chained inside a prison-bakery, like some of the others in the city, a small mercy in an Empire that rarely offered any. Slaves like them were not seen as people, but as property, no better than animals in the eyes of many.

As Petrinus passed the city's grandest bathing complex, he slowed again, watching the early bathers milling outside. He longed to join them as a free man, unburdened by errands and expectation. The baths had been hottest a few hours earlier, but now, as the workshops emptied, the bathhouses swelled with people, the city easing from work into evening life.

Today was no ordinary day. Tonight, Pompeii would come alive with spectators drawn to the amphitheatre by the promise of blood and spectacle. Games were common in the city but always timed to avoid clashes with those in Rome or neighbouring towns. This evening's games were staged by the *aediles*, elected magistrates responsible for public events and infrastructure, supported by Petrinus' master and incoming *aedile*, Pansa. He had thrown himself into the preparations, relishing the chance to impress the people before formally taking office. Petrinus had heard him practising his speech at the house, speaking in the sophisticated, measured rhythm of a man trained in the art of rhetoric from a young age.

The spectacle would showcase some of the city's finest gladiators, men trained in the barracks near the Greek Theatre, or at the

THE INVISIBLE SLAVE

famed *Ludus Magnus* in Rome, their bodies honed through years of brutal combat. Petrinus had attended the games many times as Pansa's shadow. He could still recall the glint of steel beneath the arena's torches, the sinewed grace of fighters moving with lethal precision, the roar of the crowd and the clang of blade on blade. Then that final, dreadful moment when a man's life hung on the whim of the *editor*, the high-ranking sponsor who held the fighters' fate in his hands. Those moments, so fleeting and savage, gave Petrinus something to cling to in an otherwise dull and invisible existence. But he wouldn't be going today. He had a feast to help prepare.

The life of a slave was a relentless rhythm of obedience and toil. Perhaps a quarter of all people in Rome's empire lived in bondage, though no one really knew the number. The census counted citizens, not slaves. In Egypt, where scribes kept records with meticulous care, the number of slaves was lower. But here in Pompeii, amidst opulent villas, thriving workshops and the ceaseless flow of mercantile trade feeding the ever-hungry appetites of Rome's citizens, the enslaved were everywhere, woven into the very foundation of the city.

Petrinus had once listened from the shadows as the Greek tutor, who came regularly to the *domus* to teach the younger Pansa, had recited Caesar's campaigns in Gaul with cool detachment, as though they were achievements to admire. In just 8 years, Caesar's armies had conquered vast territories and enslaved more than a million people. In 57 BCE, after the siege of the Atuatuci stronghold, the mighty Caesar sold 53,000 tribespeople in just one day.* Five years later, Caesar rewarded each of his 80,000 soldiers with a slave, a living trophy to mark their triumph at Alesia. Nameless

---

* In modern-day Belgium.

prizes. Human beings distributed like *amphorae* of wine or silver coins.

Petrinus turned the number over in his mind: 53,000. Nearly three times the population of Pompeii. An entire people, scattered like ash. Just like him.

And yet Romans like the *gens Cuspia*, Pansa's family, called it a *triumph*.

They had made slavery so routine, so abundant, that a life could be tossed away like dice across a gaming board. Petrinus was disposable and he knew it. And yet a flicker of hope always lingered. To be free meant that his children would be born as full Roman citizens, not as property but as people with rights. His child could walk through the forum without deference, vote, hold office, *be* Roman. It was a prize so coveted that foreign soldiers laboured 25 years in the legions for it, bleeding on distant battlefields in the hope of winning citizenship for themselves and securing a future where their children would never know servitude.

Some did rise from slavery to become successful. *Immensely* successful, at that. Pansa had talked of the two Vettii brothers who lived across the city. Yet judging by the tone of Pansa's guests, this wasn't an outcome they celebrated. The *liberti*, or freed class, existed in a liminal space, neither enslaved nor fully equal to a freeborn *ingenuus*, or Roman citizen. Some Romans sneered at them, dismissing them as men who had once been owned. Others resented their ambition, uneasy at the sight of freedmen who had surpassed the old families in trade, power and influence. Petrinus had watched from the sidelines as freedmen navigated a world that would never let them forget, still carrying the weight of what they had been, despite great fame and fortune.

And yet, he knew which life he would choose.

THE INVISIBLE SLAVE

If freedom came with social debts and quiet reminders of past servitude, so be it. Better a man who had to fight for his place than one who was never given a choice at all.

There were many paths to freedom, some grand and others quietly improvised. *Manumissio vindicta*, freedom 'by the rod', was a staged trial before a magistrate with absolute power, or *imperium*. After the slave was declared free, their owner remained silent, and the magistrate touched the slave with a staff, reciting the set formula that made the act official. This formal manumission bestowed full citizenship and status upon the *libertus* or *liberta*. A less formal route, *manumissio inter amicos*, involved a simple declaration of freedom spoken by the master in front of friends. It was freedom of a sort, though it lacked some of the legal weight of full manumission, creating a Junian Latin without full Roman citizenship.

In *manumissio censu*, slaves were transformed in a moment from property to person by the entry of their name into the census. Others were set free by the stroke of a stylus in a will, though by then, their master was long past hearing any words of thanks. And then there were whispers of the Christians, a new sect that spoke of spiritual equality and practised *manumissio in ecclesia*, freeing slaves in their gatherings as an act of religious devotion. But that was a distant promise, something happening in other cities, in other worlds. Not here in Pompeii.

* * *

From a nearby stall, set up alongside many others in the city's main square, a familiar voice called out; Philemon, the old fruit seller, his smile a gap-toothed crescent moon, gestured towards a pile of pomegranates and dates, their skins dusted from travel. 'Fresh from Parthia this morning,' he rasped, as if Petrinus hadn't heard the same boast every week. He nodded. He needed equal amounts of both.

The plates of the brass scale swayed as Philemon weighed the fruit, before tucking them carefully into Petrinus' basket. Six *asses*, bronze coins the size of a thumbnail, would cover it. Petrinus fished a handful out of his purse, and the face of the new emperor, Titus, stared up at him from the metal. Nestled among the other coins was an older one, a worn *quadrans*. He counted six *asses* and dropped them into Philemon's hand. Turning away from the stall, he flipped over the *quadrans* with his thumb. It was a coin from Caligula's short reign, back when the Empire still allowed his face to exist in public.* It had been minted to celebrate the end of Tiberius' rule, a tyrant replaced by a madman, or so the stories went. Petrinus had only ever known the stories.

His rough fingers traced the outline of the *pileus*, the soft cap worn by freedmen. It was wedged between the letters S.C., '*Senatus Consultum*', a mark of legitimacy and state sanction. To the free, the *pileus* meant liberty, and freedom from kingly tyranny, taxes and another man's rule. For the second time that day, Petrinus' mind turned to freedom, though now it had taken shape in the *pileus*, that small cap of liberty he one day hoped to wear.

The irony to be found on the other side of the coin was not lost on him. There were the letters *RCC*, '*remissa ducentesima*'. Petrinus knew its meaning. This 5 per cent auction tax had once been levied on everything, from furniture and livestock to people like himself. That was before Caligula had abolished it. It had been the emperor's gift to slave traders, not to slaves; not only did it make the enslaved more profitable, but it made the transaction of human beings more straightforward. A reward for cruelty.

The auction which led him to his current master had been a blur

---

* Images of the disgraced Caligula, like many Roman emperors before and after him, were defaced, destroyed and removed following his assassination, in a process now referred to as '*damnatio memoriae*'.

of noise and heat and humiliation. Buyers had crowded the forum that morning, pacing the rows like farmers at market, calling out prices, laughing, spitting, examining what they might buy. Slaves were made to stand still and turned like statues, their mouths forced open to examine teeth, their limbs bent and hair tugged. There was no dignity, no softness. Just the scratch of rope on wrists and the sharp smell of sweat and fear.

He had been just 13. His name and age had been inked on a wax tablet, along with the other property being liquidated: kitchenware, livestock, an oil lamp. He had belonged to Poppaea Note, a freedwoman who was once enslaved herself. But debt changed things. She had borrowed 1,450 *sestertii*, more than a soldier earned in a year, from Dicidia Margaris. Making the agreement, they had scratched the terms into a tablet as a lasting contract, and when Poppaea's repayment lapsed, Dicidia kept her two slaves as collateral: Petrinus and another boy named Simplex.* Dicidia had been swift and unsentimental; the two boys were already being led to auction the morning the loan agreement ended.

He had stood on a low platform, blinking in the sunlight, trying not to meet anyone's eyes. The tears had been threatening to pour over, but he knew this would only bring brutality. Instead, he attempted his best look of defiance. Beside him Simplex, a few years younger, looked at Petrinus for comfort. All day, people had turned each of them around, inspecting their muscles. Petrinus had only just begun developing into early adulthood, his knees achy from a growth spurt and his arms slim and awkward.

It was Pansa who had bought them at the auction. The slave he had brought with him, now long dead, had passed a purse of coins

---

* The two wax tablets recording this business deal were found in the furnace area of the Palaestra Baths in Pompeii, and they are dated to 61 CE.

to the auction clerk and yanked Petrinus and Simplex by the rope away from the podium and on to the next auction, where their new master purchased furniture and decorative items for the *domus* for a price higher than the two of them put together.

No one had spoken a word to them, or introduced themselves. Petrinus had sat with bated breath in the back of the wagon, wedged between two *amphorae*, a bronze tripod and a bundle of fennel stalks as they trundled through the city, petrified of the prospect of being separated from Simplex, or worse, spending the rest of their lives in vicious toil in the fields of the countryside. They wouldn't last 2 years. He'd led out an involuntary sigh of relief as they turned onto the main shopping street of the city, only for the old slave to cuff him with such force around the head that it made his ear ring. He didn't speak a word as they were led through the back entrance of Pansa's home and shown their sleeping quarters, far above any standard he had experienced in his many years of enslavement.

The bittersweet memory of that day, 18 years ago, a tangle of grief, terror and, at last, relief, had never left him. It was the second time he had been sold in his short lifetime, reduced to nothing more than a name and number scratched on a wax tablet, and still no one came to save him. He sometimes saw Poppaea in the streets. He always made sure to avoid her eye.

Snapping out of the memory, he looked again at the coin in his hand. Petrinus forced thoughts of freedom aside; dwelling on them led nowhere. The forum pressed in around him, a restless tide of voices and movement. He wove through the crowd, past men deep in debate and women balancing baskets of produce on their hips, each person's bargaining sharp and relentless. Keeping to the forum's edge, he moved past the looming bulk of the Temple of Jupiter, its shadow cutting across the square, and passed through a vast doorway into the market building, the *macellum*.

Here in the heart of it, voices clashed, hands gestured and coins changed ownership with practised ease. At the centre, a round colonnaded structure, a *tholos*, stood like a stage, its roof held aloft by a ring of slender columns. Merchants prowled around it, their voices raised in competition, each one desperate to drown out the others with promises of the freshest produce and the fairest deals. In the far corner, mosaics of fish swam across the walls, advertising the bounty below.

Fish had always been a staple in Pompeii, more so in the towns along the coast, like Herculaneum, where the bones of its

Figure 4: Marine life mosaic from the House of the Geometric Mosaics (VIII.2.16)

occupants were said to be stronger from a life fed by the sea. That morning, the fishermen had returned from the coast just beyond the town, their carts heavy with their odorous hauls. Now, the air bristled with the tang of salt and brine.* It hardly mattered what Lavinia had requested; Petrinus was at the mercy of whatever had found its way into the fishing nets. The fishmonger before Petrinus was busy replenishing his offerings: writhing octopus, sleek sea bass, crabs stacked atop one another, clams gaping in their shells, oysters still slick with seawater and rows of bream and mullet, their scales flashing like scattered coins. Petrinus scanned the selection of the region's finest mullets, a basket brimming with mussels and enough octopus to satisfy the demands of any opulent feast.

In the mix of tradesmen, Petrinus' dark eyes found Lavinia's preferred fishmonger a few stalls down, his hands moving fast as he scaled, gutted and sliced at speed. He was good at what he did; his steady churn of customers proved it.

The fishmonger barely came up for breath as his blade danced from one carcass to the next, each one dispatched cleanly to a slave's waiting hands, who laid the fillets out in a colourful display. Petrinus stepped up to the counter.

'Lucrine oysters please,' he said, adjusting the weight of the basket on his hip.† 'And I'll need crayfish, cuttlefish and an octopus, cleaned.'

---

* Dietary studies on the skeletons from Herculaneum, as well as work on the sewers, has shown that the people of this 'elite' city, regardless of social status, enjoyed a varied diet, primarily made up of fish. For more, see Erica Rowan's chapter in *The Economy of Pompeii* (2016).
† Located near Baiae along the north-western shore of the Gulf of Cumae in the Bay of Naples, the Lucrine Lake was well known for its oysters, the height of luxury.

The fishmonger didn't look up right away, but reached into a shallow tub and started pulling out oysters, slick and grey, the sea water dripping down his arms.

'It's for Pansa's feast tonight.'

The fishmonger gave a short nod, then reached for a bucket under the counter and started pulling out even larger specimens.

'How many?'

'Enough for nine, maybe 10 guests. The cook's doing a sauce.'

The cuttlefish and octopus followed, spread out on the counter on a clean wrap of damp leaves. Petrinus leaned in slightly, inspecting the glistening pink skin of the octopus, making sure that it had the pleasant fresh sea smell that indicated a good catch.

'Good quality,' he said. 'If she finds the eyes cloudy, she'll send me back.'

That earned a dry chuckle from the fishmonger. 'She knows her fish.'

Petrinus watched as his knife moved with practised confidence, separating flesh from bone in fluid strokes, the scales flashing in the light as they peeled from the fish, drifting to the floor like silver flecks. One of the town's cats, released to keep the rat problem under control, circled Petrinus' ankles, mewing hopefully. When the fishmonger had finished, his assistant tied the bundle and handed it over, taking the coins from Petrinus. The fishmonger had already turned back to his slab, his blade flashing once more.

As Petrinus pressed on, weaving through the crowd, his heart sank. Around him, shopkeepers were pulling bi-fold doors across their shopfronts as hawkers were turning into side roads and stallholders were sweeping away the debris from below their stands. Could it already be the ninth hour? In an hour, most of the city's shops would be shut. Running across the forum to the Temple of Apollo, a sundial confirmed his fears. And he hadn't even secured the most important item: the wine. Swallowing his frustration, he rounded the corner leading out of the forum at speed and slammed into a woman carrying a basket of bread. She gasped as a loaf tumbled to the dust. A heavy-jawed man with a sunburnt neck who had been pestering her rounded on Petrinus.

'Clumsy animal!' He struck Petrinus in the face. 'This is why you should all be in chains.' No sooner had Petrinus returned the bread to the basket than the man had chucked it across the street like a discus, stray dogs pouncing on it before it had barely touched the ground.

'Disgusting. As if she'd eat that now! It's been in your filthy hands.' His efforts to impress were in vain; the woman had taken the scene as an opportunity to escape.

The man straightened, looking around with irritation as he realised she was gone. Petrinus used the moment, slipping past and scuttling into the butcher's shop on the next street of stores behind the forum, praying the man wouldn't follow him through the door. The butcher, a veteran of the trade, was still at work. The air smelled of raw meat and sawdust. The boar and peacock for the feast had been delivered to the house this morning; Lavinia would already be roasting them in the big oven. He just needed to pick up the sow's udder.

As he passed the swollen mass wrapped in fig leaves over the counter, the butcher's eyes landed on the bruise already forming on Petrinus' cheek. Ignoring his gaze, he paid and dashed out of the small shop, his face flushed with shame.

With the main ingredients packed and the basket heavy on his shoulder, Petrinus turned south, slipping instinctively into the quieter backstreets. Rather than battle the end of the working day crush along the forum colonnades, he cut behind the *macellum*, past a row of dye shops and a bakery where the mules and slaves inside walked their relentless path around the millstones, turning them as they trudged. He emerged near the top of the Via dell'Abbondanza, the city's main shopping artery, and crossed it during a lull between carts, heading down the steep slope towards a quieter stretch of road.

There, nestled at the edge of a crossroads, stood a *caupona*, part tavern, part inn, with a painted façade. A vine crept over the wall at the rear, and Petrinus could just make out the clatter of plates and the low murmur of conversation in the garden behind it. To the left of the doorway, bright against the stuccoed wall, was a painting of a phoenix, accompanied by two shadowy phoenixes below and framed with trailing garlands. Beneath it, in neat white lettering, were the words: *Phoenix Felix Et Tu* – 'The Phoenix is lucky; may you be too.'

Petrinus smiled to himself. Simplex had taught him to read, and it pleased him to at least not be excluded from this part of life. His eyes landed on a political notice next to the painting, its bold red letters standing out against the wall, despite the passing of 2 years: *Euxinus asks you to elect Quintus Postumius and Marcus Cerrinius aediles, together with Iustus*. The innkeeper's name sat proudly at the top, a public declaration of his allegiance, while the signature of the painter responsible for the notice stood out below: *Hinnulus wrote this.**

Petrinus observed the freed people in the inn and remembered, like many times before, that he wasn't here to join in. Some dined

---

* Like many notices in Pompeii, this one was written by an official notice writer (*pictor*), who here records his name, Hinnulus, for posterity and self-advertisement. It was written on behalf of the inn owner, Euxinus, who clearly favoured Quintus Postumius and Marcus Cerrinius in the year 77, who were popular with tradesmen and even had women supporters, despite the latter not being able to vote.

Figure 5: The 'Lucky Phoenix' at Euxinus' Caupona (I.11.11)

in the room at the back, their laughter travelling to the counter where he now stood; others spilled into the garden space littered with tables and chairs below the vines. An attractive, voluptuous woman was busy cleaning a pot with a cloth and giving instructions to one of the inn slaves. For a second, Petrinus felt grateful for the household that he was a part of. Sure, it was hard work, but not as relentless or dirty as an inn.

Euxinus, ever the shrewd merchant, wasted no time in offering some of his finest vintages, despite Petrinus only being here to pick up spiced *mulsum*, a rich, honeyed wine. As a gesture of goodwill, or advertisement, he offered to add an *amphora* of his own homemade wine to the order, grown from the vines in the small inn garden and at the back of his house next door. Petrinus smirked; self-promotion. Not that it would make it to his master's table. Wine grown within the walls of Pompeii had a reputation for being sharp and overpowering, lacking the refinement of the prized vintages left to mellow in distant vineyards and leaving the drinker with a terrible headache the next day.* Still, the wine might find its way to the slaves or those less discerning about what filled their cups. Petrinus looked forward to that.

After confirming the arrangements and ensuring the *amphorae* would arrive in time for the evening's feast, he could only hope that Euxinus had enough to meet their needs. Running short was simply not an option.

The noise of the *caupona* fell away as Petrinus turned onto a narrow side street. He knew this warren of back streets well in the garden district, where many a vineyard and orchard had been created after the great quake 17 years ago.

This lane was quieter and cooler than the busy main streets, hemmed in by high garden walls and shuttered windows. Along the top of one wall, shards of broken *amphorae* stuck out from the mortar, a crude but effective deterrent against thieves. He followed the lane until he heard the soft rumble of carts on the Via di Nocera, and he stopped at a small shop on the corner, opposite a bustling *thermopolium* where customers were grabbing a bite before making the short walk to the amphitheatre.

---

* We hear this opinion from Pliny the Elder (*Natural Histories*, 14.8), who says: 'As to the wines of Pompeii, they have arrived at their full perfection in ten years, after which they gain nothing by age: they are found also to be productive of headache, which often lasts so long as the sixth hour of the next day.'

He was relieved to see the wide shutters of the shop still open. Baskets of fresh fruit, vegetables, herbs and nuts, alongside rows of small storage jars called *unguentaria*, spilled onto the sidewalk in a colourful display. Stepping inside, he let his eyes adjust to the dim light. No one there, though he could hear a low mumble of conversation floating through the side doorway. Grabbing a string of garlic, Petrinus walked over to a little bronze bell hanging by the door and gave it a shake – *tring* – before peering through.

The most glorious garden opened up in front of him, a tangle of vines, herbs and fruit trees bathed in the afternoon light. It was not the kind seen in his master's house, nor in the houses of Pansa's friends. This was from a bygone era, the rustic ideal of the virtuous Roman who tilled the land with his hands. Or hers, as the case seemed to be. A man was pouring water into a cistern near the back wall, while a woman stood nearby, hands on hips, watching his work with an appraising eye.

He recognised her at once: Umbricia Fortunata. She was the freedwoman of Aulus Umbricius Scaurus, the *garum* 'fish sauce' magnate and soon to be a guest at tonight's feast. He'd seen her husband, Lucius Aelius, at the house a couple of times, dropping off orders of the *garum* she sold for Scaurus. The dark, intensely flavoured sauce was made from fermented fish and salt, a delicious essential of most Roman kitchens. At other times he'd seen her in the *palaestra*, hawking fresh food. He realised now this produce must be from her garden. She turned at the sound of the bell, her gaze settling on Petrinus with perhaps a hint of recognition. He held up the string of garlic, the bulbs still dusted with a little soil where they had been plucked from the earth that morning.

'There are a couple of other things we need, if it's not too much trouble.'

She smiled. 'What's Pansa after?'

THE INVISIBLE SLAVE

As she spoke, a phrase Petrinus had once read scratched into the atrium wall of one of Pansa's friends came to his mind: 'If anyone does not believe in Venus, they should gaze at my girlfriend.' It could easily have been written about Fortunata, though for Petrinus, her beauty stirred no longing of his own.

'Pears, pine nuts. What else? Ah, yes. Coriander and parsley …' Fortunata bustled around the shop gathering the items as he listed them aloud. 'And some of your imported dates.'

The atmosphere here couldn't have been further from that of the forum or the *macellum*. There were no shouted prices, no elbowing crowds, just the tranquil virtuosity of someone in complete control of her space and business. He passed her the coins, then turned to leave. Outside, the sunlight caught the top of the garden wall, glinting on the jagged *amphora* shards set into the mortar.

As he made his way north, up the gentle slope back towards the Via dell'Abbondanza, the city was shifting. The usual noise of the day was giving way to the hush of early evening when the carts stopped moving through the streets for the few hours before nightfall, when they would begin again. Shop doors closed with soft clicks and the crowds dispersed as the sun hovered low, bathing the upper walls in an orange-gold light. But for the house of any family worth their salt in Pompeii, the most important part of the day was only beginning.

As always, Petrinus slipped into the side alley off the Via dell'Abbondanza that led to the side entrance of the house, the very one he had entered on his first day in the household.* In recent years,

---

* The most probable home of Pansa is the House of Marcus Epidius Sabinus, based on the frequency of graffiti endorsing Pansa on this house and in the vicinity. However, this is by no means a foolproof way to determine the location of someone's house in Pompeii. Nonetheless, this house is a good example of elite living in ancient Pompeii.

the alley had been pedestrianised, with the addition of a stepping stone at the far end and a fountain just beyond the house, barring carts from passing through. Yet, deep grooves remained, worn into the stone, scars created by the many years of wheels grinding over the same path.

By now, Lavinia's kitchen would be alive with movement: flames roaring, pots clattering and wastewater being chucked down the latrine, Lavinia's voice carrying over the din. Petrinus could picture it clearly: the swirl of steam, the smell of vinegar and herbs, the occasional shout when something was dropped or burned. Tonight, Pompeii's finest politicians and businessmen would gather in Pansa's *triclinium*, their laughter rising with the smoke of burning oil lamps as the slaves filled their goblets and lined their plates. They would not think of the hands that prepared their oysters, or stirred the sauce, or fetched the garlic from the garden behind a quiet shop on a quiet street.

That was simply the way of things.

* * *

Petrinus entered his master's grand house through the smaller of its two *atria*, instinctively sidestepping Martial, the imposing guard dog chained near the entrance. The sleek Laconian hound flicked his nose at the scent of meat and fish wafting from Petrinus' basket, his muscles shifting beneath his glossy black coat. With his tall frame, sharp snout and pricked ears, Martial personified vigilance: a true Spartan hound, prized for hunting prowess and relentless speed. Now, he simply stretched out his long legs without rising, lazily acknowledging the arrival.

Petrinus had seen mosaics of dogs like Martial all over Pompeii: snarling beasts, their sharp teeth bared, a frozen deterrent to any who might enter uninvited. Some carried an accompanying warn-

THE INVISIBLE SLAVE

Figure 6: A typical 'Beware the Dog' mosaic at the House of Paquius Proculus (I.7.1)

ing: *CAVE CANEM*, 'Beware the Dog'. His master preferred the genuine article, keeping a dog at each entrance, along with burly slave porters who lodged permanently in the side rooms.*

Petrinus walked into the back atrium of Pansa's home, overflowing with the scent of fresh flowers and the soothing murmur of water trickling into the *impluvium*, the rainwater pool at the centre. Its opulence was undeniable: soaring ceilings and intricately painted walls demanded awe. In a niche in the wall, the sombre

---

* Pansa was not alone in keeping real guard dogs in his home. On 20 November 1874, excavators at the House of Orpheus (VI.14.20) made a haunting discovery. Beneath the hardened ash they found the plaster-cast form of a dog, still wearing its collar, its body contorted in agony. Likely the same breed as Martial (a Laconian hound), with tall legs, a long snout and sharp ears, the animal had been trapped by its chain, unable to escape. As ash poured through the roof opening above the atrium, the dog scrambled higher, desperately trying to free itself. It was found near the entrance nearly 2,000 years later.

presence of wax death masks of the two elder Gaius Cuspius Pansas cast a reverent shadow over the space. One was the recently deceased patriarch, and father of his master, and the other was the elder grandfather. Their eyes, though closed, seemed to observe all. As he moved through the room, Petrinus kept his head bowed, his steps almost silent on the mosaic floors.

Around him, fellow slaves darted about, balancing gleaming silverware, vibrant flower garlands and luxurious furnishings in their arms. Petrinus followed one struggling with a hefty grain container into the small private bakery, or *pistrinum*, that Pansa had set up just off the atrium to boost income and impress guests with freshly baked bread.* The heat inside was stifling as the oven blazed, baking round loaves of *panis quadratus*, each marked with Pansa's stamp and divided into eight pieces.

Set into a rectangular niche above the curve of the oven, a red phallus carved from travertine watched over the bakery, a guardian against disaster, disease and anything else that might sour the day's bread. Below it, painted in neat red letters, the words *hic habitat felicitas* proclaimed 'happiness lives here'. A hopeful sentiment, Petrinus thought, but not exactly applicable to those doing the baking. To his right, a neat pile of fresh *panis quadratus* loaves were piled on a masonry bench beneath the open street-facing windows, the crusts warm and dusted with flour. These were for the household table. Off to one side a basket of coarse rolls sat cooling for

---

* The standard process of breadmaking was vividly illustrated on a grand tomb just outside Rome's Porta Maggiore gate by the famous freedman baker, Eurysaces. The marble friezes depicted the entire operation: from grain receipt and grinding by donkeys, through to sieving and kneading and to baking and delivery. Each panel was a detailed snapshot of the bustling bakery, reminiscent of today's busy pizza kitchens, showcasing a well-oiled production line that ensured each loaf met state standards before being sent off in baskets.

the slaves' dinner: small, dry and flecked with grit. The flour in these had barely been sifted; it wasn't unusual to chip a tooth on a bit of stone. If they were lucky, though, there might be leftovers from the feast. A few scraps of fish or a slice of soft white bread that had gone untouched. One could always hope.

The clamour of the bakery and the formal grandeur of the atrium faded behind Petrinus, replaced by the stillness of the peristyle, a garden courtyard ringed with elegant columns, its open centre alive with sunlight, foliage and the soft rustle of leaves. Here, the sweet scent of blooming flowers interlaced with the earthy breath of freshly watered soil, while the hazy hills of Campania

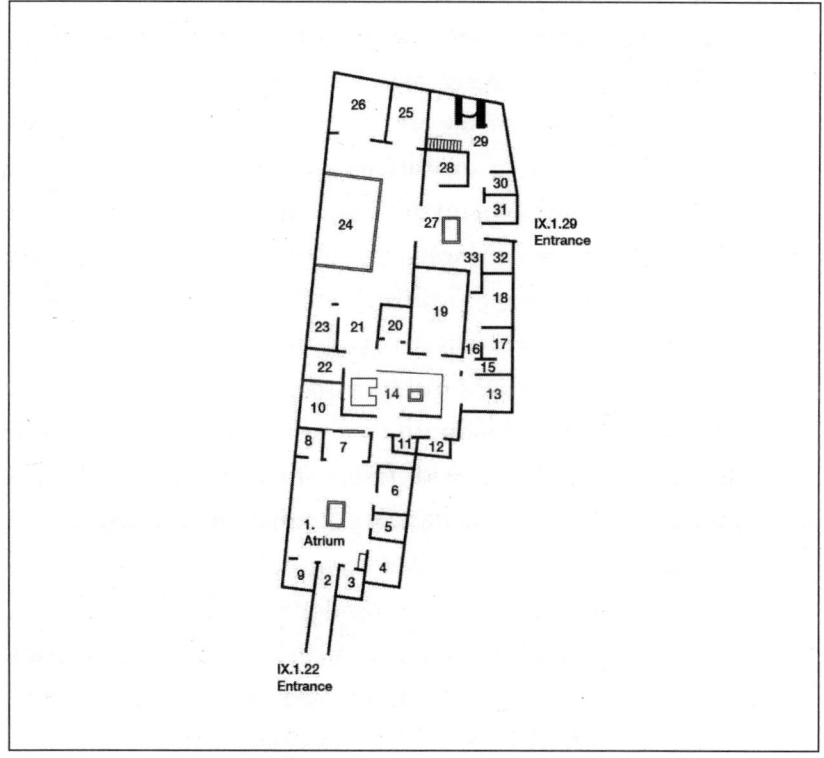

Figure 7: Plan of the House of Pansa (also known as the House of Marcus Epidius Sabinus (IX.1.22))

framed the garden beyond like a painted backdrop. Two slaves worked quietly nearby, one pruning roses with meticulous attention, the other wiping down statues until they gleamed. Petrinus kept moving, stepping lightly across the shaded walkway and into a smaller peristyle tucked just beyond. A shallow basin of water sat at the centre, encircled by thick greenery and small animal statues of frogs, pigs and a lizard curling around the base of a planter.

From ahead came the shuffle of movement, as he spotted more slaves in the adjoining grand *triclinium*, setting out the evening's feast. Low couches were being arranged for dining, their cushions fluffed and straightened, and the linen cloths laid out with care. Lamps were filled with oil, their clay mouths dark with soot.

Not keen to be dragged into setting cushions or arranging silver, Petrinus slipped by and headed for the kitchen, the basket by now unbearably heavy in his arms. As he approached the aromas intensified, an enticing mix of simmering sauces, roasting meat and freshly ground spices. He tossed a handful of herbs from his basket into the storage cupboard beside the kitchen and wiped parsley curls clinging to the sweat of his palms on his tunic.

Inside, the *culina* was in full swing.

Voices overlapped in a chorus of instructions and quick replies as the knives struck wood with rhythmic precision. Oil hissed as it met hot pans, and the fire in the hearth crackled and roared, casting restless light on the painted walls where serpents coiled around altars and guardian spirits watched from niches. Petrinus pushed his way through the controlled chaos, dodging elbows and steam, to hand over the basket of provisions to Lavinia. She was busy issuing orders with a clipped tongue and flashing gestures. As always, she moved fast and expected the same from everyone else. Under her direction, the kitchen ran with the precision of a choreographed dance.

THE INVISIBLE SLAVE

In the corner, a small slave boy knelt next to a *glirarium*, a large ceramic jar used to fatten up edible dormice, the inside complete with little shelves for them to run up and down. Reaching in, he pulled one out by its tail, its fate sealed. The little creature squirmed and squeaked. Soon it would be skewered, coated in honey and poppyseeds, and set before the guests as a delicacy. Not keen to watch the creature's cosy existence end, Petrinus turned away. He dropped the basket onto the counter, calling out to Lavinia so she knew it was there, then slipped back out into the small peristyle.

Figure 8: A gliarium, *used to fatten up dormice* (glis glis) *for food*

He stopped to catch his breath. As the corridor was teeming with all manner of stressed slaves shouting back and forth to one another, Petrinus opted for a different route back to his quarters, hoping for a short rest before the feast. He had been up before first light of day and would, no doubt, be staying up until the same time tomorrow. He peered through a sheer curtain to his left and saw that the room inside was empty.

On most days, Petrinus would find his master in the *tablinum*, or study, seated with a scroll of the latest academic text across his lap, or playing gracious host to a friend who grumbled about one politician or another. The room had a gentle warmth, lit by bronze lanterns, with the October breeze blowing in from the atrium softened by heavy curtains drawn across each side. The space struck a careful balance between comfort and show. Carved wooden furniture, richly dyed cushions and wall paintings in the latest style created a setting that was both inviting and refined. A pile of scrolls sat in a cabinet, their surfaces curling slightly, while wax tablets lined the shelves in tidy rows.

Passing quietly through the formal atrium, where guests would soon arrive to be dazzled by torchlight and polished marble, Petrinus eased into the cramped back room he shared with three others. It was part storage cupboard, part sleeping quarters: a space where old *amphorae* and broken furniture were stacked at random. Two bed frames were pushed against opposite walls for him and the other two adult slaves, plus a *verna*, a child born into slavery. A bucket of water sat in the centre of the room, intended for washing the street filth from his skin. He cleaned himself in silence before settling onto the bed, his muscles throbbing. He no longer noticed the coarse ropes that made up the bed's base in lieu of mattresses; his body had long since adapted. The household was far from sleep, but he had no more to give.

THE INVISIBLE SLAVE

* * *

The feast that evening was expected to be nothing short of legendary. It was one thing to invite a few wealthy friends or political allies for a quiet dinner, but some occasions demanded more of a spectacle. These lavish, staged affairs were designed to impress, to win favour and to remind Pompeii exactly where a man like Pansa stood. They were never just about food or wine, though both had to be flawless. They were about performance, on a metaphorical stage where reputations were made, alliances forged and futures secured.

Petrinus had only just closed his eyes when another slave came in and sent him straight back to work, scrubbing the mosaic floors throughout the house. By the time he and a young female slave had finished the final touches in the *triclinium*, polishing and laying out the family's prized silverware, the guests had begun to arrive from the arena, buzzing with excitement from the gladiatorial fights.

Petrinus and the other slaves washed the guests' feet at the entrance before guiding them into the *triclinium*. Inside, garlands were draped in loose loops across walls painted in rich reds and ochres. Beneath, the *cocciopesto* floor was inlaid with delicate lines of white stone dots.* Painted birds appeared to flit and flutter around the room, which was framed by painted foliage motifs, blending almost seamlessly with the greenery of the peristyle beyond. The upper walls, painted black to disguise the soot from the many lamps, lent the room an opulent tone. On the tables placed around the couches, polished silver dishes gleamed as the

---

* *Cocciopesto* is a type of Roman flooring made from crushed terracotta mixed with lime and sand, creating a durable, reddish surface often used in courtyards and baths.

whimsical notes of an Anatolian pipe melody danced through the air, curling like the smoke that drifted above the couches.

Some of Pompeii's most influential men were gathered in Pansa's *triclinium*. His fellow magistrates reclined around him in their appointed places, their positions chosen to balance status and favour, ensuring no one felt overlooked – unless, of course, that was the intention. The first couch, the *lectus imus*, was where the host family reclined. Pansa took his seat here, alongside Lucius Popidius Secundus, his fellow incoming *aedile* and a relative of Popidius Natalis, another of his guests, seated on the lowest couch. At the end of the *lectus imus* was Pansa's son, watching and learning the etiquette of a feast. Pansa's neighbour and friend, Paquius Proculus, reclined as the guest of honour on the middle couch, the *lectus medius*, alongside the other two *aediles* for the incoming year, Gnaeus Helvius Sabinus and Marcus Samellius Modestus. On the lowest couch with Natalis was Aulus Umbricius Scaurus, the freedman fish-sauce magnate, and Lucius Eumachius Erotis, an up-and-coming freedman in the roof-tiling business.

The masks worn in public gradually slipped as the wine flowed and the night progressed. From the shadows at the edge of the room, his back pressed to the cool wall, Petrinus remained still and unnoticed as he watched the feast unfold. When the final course was served, a dish of the imported dates from Parthia that he had picked up that afternoon, Petrinus poured watered-down Falernian wine from chilled jugs into the silver goblets of Sabinus and Modestus, his expression deliberately blank as they talked in hushed tones. Another slave knelt at the feet of an intoxicated Secundus, who swayed unsteadily as his sandals were removed.

At the centre of it all, Pansa sat with his head veiled in the manner of a priest, the attire lending him a regal air as his arm lay

THE INVISIBLE SLAVE

draped across the shoulders of his newest favourite, a short-haired boy from Mauretania, bought only that summer. The boy's eyes had glazed and were fixed on some point far away. Petrinus recognised that look, the dull retreat into a place where the noise could not reach. He remembered his own first night in the household, the tears that had brought no comfort, the silence that had met his grief.

'Come on, lad. Finish it off,' Scaurus pressed, as Erotis raised a drinking horn to his lips. Red-cheeked and hesitant, he gulped until his chest heaved, then sputtered, a spray of honeyed wine spilling down his front. Scaurus roared with laughter, striking him on the back in jovial approval, as Pansa's son looked on with glee.

Figure 9: A raucous banqueting scene from the House of the Triclinium (V.2.4)

'Make yourselves comfortable while I sing!' Sabinus suddenly shouted, sitting up and spilling wine onto the cushions.

'That's what life's all about. Go for it,' replied Scaurus, his eyes heavy.*

As Sabinus began his tuneless lament, Paquius Proculus picked idly at something in a silver dish, his gaze fixed on a dancer moving to the sound of flutes, her body swaying and bare skin glowing in the lamplight. Erotis slumped forward and retched onto the floor as Scaurus looked on at the young man with amusement, his stomach long since hardened by years of such excess. Petrinus lurched forward to push Erotis upright. Despite the mess pooling at his feet, he tried to keep his expression neutral as the man groaned, his toga slipping from his shoulder. Naked female musicians, or *tibicines*, played on without looking up, absorbed in their instruments. Two more girls, also bare, moved between the guests with lowered eyes, balancing trays of food and refilling empty cups.

Petrinus shifted his grip on Erotis, steadying him as another heave wracked his body. The stench was overwhelming. Behind him, another guest swayed as he tried to stand and clutched at a tripod for balance, knocking over a lantern. It crashed to the floor.

He glanced around at the other slaves, unnoticed figures moving through the chaos, their presence barely registered as they stooped to clean the various messes. The earlier negotiations, the laughter and the toasts, none of it was possible without them, he thought. By morning, only those clearing away the wreckage would remember the night in full. Erotis, finally regaining his balance, waved off

---

* These words I have taken from another fresco in the same room as the image seen in Figure 10 above, in the House of the Triclinium (V.2.4). A third fresco shows dancers and musicians entertaining feast-goers, in the manner I describe here. The actual reply is 'That's how life is; be well', but I choose to paraphrase.

*Figure 10: 'Make yourselves comfortable, I'm going to sing!'
A banqueting scene from the House of the Triclinium (V.2.4)*

Petrinus, who knelt down to help clear up his vomit. Suddenly, a hush spread through the *triclinium*. The flutes softened and voices fell away as every head turned towards the doorway.

The priest of Isis had arrived with his entourage.

The slaves were temporarily dismissed, and Petrinus followed the others as they melted into the shadows beyond the peristyle. From the shelter of a narrow doorway, he watched through a slender crack. The priest stood bathed in flickering lamplight, his head shaven and white linen robes immaculate. In one hand, he held a bronze *sistrum* rattle, while in the other he sprinkled perfumed water from a palm branch onto the threshold of each door. The *sistrum*, with its handle and U-shaped frame holding sliding cross-

THE LOST VOICES OF POMPEII

Figure 11: Fresco depicting a Priest of Isis from the Temple of Isis in Pompeii

bars, was designed, when shaken, to invoke the goddess Isis.* Incense curled upwards in silvery spirals from *thuribula*, or bronze incense burners, held by the Isiac slaves whose low and rhythmic chant echoed around the open courtyard. Their chants were a prayer to Isis for purity, protection and renewal, and their ceremony marked a symbolic cleansing of the household, a blessing upon those gathered within.

* *Sistra* were previously used in the cult of the cow-goddess Hathor. The name sistrum comes from the Egyptian *sekhem* or *sesheshet*, after the sound the rattles produce when shaken.

Delighted to see the rites of a goddess he, like many other slaves, revered, Petrinus stood motionless, transfixed by the scene. As the priest moved between doorways, trailing smoke and murmured invocations, his gaze swept the edges of the peristyle and, for the briefest moment, their eyes met.

There was something unsettling in that glance. It was not the usual vacant look of a man noticing a slave, nor casual curiosity. It was recognition. A quiet, disconcerting acknowledgement, as though the priest saw something others did not. Did a smile touch his lips, or had Petrinus imagined it?

The moment passed and the priest moved on, continuing to flick water over each threshold, before finally disappearing through the passage which led to the atrium. The hush that had gripped the gathering lasted only a few seconds. Laughter swelled almost in communal relief, and cups clinked once more. It was as though nothing had changed.

But Petrinus felt it, a shift. A subtle unease in the air, like the stillness before a summer storm. The guest who had been unwell staggered again and knocked a glass cup to the floor, its shards scattering across the mosaic. Kneeling once more onto the cold floor, Petrinus gathered the pieces, one sliver nicking his skin and drawing a bead of blood. Above him, Pansa stepped forward before his guests, steady and composed, and launched into his second speech of the evening.

'My honoured guests,' he began, spreading his arms wide, 'you are familiar with the generous streak that runs through my family, the *gens Cuspia*, as it has for generations. All over this town, you will see the signs calling for me to be made *aedile*.'

Pansa's son sat forward, eyes bright with admiration, as his father began to speak of ancestors and honours, of the family's hand in rebuilding the amphitheatre, of his own generosity to Pompeii. The guests murmured their approval at each well-placed boast, the rhythm of his words rehearsed. Petrinus had heard it all before. But then the speech turned. Pansa invoked Feronia, the goddess of liberty, whose festival would fall on the Ides of November. Petrinus' hands slowed.

'Step forward, Petrinus.'

Leaving the shards where they lay, Petrinus edged towards his master, a tremor running through him as he braced for the rebuke. Too loud, too slow, never quiet enough.

But no punishment came. Instead, the words 'Petrinus, be free' met his ears. He was stunned as he looked at Pansa, who beamed at his now applauding guests.* Anticipation surged through him, hot and dizzying, as he became incredibly aware of how *visible* he was.

'I also give the *peculium* that Petrinus has thus far saved and any items he has gathered under my ownership in the preceding years. Simplex, please undertake the necessary ceremony of shaving Petrinus' head.'

A hush of anticipation fell over the room as a female slave hurried away to fetch the shears for the ceremonial shaving, a formal rite marking the process of manumission. When she returned, she placed them silently into the hands of Petrinus' truest companion, the one who had stood beside him longer than anyone, steady and constant in the way few are. The man who had come to mean everything to him. As Simplex stepped forward,

---

* *Servus meus liber esto*, or 'Be free my slave', was the proper way to declare that a slave was now free in the presence of friends. We see this spoken by the fictional freedman Trimalchio, in Petronius' *Satires* ('Dionysus, *liber*'), when he frees a slave dressed as Dionysus in the presence of the friends (inter amicos) at his feast. The newly freed slave would then don the pointed *pileus* hat as an act of 'being free'.

THE INVISIBLE SLAVE

something in his gaze had shifted, his eyes no longer quite meeting those of Petrinus. He raised the shears, and with careful movements began to cut. The metal scraped softly against Petrinus' scalp, and tufts of hair drifted to the floor, each one a token of a life being left behind.

When the ritual was complete, Petrinus remained still, the warm air of the *triclinium* tingling his bare scalp. Pansa stood in front of Petrinus, his expression a strained imitation of benevolence. In his hand, he held a small, pointed red cap, the *pileus*, just as it had appeared on the coin. With care, the master placed it on his former slave's head.

'Now let deserving slaves sit down so that they may stand up free.'*

Petrinus obeyed, lowering himself onto the nearest couch before rising again in a single motion.

'Go forth, Gaius Cuspius Petrinus, and serve in the name of the Emperor, the Senate and the people of Rome.'†

The guests roared in approval – but not for Petrinus. Their cheers were for Pansa, the magnanimous master, the gracious benefactor. Petrinus' name, though newly granted, was of no importance to

---

* This rather fabulous phrase was written on a stone beside a shrine in Feronia, Terracina, just south of Rome on the coast. This temple site had long been associated with the freeing of slaves. Varro, the ancient writer living in Italy between 116 and 27 BCE, associated the goddess Feronia with *libertas*, or 'freedom', something which a slave earned upon being freed.

† Slaves were given a single name upon their birth or capture, which erased any identity they may have had before captivity. Petrinus' name is fictional, as no records of slaves from this household, or most others, survive. Romans usually had three names: a *praenomen* (personal name), a *nomen* (family or clan name), and a *cognomen* (a nickname that became a hereditary surname). Upon being freed, slaves preserved their *cognomen* and adopted their master's *praenomen* and *nomen*. Thus, Petrinus would have become Gaius Cuspius Petrinus, marking him as part of Pansa's extended household.

them. Only Simplex was looking at Petrinus, a mixture of pride and sadness in his eyes. What would they do without each other?

The hand of another slave pressed against his back, guiding him out of the *triclinium*. The air in the small peristyle garden outside struck him like a wave, cool and free of the impenetrable musk of wine and bodies. The first pale light of dawn was now creeping over the horizon, soft against the looming silhouette of the mountain. A day of promise and new beginnings was on its way.

For the first time, Petrinus belonged to no one, and yet he knew that didn't mean he was truly *free*. His manumission had been theatre, an informal gesture staged for Pansa's guests, not a solemn act before a magistrate. It left him in a strange, uncertain space: no longer a slave, and not yet a citizen, but a *Latinus Iunianus*, or Junian Latin. The name carried a certain dignity, but he knew the restrictive truth behind it.

He couldn't vote, and he didn't possess *conubium*, the legal right to marry in the eyes of the Roman state. Any children he might one day father would be illegitimate and have no legal claim to his name or property. They would not be recognised as citizens, and unless he later gained full citizenship himself through a second, formal, manumission known as *iteratio*, he could not legitimise them or pass on any rights. And when death eventually came for him, everything he had built, every saved coin, every modest possession, would revert to the man who had once called him *servus*, regardless of the family he might leave behind. He had been so close. What a bittersweet moment it was.

The familiar knotting feeling rose up again in his stomach. He turned the unfamiliar words over in his mind: Gaius Cuspius Petrinus. He had always been Petrinus, but now he had a *nomen*, Cuspius, the mark of the man who was now his patron. Yet to those who knew him best, he would always just be Petrinus.

He whispered the name once more under his breath, as if trying to make it fit. *Gaius Cuspius Petrinus.* The name would follow him for the rest of his life. But as he stood at the threshold of the new day, the name of Pansa felt more like the chain he had yet to unshackle.

* * *

The feast had stretched into the morning, as all good feasts do, and by the first hour of the day, *prima hora*, the city was alive with the sound of carts, horses and people going about their daily business. After his manumission, Petrinus had moved awkwardly about the house, trying to help in any way he could, though none of his slave family would allow him to. It felt wrong to him, like clothes that were too tight. Eventually, he'd given up and returned to his bed, falling asleep as soon as his head touched his poor excuse for a pillow, his first rest in 24 hours.

When he woke, there were a few disoriented seconds where he sensed something important had happened but he couldn't recall what, until he saw the red cap sitting neatly at his bedside. The room was flooded with sunlight. He was alone, the others already busy at work. It must have been late morning by now, he thought. Washing and dressing quickly, he smoothed out the folds of his tunic. As he sat down on the edge of his bed, holding the pileus in his hands, the door creaked open.

Simplex.

Sitting beside Petrinus on the bed, he said nothing at first, but only reached up to touch Petrinus' cheek, his hand warm and carrying the earthy scent of the soil he had spent the morning tending. Though he was Pansa's scribe and bookkeeper, he still helped out with chores around the house before the master rose for the day. Their eyes met, holding more than words could carry. Simplex's thumb stroked the small bristles of Petrinus' morning beard, as if committing the moment to memory. Then, with a small smile that almost masked the sadness behind it, he whispered, 'You'll do well.' They sat in peace for a moment, their foreheads pressing and hands clasped, aware that this might be the last time they could be alone together. Petrinus let Simplex's hand drop as he watched him leave.

In the atrium, many of Pansa's clients, men Petrinus had known for years, were already gathered, waiting their turn to be admitted to see him. Moving through the crowd, Petrinus made his way to the steps and passed behind the curtain of Pansa's *tablinum*. Inside, Pansa sat on his usual stool beside the strongbox holding his money and accounts, discussing the day's affairs with Simplex. The moment he saw Petrinus, Pansa's face lit up with a grin. Simplex avoided his gaze.

'Gaius Cuspius Petrinus, come in!' he beamed, gesturing to a stool before changing his mind and smoothly motioning to the stone step. 'Please, sit.'

Petrinus' face reddened with embarrassment as he lowered himself onto the cool marble. Even now he wasn't good enough for the furniture. He felt suddenly all too aware of his limbs.

'So, freedom, eh?' Pansa said. 'Welcome to your first patron-client meeting, the first of many. How does it feel?'

Petrinus cleared his throat. 'I am truly grateful, *domine*. And I will endeavour to continue to serve you as your client.'

'It's just what I do,' Pansa replied, adjusting the folds of his tunic. 'I'm a generous man. So, let's talk arrangements.'

He formally relinquished ownership of Petrinus' *peculium*, a respectable sum by any measure, then launched into a stream of practical advice, unsolicited but confidently delivered.

'You'll need somewhere to sleep,' Pansa said, leaning back. 'Try the rooms above my cousin's bakery. Clean enough, and cheap.

Though I'm not sure what the going rate is these days. I heard even that woman, Julia Felix, has some going these days. Bold creature, living off rents like a man. I wouldn't be seen dealing with her myself, but it's not like it'll besmirch your reputation.' A booming laugh escaped his mouth. Petrinus remained silent.

'Ask for the cheapest she's got, if there's any left. She began advertising in August so there may not be. You can stay here for the next day or two, while you look.'

Petrinus nodded, though this last part planted a seed of worry in his mind. 'Thank you, *domine*.'

'As for work, speak to the men at the *Forum Holitorium*. The vegetable traders there need hands, and you've a good head on your shoulders. It'll help that you can read. You *can* read, can't you?'

'Yes, *domine*.'

Pansa lowered his voice slightly, as though imparting something of real value. 'And wash properly. Hot water, not cold. Use oil and get a scrape down every now and then. You're a freedman now, you can't smell like the stables. And eat well. Perhaps ask Lavinia for some advice about cooking before you go.'

Petrinus managed a small, respectful nod. Clearly Pansa had no idea that he was capable of all these things. Petrinus caught the eye of Simplex who smiled a little, so small you could miss it.

'Anyway.' Pansa stood and gestured towards the door. 'That'll do for now. I've got real clients to see. I'd explain more to you, but it'd take all morning, and I haven't got that kind of time.'

Petrinus was surprised when Pansa followed him to the curtain leading into the atrium. A slave opened it as he approached.

'*Bona fortuna*, Gaius Cuspius Petrinus,' he declared as he passed through the curtain first, his voice booming and performative. 'I wish you all the best in your new life as a freedman bearing my name.'

The crowd of clients broke into applause, heads nodding and voices rising in praise of Pansa's generosity.

No one was looking at Petrinus. Nothing had really changed.

* * *

Since the meeting, Petrinus had been wandering the streets in a daze. No longer bound to work for Pansa, he spent his new free time dedicating an offering to Feronia in thanks for his freedom, and to Isis, for the memory of the priest's gaze lingered in his mind. But his first selfish act would be to revisit the *Caupona* of Euxinus, this time as a freedman.

The familiar smells of roasting meat and sour wine drifted into the street as he opened the door. Inside, the tavern was beginning to stir with the hum of early patrons and the clatter of cups on wooden tables. He hesitated as he crossed the threshold, awkward without a task or a basket in hand. Euxinus looked up, his eyes settling on the red *pileus* perched on Petrinus' head. His expression flickered with amusement.

'Well I never!' Euxinus threw his arms up in joy. 'Marvellous news. Congratulations on your manumission–' He hesitated.

'Petrinus.'

'Yes, of course! Gaius Cuspius Petrinus, now.'

The innkeeper reached for a jug and poured a cup of his homemade wine, before setting it down in front of Petrinus. 'An offering on the house, and a welcome into the world of the free.'

The wine was deep and mellow, not the kind he had most often tasted in slavery. He drank slowly, letting its warmth spread through him. The taste of freedom. A fresh portion of bread followed, no grit, no rough texture, just soft, well-baked loaves. As

THE INVISIBLE SLAVE

he left, Euxinus leaned out from the garden doorway and called after him. 'Take care, now. The ground beneath you isn't always as solid as it seems.'

As Petrinus walked through the streets, now approaching the seventh hour, words of congratulations reached him from passers-by. For years he had moved unnoticed, a presence without recognition. Now, the *pileus* both set him apart and made him one of them, one of the people. Freedom had made him *seen*.

His eyes skimmed the walls of each house he passed, looking for freshly painted tenancy notices. The irony struck him then. Only yesterday he'd been thinking about how gruelling the existence of the poor of Pompeii was, long hours simply to keep the wolf from the door, and sometimes even that wasn't enough. Unlike Simplex, trained as a scribe, Petrinus had never mastered a trade. Whatever work he found would have to be simple, though with luck he might make use of his one advantage, the ability to read, a skill uncommon even among the free.

He would go to the *Forum Holitorium* later, at the end of the working day when things were likely to be a little quieter. For now, the anxiety of having nowhere to live was pressing down upon him. After circling the nearby neighbourhoods, he turned back towards familiar ground, arriving at the estate of Julia Felix. Best to start high, even if disappointment was almost certain, and only then lower his sights to Pansa's cousin's cramped rooms above the bakery.

Julia's property took up an entire *insula*, its scale and grandeur vast and imposing. Behind high walls, the tops of fruit trees swayed in the breeze, offering glimpses of the verdant gardens beyond. Turning onto the narrow side street that led to the public entrance, Petrinus spotted what he'd been looking for. Scrawled across the façade in bold black letters, the notice stood out starkly against the sun-bleached plaster:

To let, in the estate of Julia Felix, daughter of Spurius: elegant Venus baths for respectable people, shops with upper rooms, and apartments. From 13 August next, to 13 August of the sixth year, for five continuous years. The lease will expire at the end of the five years.

It seemed ideal, if any apartments were still available. The month of Augustus had long passed, and the rent might be steep, but a businesswoman like Julia Felix likely had smaller lodgings elsewhere, tucked above shops or along quieter streets.* Stepping through the main entrance, Petrinus found the porter and stated his purpose. The man's eyes flicked to the *pileus*, then back to his face.

'You're in luck. *Domina* is open to receiving new business enquiries today. Out this way, turn left, and it's the last door on the way to the amphitheatre. Or,' he added, 'you're welcome to walk through the house and gardens. Follow the columns after this room.'

The porter turned to a small slave and told him to carry word to Julia that a freedman was on his way to discuss room rentals. Surprised to be welcome anywhere, and curious for a glimpse inside, Petrinus crossed into the peristyle as a slave ran past him towards the direction of Julia's private rooms. The air smelled of box hedge, flowers and damp earth, a welcome relief from the odours of the streets. Birds flitted between the branches of well-tended trees, their song blending with the trickle of water and the murmur of voices drifting over the walls. The plaster shone a vibrant yellow, its painted details fine and intricate, reminiscent of

---

* August was originally called *Sextilis* (the sixth month, because the year used to begin in March) but it was later renamed Augustus in 8 BCE in honour of the first Emperor of Rome.

THE INVISIBLE SLAVE

Figure 12: Advertisement outside the Estate of Julia Felix (II.4.2-3) advertising properties for rent and use

those in Pansa's house. A long, elegant water feature, much like a river, stretched along the garden's centre, its marble surfaces gleaming in the early golden sun. Beneath the rippling surface, fish darted in and out of the shadows, their movements quick and fluid, vanishing as suddenly as they appeared.

For a moment, Petrinus let it wash over him: the hush of shaded colonnades, the shimmer of painted walls, the scent of earth and blooms, a beauty meant for leisure, not labour. But just as quickly, reality came crashing back, panic tightening in his chest. He was out of place, completely beyond his depth. He had known nothing beyond the walls of Pansa's household. What was he doing, enquiring after a property on Julia Felix's estate? He might have his *peculium*, but he had no job, no income, no plan. What was meant to be a new beginning suddenly felt vast, a gaping and terrifying hole of uncertainty before him.

The ground beneath him seemed to shift. Petrinus steadied himself against one of the columns, his breath shallow and uneven. He told himself it was just the panic, the rush of uncertainty, the weight of everything changing too fast. All of it felt unreal, as if he were slipping out of step with the world around him.

Then came the sound.

Low at first, a deep, rolling tremor that seemed to press in from all sides. The birds shrieked, bursting from the trees in a frantic swarm; another earthquake, Petrinus thought with dread. To his right, a figure stumbled into view.

Julia Felix.

She erupted from the private wing of her house, the controlled feminine elegance and composure of one of her station gone as the tremor grew underneath them. Her *stola* twisted around her legs as she moved, her chest rising and falling in sharp, shallow breaths as her trembling hands reached out to the wall. He'd seen her many times before, but not like this. Their eyes met briefly, and he saw the panic in them.

Then, the world of tranquillity around them ripped open.

A deafening crack tore through the air, and the ground buckled. Slaves darted from doors, their eyes ascending to the sky above them. Somewhere behind Petrinus, stone groaned and shattered as a column crashed down, sending shards of marble skidding across the floor. Another tremor, violent and unstoppable, split the ground below his feet.

Run.

He didn't think, he just moved, dodging falling debris as the walkway collapsed around him. He barely made it to the open space of the garden before the next tremor struck, the earth rippling like a storm-tossed sea.

Breathless, his heart hammering, Petrinus turned to see Julia standing amidst the hedges, her hands clutching the folds of her *stola* as if holding herself together. But she wasn't looking at him. She was looking up.

Her lips parted and her whole body seemed to shrink at what she saw before her.

Petrinus followed her gaze.

A monstrous column of black smoke was unfurling from the mountain, twisting ominously into the heavens, swallowing the sun in its thick, churning mass. It rose higher and higher, unstoppable, and devoured the world above.

CHAPTER TWO

THE WEALTHY BUSINESSWOMAN

THE SEVENTH HOUR (12 NOON), 23 OCTOBER 79 CE

Julia Felix went against the grain of what was expected of a female in Roman society, which only made her more determined to make that grain into bread. It had been three centuries since the law was passed enabling women to be named as the sole beneficiaries of another's will and therefore to own property. Yet it had done little to change the role women played in a society built by men.

As a highly spiritual woman, Julia found this disparity odd. Though Jupiter reigned supreme on Mount Olympus, it was Juno, his queen, who called the shots. It was she who manipulated her husband to get her way, she who took out enemies at will. It was Helen whose face launched a thousand ships, beginning a war that would change history. It was Minerva, the goddess of wisdom, skill and strategy, who shaped outcomes not through force, but through careful planning and foresight. Dido, though mortal, was a queen in her own right, founding Carthage by turning words into walls and negotiation into power. She had carved her own path and built her own city, proving that tenacity and wit could achieve what an army could not.

Julia saw something of herself in these women, in the subtle mastery of influence. She had not become this way by choice, but by necessity. In business, and in the Roman world more generally, a smart woman let others believe they held the upper hand while keeping her true power just beneath the surface.

In the shade of a plane tree, Julia sat on the curved bench of an imposing, multi-tiered tomb, an *exedra*, just beyond Pompeii's southernmost gate. It did not belong to her, nor to her family, but to Eumachia, one of the city's most formidable women. The terrace overlooked the burial enclosures of Eumachia's kin, where stone herms, slender pillars topped with weathered faces, kept their eternal vigil among the dead. A frieze of Amazonian warriors in battle stretched across the space, locked in a struggle that embodied feminine strength and defiance. It was a fitting tribute to a woman who had secured her place in Pompeii, navigating the constraints of her station with skill and resolve.

Eumachia's influence had peaked some 40 years ago, when she had held the prestigious role of priestess of Venus, the patron goddess of Pompeii, a position which brought its own unique status and power. But Eumachia had been more than just a religious figure. She had inherited a considerable fortune from her father, Lucius Eumachius, whose success in large-scale brick manufacturing had come at the perfect moment, just as the Empire expanded under Augustus' direction, and colonies across Italy and beyond required Roman builders to shape their new cities. Not content to rest on her inheritance, Eumachia had secured her future by marrying into one of Pompeii's oldest families, the Numistii Frontones. Her wealth and their connections had left a mark on the city in the most prominent of places: the forum.

THE WEALTHY BUSINESSWOMAN

Together with her son, Marcus Numistrius Fronto, she had gifted Pompeii a forecourt, crypt and portico walkway with an elegant façade and dedicated it to *Concordia Augusta* and *Pietas*, goddesses of harmony within the imperial family and religious devotion. The symbolism had not been lost on Julia, nor on any member of the elite who understood the language of politics.

The building itself spoke volumes. The carved acanthus leaves around its entrance echoed the famous *Ara Pacis* in Rome, Augustus' great altar of peace. The statues inside, including one of Eumachia dedicated by the town fullers, emulated Rome's grand Portico of Livia, built by Augustus for his wife some 50 or so years before.* Aligning herself with the emperor's family was a bold statement. Many thought her ambitions unusual, even improper, but Julia understood. The building was not only a gift to the people: it was a declaration of Eumachia's role in Pompeii's economy, and her lasting legacy.

Eumachia had become close to a local legend, evidence of what a woman *could* achieve within the empire's rigid structures. And yet, Julia had always found Eumachia's tomb curious: the inscription stated she had paid for it herself. This woman of status, a public priestess of Venus and a benefactor who had given the city a grand hall in the forum, had been left to finance her own burial.† Others, who had done far less for Pompeii, had been honoured with public tombs, their names immortalised at the expense of the

---

* Construction of the Portico of Livia began in 15 BCE and it was dedicated in 7 BCE. A symbolic theme which ran throughout the rule of Augustus and Livia was abundance, signified by verdant plants and fruits. The same symbolism can be found on Eumachia's building.

† Eumachia was also the matron of the fullers' guild, launderers responsible for cleaning and dyeing clothing. This has traditionally given the Eumachia Building its supposed use. However, historians now think that this large space in the forum was likely being used as a slave market in 79 CE.

people. Power, it seemed, did not always guarantee remembrance. Unless you were a man.

As Julia sat on the bench belonging to the woman who so often crossed her mind, her fingers traced the cool stone, which had grown rough over the years. For the first time in a long while, Julia was alone. She had left behind her usual entourage of slaves and advisors, taking only her most trusted slave, who lingered a few paces away. The steady rhythm of mule-drawn carts passing in and out of the city was a welcome reprieve from the din of Pompeii's streets, the shouting of merchants, the wails of children and the ever-present cacophony of competitive traders. She breathed in the warm, dusty air and allowed herself a moment of stillness.

To the people of Pompeii, Julia was an enigma. Her name hinted at a link to the Julian family, to Julius Caesar himself, deified and distant, but also to a past shaped by servitude and freedom. Felix was a name often chosen by freed people, and Julia bore it proudly. She called herself the daughter of Spurius, a name that could mean illegitimate, or simply unknown; she liked to let people draw their own conclusions. Some said she was born outside of marriage, others that she was once enslaved. Either way, she stood apart from most Roman women: unmarried, wealthy and in control.

Speculation about her birth followed her, but so did the evidence of her success. In the aftermath of the great earthquake 17 years before, Julia had spotted an opportunity. She had built apartments, bathhouses and gardens in a sprawling complex opposite the amphitheatre, drawing residents from across the city and catering to Pompeii's social elite and expanding merchant class alike. Those who rented the spaces of her *praedia*, or estate, as well as those who walked or drove past it daily, understood that Julia had defied the expectations of what a woman might achieve in Pompeii by build-

THE WEALTHY BUSINESSWOMAN

ing this subtle empire. Though her origins remained a mystery to most, her impact on the city was undeniable.

Leaving Eumachia's tomb behind, Julia took the short walk back into the city, following the uneven stones worn smooth by many years of use. Carts groaned past her, their iron-covered wheels jolting over the ruts and clattering with goods destined for the bustling markets. Travellers moved in both directions, some alone, others in lively groups, bantering as they went. From the arch of the city

Figure 13: Detail of a fresco showing Omphale from the House of the Prince of Montenegro (VII.16.10)

gate, a shepherd emerged guiding a flock of sheep he had been trying to sell at the market in the forum. His crook rested on his shoulder as his sharp-eyed dog crouched low, darting at the edges of the flock to keep the ewes in line. Together, man and beast were a perfect tableau of the rustic ideal so beloved by Rome's poets and philosophers, a vision of simplicity and order.

Julia's home lay close to the great expanse surrounding Pompeii's amphitheatre in the south-eastern corner of the city, the neighbourhood known for its many lush gardens, vineyards and orchards. The streets buzzed with activity as she passed through them, the air alive with the anticipation of the impending games that evening.

Julia stood out from the average person on the street. Her coiffed hair was delicately arranged and tied with a soft silk ribbon at the nape of her neck, creating a colourful band across the top of her head. Her earrings, gold with two white pearls dangling below, framed her long, round face and soft jawline, and a simple gold chain necklace adorned her slender neck. As she passed below the arch into the open area near the amphitheatre, Julia adjusted her buttercup-yellow *palla*, a light cloak which provided modesty in public, which she wore over a simple light-blue *stola*. The scent of roasted nuts and spiced wine blended with the earthy tang of dust dampened by the previous night's rain.

Years earlier, Julia had had a hand in transforming the bustling thoroughfare outside her property. Removing the noisy road that once brought the clatter of carts and the chaos of traffic, the town had pedestrianised the space, creating a tranquil environment for walking, socialising and trading. Vendors, drawn by the games, now filled the broad, inviting area with temporary stalls, adding colour and life to this carefully curated corner of the city.

Framed by two cypress trees, Julia's garden entrance faced the amphitheatre, the gate thrown wide today as a deliberate invitation to passers-by. Opening her lush grounds served a dual purpose: it flaunted the estate's beauty and advertised the baths and apartments available to rent. The gardens, planted in orderly rows, were tended by a small team of skilled gardeners. Flower beds bloomed beneath canopies of fruit trees of fig, pomegranate, pear and apple, all of which were bare after the recent autumn harvest.* Just weeks earlier, their branches had been heavy with fruit and the estate's kitchen had worked for days preserving the bounty in honey and oil, stockpiling for the winter. They had steeped the pomegranates in hot seawater, the salt helping with preservation, before hanging them up to dry from rafters and doorways.

Even in mid-October, Julia's garden was a masterpiece. Bursting with life, its late-blooming flowers wove a tapestry of colour and scent. Beyond the fruit trees, trellises of grapevines stretched across sunny patches. Near the entrance, neatly arranged beds of thyme, rosemary and other herbs released their fragrance, waiting to be used by the cook, or as a sacrifice at one of the house altars. The pathways wound throughout the garden, and the box hedges, shaped by her trusted *topiarii*, topiary trimmers from Rome, exuded a woody, fresh aroma. She inhaled deeply, closing her eyes. That scent had always been one of her favourites.

As Julia passed through the gate, she turned to the young female slave beside her.

---

* We don't know the exact kinds of trees that were in this garden. When excavators examined this area, their reports did not mention the nature of the root cavities found here and they were not preserved for later excavators, nor was pollen analysis possible. However, regular flower beds were noted with tree cavities around their edges. We do know, however, what types of trees and plants were likely growing here from archaeological remains and wall paintings elsewhere in the town.

'Make sure the stewards are ready,' she said. 'I'll be inspecting the baths shortly.' The slave nodded.

'Once the inspection's done,' Julia added, her voice lifting with a hint of excitement, 'I'd like you to walk through the whole estate and note anything that needs my attention. I want nothing out of place.'

'Yes, *domina*.' The slave's pace quickened to overtake Julia.

Julia's gaze drifted across the courtyard, already picturing the space transformed. 'Tomorrow will be important. The worshippers will gather here, to initiate Octavius Quartio into the cult of Isis.'

The slave looked up, eyebrows raised. 'Your neighbour?'*

Julia gave a satisfied nod. 'Yes. Priest Amisusius said he has received the call. They'd planned to use one of the public baths for the sacred rite, but when I suggested our own …' She smiled. 'He agreed without hesitation.'†

'That is a great honour, *domina*.'

'It is,' Julia said simply. 'And one I have earned.'

The baths on her estate had once been a private luxury for the household alone, but opening them to paying clients had been one of Julia's shrewdest decisions. With the nearby public baths still in disrepair after the great quake, she had spotted a gap in the market and filled it quickly. The investment had been worth every *sestertius*. The rooms were elegant, the service impeccable, and those who came paid well for the privilege of exclusivity. Her slaves ensured that every visitor left feeling indulged.

---

* Initiation into the cult of Isis marked a personal commitment to the goddess, though priesthood was a separate, higher role that required additional status, training and often a public position within the temple community. Most initiates were ordinary people seeking a deeper spiritual connection or divine protection.

† The initiation rite required the cleansing of the initiate at a public bath. Julia's estate, with its own public baths, strong signs of Isis worship, and close location to the Temple of Isis, would have been a perfect candidate for such an event.

THE WEALTHY BUSINESSWOMAN

Along the far garden wall stood Julia's private shrine to Isis, a narrow-arched *sacrarium* no more than a step or two across, its walls alive with colour and meaning. On the shelf at the back, a terracotta lamp burned low, its fragrant smoke curling upward to the vents in the vaulted ceiling. Painted serpents slithered through lush green foliage towards an altar beneath Isis, crowned with a crescent moon and lotus, a *sistrum* in one hand and a vase in the

Figure 14: The sacrarium *found in the inner garden of the Estate of Julia Felix (II.4.3)*

other. She was flanked by Anubis with his jackal head and palm frond, and Serapis with the horn of plenty, the *cornucopia*. On one wall, another serpent kept watch beside an image of Julia offering fruit and eggs; on another, Fortuna balanced on a globe beside Harpocrates, keeper of secrets, his finger held to his lips in secrecy. Lighting the lamps, Julia lingered over her favourite piece: a silver-leafed bronze tripod lantern, its three legs imitating those of half-men, half-goat satyrs, who leant forwards in mischievous defiance, their cloven hooves poised as if guarding the sacred space. In the warm glow of the *sacrarium*, the world beyond seemed to melt away.

Julia moved her fingers along the slender marble shelf on the wall and adjusted each object in its place. A glass vase with a delicate handle stood at the centre, flanked by a crescent of polished silver and a round gold *fibula* brooch that caught the light. Nearby, two coins bore the resolute face of Emperor Vespasian, with three more showing the worn profiles of his family. A headless marble woman with Cupid on her shoulder stood beside a small ivory figurine inscribed as a gift from a dear friend. But her favourites were a bronze Priapus, guardian of the garden and an emblem of luck and fertility, and a silver Harpocrates. Smiling, she stepped back to regard the shrine, each piece chosen with care to reflect her devotion to the goddess Isis.

* * *

Julia stepped out onto the bustling street through her property's main door. This entrance, located on the quiet end of the Via dell'Abbondanza, was closest to the shops and baths that formed the northern part of her estate. Passing a public fountain on her way to the city centre, its cool water trickling over worn stone, she nodded a greeting to a woman with children about her feet who

THE WEALTHY BUSINESSWOMAN

Figure 15: Marine fresco from the House of Venus in the Shell (II.3.3)

was filling a terracotta *amphora*. Just beyond the fountain stood the house of Julia's friend, Decimus Lucretius Satrius Valens. His father, a man who shared his name with his son, had once been a perpetual priest of the Emperor Nero, though he had quietly dropped this title after the emperor's downfall, brought on by excess and cruelty. Julia considered his garden to be among the most beautiful in Pompeii. Decorating the far wall was a painting of Venus reclining in a vast clam shell, her ankles kissed by the bright blue waters of the Mediterranean. Around her, cupids frolicked on the crests of the waves, astride leaping dolphins, their playful forms frozen in paint and plaster.

Further down, on the opposite side of the street, the doors to the headquarters of the military association, the *Schola Armaturarum*, stood wide open.* From the shade of the entrance corridor came the gritty scrape of blades drawn across whetstones and the metallic

---

* This property was heavily bombed during the Second World War and suffered significant damage in 2010 due to rainfall, and other parts are still to be excavated. However, multiple amphorae with written labels on them were found in rear rooms of the property.

chime of armour plates being fastened. A pair of sun-browned veterans with weathered faces stood near the doorway, oiling helmets in slow, practised strokes. Further inside, shadows moved as men hauled in a delivery of *amphorae* and *unguentaria* holding wine and fish sauce, the jars knocking dully together as they were shuffled along.

Julia's glance lingered a moment too long. One of the younger men near the door caught her eye and grinned, pushing away from the wall with a confident swagger. The mood shifted; a whistle cut through the voices, followed by a loud, mocking toast. From somewhere inside came the shout: 'Take off your tunic and show us what's underneath!'

Before he could reach her, one of the older veterans called him back, his tone clipped: 'Leave it, that's Julia Felix.' A ripple of recognition passed through the group, met by another crude remark. She tried to ignore it as she stepped up to the home of her friend, Sutoria Primigenia, its doorway open to the afternoon light.

Just inside, Sutoria's old porter slave, Astylus, sat slumped in his chair, snoozing peacefully. As she stepped over the threshold, her gaze drifted to a notice on the wall beside the entrance, a painted election endorsement by Sutoria calling for the election of Lucius Ceius Secundus to *duumvir* from the previous year. Below it, someone had hastily scrawled: 'Astylus, are you sleeping?' Clearly, the *scriptor* hired to write the original notice had been met with much the same scene as she was now. The corner of her mouth lifted as she passed out of sight of the street, and the whistling men, behind her.

A fellow worshipper of Isis, Sutoria had shaped her house into a statement of devotion and tradition. The air inside was cool and scented with fresh flowers, and from inside wall niches, lamps flickered. Beyond the atrium, a wide window opened into the dining room where she and Sutoria had so often recreated their own

THE WEALTHY BUSINESSWOMAN

female *symposia*, nights of wine and debate, free from the scrutiny of men, their talk turning freely to politics, trade and the hazards of business.

To the left of the window, a door revealed Sutoria's small rear garden, its vine-shaded *triclinium* a private refuge. In the rear wall stood a shrine to Athena, the ash now cool from the recent offering. Julia could see the words THEODOR MAS across the front of the shrine, referring to the virility of Sutoria's son, Theodosus. In the corner, Sutoria had also installed a second shrine fashioned like a small building, much like the one in Julia's own garden, complete with a small altar inside. From where she stood in the atrium, Julia could see the door to the kitchen. She could picture the fresco above the hearth in her mind's eye.

A saddled mule and a bull processed solemnly towards a sacrifice, where Sutoria and her husband reigned as *materfamilias* and *paterfamilias*. Sutoria was in the guise of Juno, leading their family

Figure 16: Fresco depicting the Caristia festival from the kitchen wall of the House of Sutoria Primigenia (I.13.2)

in the *Caristia*, the day that followed the *Parentalia*, the feast of the dead, when families would come together to share a meal and honour the *lares*, or household gods. Julia knew this was no ordinary decoration. It marked a reunion once celebrated in the past, and now, with her husband gone, it stood as a memorial to that moment, a tribute to the unity Sutoria had lost, and the bond she was determined to preserve.

The city had whispered, expecting Sutoria to remarry after observing the 10-month mourning period, as custom dictated. But instead, she had seized her widowhood as an opportunity, choosing independence over convention. With only a guardian to oversee financial transactions when required, Sutoria had relished the freedom that came with it.*

When Sutoria appeared, she looked radiant, her cheeks aglow with homemade rouge and a light kohl around her eyes. 'You look well,' Julia said, leaning in to kiss her cheek. 'Rested. Better than I last saw you with that chest cold you were developing.'

'I had an early bath late morning, before the crowds arrived,' Sutoria replied, smiling. 'It helped. My physician prescribed chicken soup and a concoction of horse saliva and honey. It goes without saying that the soup was the better of the two.'

She crossed to the wooden cabinet in the atrium and opened it, revealing a collection of colourful glass perfume bottles. Her fingers moved carefully along the rows until she found the one she was looking for: a dark violet *unguentarium* bottle, shaped like a cluster of grapes. It caught the light as she held it out. '*Kyphi*,' she said.

Julia took it gently and, pulling out the stopper, breathed in deeply.

---

* As with many people in the city, we have no idea whether Sutoria Primigenia was unmarried or widowed, but the political endorsement in her name suggests that she was not attached to a male figure, much like Julia.

THE WEALTHY BUSINESSWOMAN

'It smells like the temple.'

Sutoria nodded. 'I bought it in the perfume garden near the amphitheatre, the one with the grapevines growing over the *triclinium* in the garden. The woman who sold it to me said it was blended in the Egyptian style. Frankincense, honey, myrrh, cinnamon, saffron … raisins soaked in wine. All pressed together with resins.'* She smiled. 'It's made to rise slowly, like a prayer.'

Julia closed her eyes, letting the scent settle over her. 'It carries Egypt with it,' she whispered.

After taking some watered-down spiced wine together, the pair left the calm of Sutoria's home and stepped onto the bustle of the Via dell'Abbondanza, the street narrowing as they went. A familiar voice called out, and Julia turned to see Faustilla the moneylender striding towards them, a slave close behind her, his arms full of wooden writing tablets.

'*Salve*, ladies. Have either of you seen Pomaria of late? She left a gold earring with me as collateral for 32 *asses* on the fifteenth of July, but I've not heard from her since.'

'I've not seen her trading at the market for weeks. Perhaps it's time to sell to the goldsmiths,' Sutoria said.

'I heard she'd started working at the *lupanar* to pay off her debts,' Julia added. 'One of my tenants swore he saw her by the main brothel by the forum the other week.'

Faustilla shook her head. 'I can't say I'm surprised. What choice does she have? Two kids at home and her husband away on campaign.' She hesitated before adding, 'Better the brothel than being forced to work the streets and inns. At least she'll have a room there.'

---

* The earliest recipe for *Kyphi* comes from the Ebers Papyrus (c. 1500 BCE).

They both knew what that meant: a narrow cell with a hard bed, a small oil lamp, and little else. Gods only knew where the children went during working hours. The *lupanar*'s walls were crowded with crude graffiti: boasts of clients and prices scrawled beside names, below paintings of various positions to try out with a girl. Prostitution was a trade without honour. Most of the women inside were slaves, but debt could drive a freeborn woman there too. Sometimes it was a temporary measure, though leaving was not always as simple as entering.

'Well, that's life.' Faustilla shrugged as she carried on her way.

The two friends watched her go, then walked on in companionable silence. Following an alleyway that sloped gently downhill, they emerged onto a backstreet near the garden district. At the crossroads, carts rattled past in both directions and drivers shouted over the din of wheels on stone. Julia and Sutoria stepped across on the raised stones, their hems lifted clear of the muck. Ahead, the

Figure 17: The Temple of Isis, with its alleyway to the left, leading down to the Greek Theatre District

temple and theatre district rose in stately prominence, the roof of the Temple of Isis coming into view. Its upper edges shone in the bright afternoon light, and behind it, the grand Greek Theatre loomed. At the far end of the street, people streamed in and out of the garden beside the Triangular Forum, and from the small public baths next door. As they approached the temple doors – large, wooden and folded back to welcome worshippers – Julia and Sutoria ascended the two low steps, leaving the restless pulse of the city behind. In the courtyard, the familiar rhythms of the afternoon ceremony were already beginning.

* * *

After seeing the daily veiling of the statue of Isis, now to remain shrouded until the next morning, Julia returned home to find her garden transformed. During festivals and games, it was not uncommon for such spaces to be temporarily given over to vendors, especially this close to the amphitheatre. Makeshift stalls lined the pathways, taking advantage of the passing crowds drawn to the games, and smoke curled into the air from small braziers, the rich smells of roasting nuts and meat ascending to the heavens. The rumble of voices was punctuated by the jingle of money in pouches hanging from belts and the occasional bark of laughter.

Julia sliced a path through the throng, nodding here and there to familiar faces, her attendance both commanding and warmly received. She moved towards her preferred sunny area in the main garden, just beyond the stalls, where the steady movement of visitors offered a natural point for business. Here, tenants, bath patrons and acquaintances could approach her openly, to exchange news, petition for help, or request a loan. Her financial guardian was supposed to be there to approve large financial transactions, though in truth his role was a legal formality few independent women bothered to observe. Secundus, her round-bodied head slave with red, calloused hands, sat on a cushion in the grass nearby with a double-leaved wax tablet balanced on his knee, ready to record whatever was agreed. Julia took a seat on a wooden stool next to him.

As she discussed arrangements for the ceremony tomorrow, Secundus etched the words she spoke into the surface of the wax, using the flat end of the stylus to erase any mistakes as he went. As Julia finished praising them for their work, a ruddy face appeared before them. It was one of her less fortunate tenants, Marcus, who cared for one of her orchards in the city. This was yet another of Julia's ingenious adaptations of city space, when she had repurposed it from a collection of houses into an olive grove.*

'Afternoon, *domina*,' he greeted her, eyes shadowed with worry. 'The press has given out. Won't turn a drop until I have the carpenter replace the beam, and he won't work without coins in hand first.'

Julia listened as he detailed the effect this would have on production and thought of her profits. Gesturing to Secundus, she instructed him to count out the required coins and pass them to Marcus. Seeing this, a man passing through the garden slowed his step, frowning. 'Financial business without your guardian?' he remarked, loud enough for others to hear.

Julia offered no reply, but rose from her chair, leading Secundus and Marcus through the arch to the inner garden, away from curi-

---

* Though we have no idea what other businesses Julia ran, aside from the baths, shops and apartments, it is plausible that she would have a hand in some nearby orchards. Clearly she had a keen interest in gardening, so it would be nice to think she would have been one of the many landowners and landlords to invest in the gardens just a stone's throw from her home. Sadly, though, we do not know the names of any of the owners of the gardens in this neighbourhood.

ous ears. There was always one. There was no use in replying to their ignorant comments; it would only draw more unwanted attention. She came to a stop within the high walls of her secluded inner garden, reserved for her guests and tenants. At the far end, two stools and a small table waited for occasions that required discretion. Upon one sat her guardian, his posture stiff and ceremonial.

'Nice of you to show, Titus. Just in time to prevent the obnoxious comments of the wonderful Pompeian public.'

'If I'd known you planned to scandalise the city before the end of the working day, I'd have come earlier.'

She smirked but said nothing more. The business at hand was concluded quickly; Marcus left with the pouch of coins. For a little while after, Julia concluded the signing of contracts for her purchase of a property across town. Once the final signatures were scribbled into the wax of the writing tablet, her guardian withdrew to see to other matters. The courtyard fell quiet again, the only sound the trickle of water from the central fountain. Julia remained still for a moment, her gaze fixed on the rippling water at the centre of her inner sanctum. Sometimes her loneliness hit her. Life was difficult for men in power, certainly, but for women on their own it took so much energy just to maintain the composure and dignity expected of them while also remaining successful. The effort was exhausting. How did women like Eumachia do it?

The last streaks of gold faded from the sky, and Julia retreated down the steps into the private living area of her home, where her slaves were already waiting to change her attire for the cooler evening air. She allowed them to replace her lighter day tunic with a more elegant *stola* of a soft but thicker fabric. A delicate *palla*, pinned with a gold *fibula* brooch, was draped over her shoulders as a final touch of refinement.

At her cosmetic table, a polished bronze mirror reflected Julia's face in the flickering lamplight. Her maid opened a small glass jar of powdered malachite, tracing a fine line of green along Julia's eyelids, enhancing the depth of her gaze. A hint of rouge brightened her lips and cheeks, its subtle flush mimicking the glow of a younger woman. She dipped her fingertips in scented oil, a rich blend of myrrh and spikenard, and dabbed it lightly at her wrists and throat.

By the time Julia emerged, the Egyptian *triclinium* overlooking the garden was aglow, the warm light of lanterns casting soft shadows over the frescoed walls. Tonight, she had invited her circle of female friends to dine, a welcome opportunity to gather and let their conversation flow while the rest of the town enjoyed the games. As the evening's guests began to arrive, they absentmind-

Figure 18: Marble triclinium in the Estate of Julia Felix (II.4.2-3) with Egyptian motifs decorating the walls

edly slipped off their *pallae*, knowing that a slave would catch them, and exchanged easy laughter as they settled on to the low couches, each covered in the most beautiful array of fabrics and cushions.

Among them was Lucretia Valens, a woman of considerable influence whose family gave much to public life in Pompeii, including some of the most legendary gladiatorial games in the city's history. It was her family member's neighbouring home that Julia admired so much, with the fresco of Venus in the shell. Then there was Cornelia, of the powerful Cornelii family, renowned for their political influence in Rome and their sponsorship of local events, and Holconia, priestess of Ceres and daughter of the politician Marcus Holconius Rufus. She was among the lucky few women who had been memorialised in stone in the city. At the main crossroads on the Via dell'Abbondanza, in the arch dedicated to the legacy of the Holconii, her father had devoted a statue with the inscription, 'To Holconia, daughter of Marcus, public priestess'.

Sutoria Primigenia was at the feast too, alongside Trebia, a matron from the Trebii family, one of the city's wealthiest whose roots stretched back to before the Roman conquest and whose influence had seen a resurgence in recent years. Then there was Caecilia, daughter of Pompeii's former leading banker, Caecilius Iucundus, who had died in the great quake, and Obelia, of the ancient Oscan family, still highly respected in the town. Completing the gathering was Naevoleia Tyche, the widow of a suburban official, prosperous merchant and a beloved member of the *Augustales*, Gaius Munatius Faustus.*

---

* Aside from Holconia, Sutoria Primigenia and Naevoleia Tyche, whose lives are all attested, the women in this gathering are fictional composites. Their names are drawn from prominent Pompeian families, reflecting the type of inherited status that shaped the city's social fabric.

Julia's female slaves, each chosen for their beauty, moved with precision as they brought in platters of roasted meats, dishes of lentils spiced with cumin, and fruit piled high in intricate arrangements. The first cups of wine were poured, their sharp tang mellowed with honey and perfumed with herbs. Behind the couches, water cascaded from a small fountain, its trickle blending with the music and conversation before pooling into a shallow basin within reach of the diners' outstretched hands. Small plates of dishes were floating there, a delightfully whimsical addition to the ambience of her very own *nymphaeum*.*

Julia reclined at the uppermost position of the host's couch to the left, the *lectus imus*. From here, she had a clear view of her eight guests, seated to face inwards in a circle of conversation and camaraderie. As the evening unfolded, her expression softened, the weight of the day's transactions, planning and jibes slipping away, replaced by satisfaction as her friends laughed and clinked glass goblets of deep blues, vibrant yellows and sharp greens.

Julia watched Naevoleia Tyche, resplendent in a light blue *palla* over a *chiton stola*, her wavy hair framing her face and her earrings rattling, as she quizzed Sutoria on her new Roman hairstyle.† She was the embodiment of female ambition in Pompeii. Her husband had built a twin tomb, complete with an interior courtyard, alongside a fellow *Augustalis* as a public display of status and political alliance around 19 years ago. Though that tomb had space for her, and despite her unquestioned devotion to him, Naevoleia had commissioned a separate one across the city for herself and her freedmen and women.‡

---

* A *nymphaeum* was a monument dedicated or consecrated to water nymphs, especially those of springs. They were usually designed to have a grotto-like feel.
† This is how Naevoleia Tyche is depicted on her tomb.
‡ Naevoleia Tyche's tomb was a large, accessible enclosure with a marble funer-

THE WEALTHY BUSINESSWOMAN

Figure 19: Female banqueting scene from the Fullonica of Sestius Venustus (I.3.18)

It was no vanity project but a masterstroke of self-definition. Naevoleia had paid for the monument and overseen its construction, and had ensured her authorship was unmistakable, placing her name first in the inscription, before her husband's. This was her tomb, designed to showcase the role she had played in the achievements of her *familia*, and to record her status and benefactions on her own behalf, just as a man might. Because like all of them, her

ary altar on a pedestal, featuring reliefs depicting a public distribution of money and a ship under sail, likely referencing her wealth and trade connections. No remains were found in the tomb, suggesting that she had not yet died at the time of the eruption.

story mattered too, and now she was shaping it, stone by stone, ensuring no man's name would shield her from memory.*

The conversation soon turned to the mysteries of Egypt as the scenes of lush gardens, fearsome crocodiles and mischievous pygmies adorning the walls drew the eyes of Julia's guests. Julia traced the rim of her glass with a finger as Cornelia knelt up on the plush cushions to inspect a scene of pygmies in a boat, destined to be victims either of the crocodile which loomed out of the water below, or of the menacing pygmy pointing a bow and arrow in their direction.

'Did you know,' Cornelia began, her tone hushed yet eager, 'that the Nile rises every year with the tears of Isis as she mourns Osiris?'

Holconia tilted her head, considering the image. 'Then her grief must be a blessing,' she said. 'For those tears bring the flood that feeds Egypt's fields and fills Rome's granaries.'

Trebia added with a sly smile, 'As long as it's enough to keep half of Rome from rioting. That's all we care about really.'

Laughter rippled through the room. Sutoria, always one for practicality, gestured towards a fresco of Isis draped in flowing robes. 'I wonder how many of those Alexandrian merchants owe their fortunes to our goddess,' she said. 'The cult of Isis protects the men of Rome as they travel on the oceans, after all.'

'Speaking of which,' Obelia cut in. 'My linen shipment is still sitting at Puteoli. The dockmaster wants a bribe before it will leave port.'

'I'll speak to my father for you, Obelia,' Holconia declared as she plucked an oyster from the tray of a passing slave. 'He should be able to call in a favour with his client in the shippers' guild. They're

---

* Naevoleia's reception in modern scholarship has often carried a negative undertone, with her ambition interpreted as overreaching.

THE WEALTHY BUSINESSWOMAN

apparently meeting at Herculaneum next week. Otherwise, he knows plenty of merchants who will be able to pull a few strings. I'll send a slave to you to let you know when it's arranged.'*

'If only the wool merchants were as easy to sway,' Naevoleia said, rolling her eyes. 'The Tarentine ship with my last order never even made it to Pompeii. They sold the whole cargo in Naples for a better price. I knew I should have kept my husband's name on the contract. They'd rather sell to some low-born merchant than to a woman.'

Caecilia chipped in: 'My father always did warn me, "Never count a coin until it's in your hand."'

'I should probably take his advice,' Julia replied. 'One of my tenants claims his olive press needs repair, but we all know he could just share the press that all the other gardeners use in town. I gave him the loan, but it'll cost him. Which reminds me …'

Julia began to relay the story of the passer-by reprimanding her for conducting financial business without her guardian present, which brought up a whole series of similar experiences from her companions. This was why she enjoyed evenings like these, gatherings where business mixed seamlessly with myth, and where the wealth of stories was as rich as the wine in their cups. Laughter and talk flowed as free as the wine as they wound their way from the gossip of elite circles to practical advice about managing unruly suppliers.

These were women who, like Julia, had secured their place in Pompeii. Most of them had done so not only through wealth and family connection, but through shrewd business acumen and an unblinking awareness of the reality of the world around them.

---

* A graffito in Herculaneum appears to advertise 'the meeting place in Puteoli – the Herculanean small-boat owners', perhaps referring to a meeting ('conclave') which will happen in the major port.

Most of their families were as old as the city's stones, their names woven into the fabric of Pompeian politics, trade and religion. Yet, for all their inherited status, these women had not simply drifted in the wake of their ancestors. Each, in her own way, had worked the rules men had set, playing the game as it was written, and winning more often than those same men liked to admit. They did not seek to overturn the order of things. Why would they, when they had learned to make it serve them? For all its flaws and fragility, this city, with its gardens and streets, still offered them opportunities.

As the feast drew to a close, Julia's female companions said their farewells and left en masse with their lantern-carrying slaves for safety and modesty. When the large door eventually shut, Julia gave her slaves final instructions for cleaning up after the meal, ensuring that they understood the arrangements for the initiation tomorrow morning.

'Everyone will be arriving at dawn for the ritual bath,' Julia reminded them, as they busied themselves cleaning and preparing. 'Everything must be ready before then. If you have to work through the night, so be it.'

The faint sound of straggling street revellers and carts carrying late-night deliveries drifted over the walls into the columned portico of Julia's garden. The lamps flickered as she swept past them towards her sleeping quarters. Her personal attendants, all young women, began to prepare their mistress for bed; one helped untie her sandals, kneeling as she worked the knots loose and set them aside. Another brought a shallow bronze basin of water, its surface rippling as fragrant oils were added. Julia dipped her hands in, the soothing scent of lavender and rosewood rising gently as she washed away the day.

While one slave attended to the basin, another unfastened the delicate brooch that held Julia's *stola* in place. The garment slipped

THE WEALTHY BUSINESSWOMAN

from her shoulders, and the attendant neatly folded it and set it inside a wooden cabinet in the corner of Julia's private *cubiculum*, where she slept most nights.* Julia stood silently as the soft linen of her undergarment was replaced by a looser, more comfortable tunic for the night. A third slave approached with an ivory comb and a small flask of oil. Julia sat on a low stool, and the woman began to smoothly untangle her long hair, adding oil which lent a faint sheen to Julia's dark locks. Occasionally, Julia winced at a stubborn knot, but the slave's hands were gentle. With her hair braided loosely for the night, another attendant approached with a small box of clean rags. She offered Julia one soaked in rosewater to remove the kohl from her eyes and the faint blush from her cheeks. Their mistress moved sluggishly after the long evening of wine and heavy food as she wiped away the remnants of her face paint.

The distant sounds of slaves finishing their work throughout the rooms and the garden drifted through the walls to her quarters. Her bed, covered with fine woollen blankets and soft cushions, awaited her. Julia slipped beneath the covers and her attendants extinguished all but one lamp, leaving the room bathed in a low, dim glow. One slave remained by the doorway until Julia mumbled her dismissal. As the god of sleep, Somnus, came to claim her, the gentle rhythms of the household and the soft footfalls of slaves faded into nothingness.

* * *

Lantern light twinkled in her chamber as Julia began her morning. Her three *cosmetae* slaves, chosen for their skills in beautification, moved quietly as they poured jasmine-infused water over Julia's

---

* Room use in Roman houses does not appear to have been fixed in the modern sense; sleeping arrangements, in particular, were likely to be fluid and adaptable.

hands and used soft linens to dry them. As one slave brushed out Julia's hair, another removed the lid of a delicate alabaster jar, revealing a creamy substance of white lead and animal fat mixed with beeswax and olive oil. The slave smeared her fingers through the mixture and applied it to Julia's face in even strokes, creating the pale, smooth complexion desired by Roman women of her status.

Once Julia's complexion was smoothed, a small shell containing the ground powder of expensive red ochre, imported all the way from Belgic Gaul, was gently blended with fat and rubbed into her cheeks and lips, lending them a healthy flush of colour. Behind Julia, the third slave busied herself by tonging Julia's hair into structured curls with a *calamistrum*, a hollow iron curling rod heated over a brazier. As she carefully wound sections of Julia's hair around the rod, coaxing each strand into shape, another slave worked in tandem to secure the emerging style with delicate bronze pins tipped with tiny beads. A cascade of glossy brown curls framed Julia's face, while the rest was gathered into a half-up style, with small plaits folded and pinned into place to create a look that was fashionable, composed and effortlessly imperial.

Meanwhile, the make-up girl held a spoon over a lantern flame, allowing soot to gather on its polished surface before mixing it with beeswax and olive oil. With swift precision, she darkened Julia's brows and traced her eyelids with *fuligo*, the Roman answer to kohl. The 'black smoke' charcoal, scented with crushed rose petals to remove the unpleasant smell, was then added to her eyebrows and the contour of her eyelashes with a slender bronze probe, enhancing their almond shape and giving her gaze a subtle intensity.

The scent of saffron oil lingered in the air, its rich fragrance filling the room as Julia inspected her reflection. By the time her

THE WEALTHY BUSINESSWOMAN

toilette was complete, the sun was already beginning to peak over the horizon. Aware of the passing time, Julia's *cosmetae* began swiftly dressing her in a finely woven Ionic *chiton*, fastened with pins from neck to wrist and drawn in around the waist with a slender tie. Red-dyed leather sandals were slipped onto her feet, a gold garnet bracelet clasped at her wrist, and pearl earrings placed on her ears. A final dab of iris-petal perfume from the local perfume garden scented her skin. Rising with poise, Julia stepped into the early light of day.

By the time Julia entered the area outside the baths on her estate, a group of Isiac worshippers had already been admitted to the atrium. They stood in solemn quietness, some talking in hushed voices to their neighbours, others with their heads bowed in silent thought. Below their feet was an elaborate black and white mosaic. It depicted a *fornacator*, or fire stoker, as he stoked the unseen fires

Figure 20: Geometric mosaic from the bathing complex in the Estate of Julia Felix (II.4.2-3)

that warmed the baths. Around him swam fantastical creatures: a twisting *ketos*, a sea-griffin, a hippocampus with hooves lost in curling tendrils of water, and a spotted sea-panther on the hunt. Dolphins leapt between them, framed by a labyrinthine border enclosing a miniature cityscape of Pompeii's walls and towers. At the centre of the mosaic, the water in the decorative *impluvium* pool lay perfectly still.

Julia walked around the portico, greeting each of her fellow worshippers who were to witness the initiation of Octavius Quartio. Once she had made the rounds, she passed into the adjoining bathing complex for a final check. The first, warm room, the *tepidarium*, was a sight to behold. Along the walls, her slaves had hung garlands of flowers and palm fronds, their vivid colours and lush greenery a tribute to the goddess they honoured. Rose petals lay scattered across the floor, and in each corner, lanterns burned on bronze tripods and cast restless shadows across the mosaic floor. The oil of the lanterns released an intoxicating blend of frankincense, myrrh and sweet marjoram.

She continued into the *frigidarium*, the cold room where the ceremonial bath would take place. Like the warm room, it too was dressed with garlands. The water of the plunge pool lay still and clear, catching the pale dawn light coming in from the window above. Julia dipped her hand in; cool but not biting. Just right. Back in the portico, yet more worshippers had gathered. Their voices, low with anticipation, were soon pierced by the soft, rhythmic *ting* of cymbals and the rattle of *sistra* drifting in from the street. Her heart quickened as the sounds grew louder: the priest, the initiate and their entourage were nearing.

The ceremony had begun at first light in the temple, as tradition required, and now the next stage of the sacred bathing rite was about to take place. This was the moment she had prepared for. As

THE WEALTHY BUSINESSWOMAN

the procession entered the *tepidarium*, accompanied by the shimmer of *sistra* and the soft shuffle of sandals on mosaic tiles, Julia stood aside to allow the worshippers to file in in anticipation of the arrival of the main procession.

A worshipper at the rear let his gaze sweep the space and remarked, a little too loudly, 'A statue of the goddess would lend this place more dignity.'

Julia's composure did not falter. 'Indeed,' she replied warmly. 'And in her wisdom, the goddess Isis requires no stone likeness to remind her of our devotion, for she is omnipotent and all-knowing. Only our deeds and faith need do that.' She inclined her head towards him, a soft smile gracing her lips, as though he had paid her a compliment. 'But you honour her simply by being here.'

The man gazed back at her stoney-faced, opening his mouth to reply, only for the procession to arrive in a cloud of incense.

Figure 21: The frigidarium in the Venus Baths of the Estate of Julia Felix (II.4.2-3)

* * *

After the initiation, Julia had made a private offering at the Isis *sacrarium* in her garden before changing into day clothes and jewellery and heading out to shop at the forum. She had chosen not to join the rest of the Isiaci for the remainder of the ritual; it had been a long week, and she had already played her part. Besides, the generous donation of food she had sent to the temple for the occasion should make up for her absence. On Julia's ears, hemispherical gold ball earrings glinted in the afternoon sun, and around her neck she wore a delicate gold-filigree necklace finished with a green pendant, its hue reminiscent of fresh spring leaves. Her fingers bore two gold rings: one a simple, smooth band, and the other set with an oval carnelian stone engraved with an image of Mercury, a talisman of protection and good fortune.

Her *cosmetae* slaves had retouched her hair, ensuring the curls formed earlier in the morning remained intact. They wove a plain ribbon through it, securing her curls into a neat arrangement that would hold through her errands. As they worked, she thought through the items she needed: a new cosmetic mirror, preferably silver, silk clothing from India, a decorative box to hold her writing implements, and maybe some of that perfume Sutoria had showed her yesterday.

By the time Julia had finished her short shopping trip, the warm autumn sun was spilling through the columns of the portico in her inner garden. The buzz of activity around the estate echoed the order she had built. Slaves carried freshly picked produce from her walled vegetable garden to the kitchens, swept and scrubbed floors and carried wood to braziers as tenants passed through with nods of respect. From beyond the atrium, the soft splash of water and low voices drifted from the baths, now reopened to the public.

THE WEALTHY BUSINESSWOMAN

Figure 22: The still-life xenia *paintings from the Estate of Julia Felix (II.4.2-3)*

Stepping into the *tablinum*, Julia readied herself for the day's business. Marcus was already in there, arranging wax tablets in the cabinet, each one filled with years of transactions. The walls around her were painted in rich red and yellow panels and adorned with floating scenes of rustic landscapes and small household deities. But it was the large display above that held the most meaning: a set of four still-life paintings known as *xenia* had been commissioned to carefully reflect her identity as a woman, business owner and head of a thriving estate. As was typical, the scenes depicted acts of hospitality; how a host might receive a guest, and the gifts traditionally offered in return. It was one of the many Hellenistic hangovers passed down from the Greeks who once occupied the area, long before the Roman Pompeians.

Following the scenes of everyday items, the tools that underpinned Julia's life and business were displayed: piles of coins in bronze, silver and gold, bulging money bags, an inkwell, a stylus and two wax tablets. Together with the other panels, they formed a carefully balanced portrait. Julia was the generous hostess who honoured tradition, a cultivated woman who understood the rustic ideals her male counterparts so revered across Italy, and a shrewd businesswoman who came toe-to-toe with men in a man's world.

A young widow stood waiting near the *tablinum*, her baby balanced on one hip, gumming a teething toy. She ran a modest *fullonica*, a laundry and dyeing workshop, near the forum and had come to ask Julia for assistance. Julia gestured for her to sit and the woman obeyed.

'*Domina*, I require your assistance and guidance, if you would be so kind as to offer it. I was in a bad way, needing to feed my children. I have two others, my husband's gone, and we are struggling to get by with only the help of my widowed mother. We have a loan from Faustilla—'

Julia stopped her breathless explanation. 'Let me guess, Aemiliana. You accepted a loan without thinking of the consequences of the high interest and now you cannot pay.'

A pause. 'No, *domina*. My late husband did.' The young widow looked down with shame and Julia was struck with pity.

'I had no idea he had done it, and then he passed away. He took the loan out in an inn, wrote the agreement on the wall. I can't blame him; we were on our knees at the time. He was desperate. But now I am left with the burden.'*

'How much did Faustilla loan your husband?'

'Fifteen *denarii* for eight *asses* interest.'

'And how long ago was this?'

---

* Found scribbled on the wall of an inn in Pompeii were the words: 'November. From Faustilla, 8 asses in interest for 15 *denarii*'.

THE WEALTHY BUSINESSWOMAN

'Last November, *domina*. I've been working to repay it, but if I can't, they say I could be forced to sell everything. Some even talk of being taken back into bondage. I can't bear the thought of what would happen to Aelia ...' The baby cooed as if listening.

'That won't happen. Marcus, give Aemiliana 20 *denarii* and eight *asses* to cover the principal, plus the 11 months of interest.' Marcus counted coins from a strong box before handing over a small pouch of money to Aemiliana.

Julia stopped to look at the mother before her, and considered her young face. She looked tired. 'I have heard that you are an excellent painter, Aemiliana. There aren't many female painters.'

'Yes, *domina*. My late father was a *pictor*.'

'Ah, him too? How wonderful. Well, a couple of my apartments could do with redecorating. Arrange a time with Marcus to discuss the designs next week and bring some sketches. This will cover your debt with me, and I'll sort the rest out with Faustilla.'*

As Aemiliana departed, a small slave stepped into the room, slightly breathless. His tunic was dusty from standing by the front steps with the porter. '*Domina*,' he announced. 'A freedman has just arrived at the front door. He wishes to discuss renting a small room.'

Julia nodded, adjusting her *stola* as she prepared for her next negotiation. 'Show him in,' she said, her voice steady, betraying nothing of the fatigue settling into her body. While she waited, she rose and moved towards the wooden cabinet pressed against the wall, its doors painted with gold-leaf floral motifs. Opening it, she searched inside for the wax tablet detailing available accommodation. The air in the room felt cooler than it had earlier in the week.

---

* The decorations on Julia's walls tell us that she was into moneylending, as were a number of other women in Pompeii. Faustilla is mentioned in two inscriptions from the city.

Reaching for the tablet she had been looking for, her gaze settled on a small bronze figure of Isis nursing Horus on one of the cabinet shelves. The goddess stood serene and regal, her hand to her breast as she cradled the youth in her arm. As her eyes lingered, a subtle tremor passed through the floor beneath her feet. She frowned. Another minor quake, no doubt. But it grew stronger. The statue of Isis began to shake violently, toppling over onto its side. A second later, a deafening explosion shook the room.

The frescoed walls seemed to ripple with the force, distorting the painted figures as though they too were recoiling in terror. Julia staggered, her fingers digging into the smooth wood of the cabinet as she pushed herself forwards out of the *tablinum* and into the atrium and beyond.

The world around her was chaos. Servants and clients stumbled through the garden, their shouts lost in the thunderous noise. Somewhere nearby, a child was crying, the wail sharp and thin against the rumbling ground.

Amidst the blur of panicked figures, one stood out: a man in a red *pileus*, stark against the sea of dust and confusion. He was standing in shock, his face turned towards her. She saw in his eyes the same fear that gripped her own body.

The portico columns trembled, their weight straining against the ferocity of the tremors. Julia reached out for the wall, her hands trembling. For a breathless moment the columns held, and then … with a sharp, sickening snap, they fractured. Stone and mortar gave way in a deafening cascade, shards slicing through the air as a storm of dust erupted around her.

A jagged fissure ripped through the mosaic floor, the fine tiles shattering as it carved a path towards her feet. Julia lurched back, her breath coming in sharp, ragged gasps.

She ran.

THE WEALTHY BUSINESSWOMAN

Pushing forwards, past the collapsing portico, past the suffocating press of walls that were coming down around her, she burst into the garden, her sandals slipping on the disturbed earth as she gasped for air. The open sky should have brought relief, but it didn't.

Turning to face her estate, her stomach lurched as her eyes lifted to the scene above.

The mountain had erupted.

CHAPTER THREE

THE EVERYMAN

ONE DAY IN 75 CE

No father should have to bury his son.

Aulus Umbricius Scaurus stood in the walled garden of the family tomb, outside the fortifications of Pompeii, and watched the flames rise. Smoke curled into the twilight, heavy with the scent of burning resin and bitter herbs, but it could not smother the stench of death that clung in his memory.

The younger Scaurus lay on the pyre, his face still. First, the fever had come, wringing the sweat from his body until the sheets beneath him were soaked. Next the chills and the tremors, the violent shivering that wracked his frame as if the air had turned to ice. And then, the worst of it: delirium, the eyes that no longer focused and the mouth that whispered half-formed words to people who were not there.*

And finally, silence.

Scaurus' son had been everything he had hoped for: sharp and

---

* We do not know what Scaurus' son died of, but malaria was a common cause of death in Rome and places like Pompeii, both of which were close to rivers.

ambitious, with the confidence of a good Roman man, expanding the family legacy beyond what even Scaurus himself had achieved. His hands had forged deals with traders as far as the Germanic frontier, his voice had carried weight in the market halls of Pompeii and his presence had turned heads in the forum.

He had been honoured in death with *laudatio funebris*, a funeral oration, by virtue of his high status as *duumvir*. After lying in state at the home of the Umbricii, the family, freedmen, merchants and political allies of the family had moved in the *pompa* procession, led by eight men carrying the deceased to the forum. Quintus Postumius Modestus, one of the *duumvirs* for that year, had delivered the eulogy, praising the political achievements of the young Scaurus. The procession of the bier, musicians, professional mourners, and family and friends had filled the air with music and wailing, the haunting melody of trumpets, horns and flutes carrying across the rooftops of the city.

The waxen mask Scaurus the Elder wore could not hide his sorrow. He, like the other male members of the funeral procession, donned the masks, or *imagines*, of his ancestors, and in the flames and shadows, the rigid visages seemed to stir. Among them was the newest mask, cast just after death from the face of the Younger Scaurus, his features caught between waxen silence and the illusion of a man alive once more. The tomb seemed crowded by ghosts.

The grief-stricken wails of the women filled the night, their cries rising into the star-dotted sky in a chorus of grief. The Elder Scaurus' wife, draped in *lugubria*, the dark, unbelted mourning garb that marked her altered state, stood close to the pyre. She let her unbound hair fall loose around her face to mirror her inner turmoil. Beside her, the pregnant, widowed young wife of Scaurus' son kept her veil pulled low across her brow, her voice shaking as she called out a last farewell to her husband.

THE EVERYMAN

Then came the moment to open the deceased's eyes so that they may be displayed to the heavens, and his eldest son, just 6 years old, stepped forward to set a torch to his father's pyre. His face was set in resolute seriousness; his slight frame strong beyond his years. The flames caught and spread quickly through the arrangement of wood, grasses and papyrus, and the scent of cinnamon, cassia and cypress, disguising the smell of decay beneath, lifted into the air.

For Scaurus the Elder, the moment was almost unbearable: forced to outlive the heir he had raised with such pride, the son who had carried his family's future upon his shoulders. All his life he had worked to maintain his family's place in Pompeii and carve their name into the city's history. He had watched his son step into spaces no Umbricius had ever ventured, driven by the same relentless ambition that had fuelled his family's rise. Now he would turn his energies to the young boy who stood shaking in the chill of the evening before his father's body, and lead him into manhood in his son's stead.

Like his father, grandfather and great-grandfather before him, Scaurus had hoped his son would inherit not only their business, but their legacy. Each jar of *garum*, marked with their name, carried more than the pungent flavours of the Mediterranean Sea: it carried memory, reputation and the family name. Yet his son had refused the narrow inheritance of trade. Instead, he had altered the course of the Umbricii, lifting them from mere merchants of fish sauce to arbiters of civic power. With the wealth of their fish-sauce vats behind him, his son had bought influence in the forum, first as *aedile*, dazzling the crowds with games and festivals, then as *duumvir*, rising to one of the highest offices a Pompeian could hold.*

---

* At the very least, Scaurus' son would have been 39 years old. *Aediles*, who held office for 2 years, had to be at least 36 years old, and the length of office for a *duumvir* was 1 year.

Yet now his son's hands, which should have been ink-stained from signing contracts, were cold and lifeless beneath his funeral wrappings. The flames snapped and crackled and the heat warped the air, distorting the black letters carved into the waiting funerary altar:

> To the memory of Aulus Umbricius Scaurus, son of Aulus, of the tribe Menenia, *duumvir* with judiciary authority. The city council decreed him the space for this monument, plus two thousand *sesterces* for the funeral and an equestrian statue to be set up in the forum. Scaurus the father, to the memory of his son.*

His son's name should not have been carved there yet. It should have been his instead. But Scaurus knew now that the Fates cared little for the order of things. As he stared at his son's name in stone, at the finality of it, a thought coiled deep in his mind. Nothing lasts forever. Not names, nor monuments. Not even cities.

THE SEVENTH HOUR (12 NOON), 23 OCTOBER 79 CE

Golden shafts of October sunlight spilled through the open *compluvium*, the central opening in the roof that let in light and rain, casting shifting patterns across the marble floor of Aulus Umbricius Scaurus' atrium. The atrium was the beating heart of his *domus*, every detail designed to send a clear message: here lived a man of wealth, power and ambition. At its centre, the still waters of the *impluvium* pool mirrored the sky above, an unbroken reflec-

---

* Both Scaurus and his son were called Aulus Umbricius Scaurus. Aulus was the personal name (*praenomen*), Umbricius the family (*nomen*, identifying his *gens*), and Scaurus their branch of that family (*cognomen*).

THE EVERYMAN

tion of the world beyond. But it was the terracotta figures that usually caught visitors' attention: leaping dogs, each uniquely crafted, were perched along the edge of the *compluvium*, frozen mid-bound in playful defiance of their inanimate state.

The sheer scale of Scaurus' house spoke for itself. Stretching the length of an entire city block near Pompeii's harbour gate, it was a product of his and his family's calculated spirit and determination. After the great quake, Scaurus had wasted no time in acquiring the neighbouring properties, merging five houses into the one first settled in by his great-grandfather after migrating from Rome. His *domus* was perfectly placed: close enough to the bustling harbour to oversee the flow of his fish-sauce business, yet distant enough to maintain an air of exclusivity.

Back in his early years, when they were still producing *garum* in workshops inside the town, Scaurus was hauling old *amphorae* for cleaning and reuse when the faded letters painted on one of the terracotta containers in his hand caught his eye: '*The tree, which is from Scaurus' estate.*' He had traced the name with his fingers, rough against the grain of the vessel, and felt the presence of those who had come before him.

His father used to speak of the upheavals that had reshaped Italy in the late Republic, when the Social War and Sulla's dictatorship brought confiscations and colonies in its wake. Across the peninsula, rebel towns were razed, their families erased from the land. In Pompeii too, after years of resistance, the proud Samnite elite were stripped of their estates, their houses seized and repurposed for Roman veterans when Pompeii became *Colonia Cornelia Veneria Pompeianorum*.*

---

* Pompeii was made into a colony in 80 BC, 9 years after its defeat by Sulla during the Social War.

THE LOST VOICES OF POMPEII

The Umbricii had been enrolled in the ancient Menenia tribe, one of the oldest of Rome's rural tribes, for many a generation, a membership which told of their deep ancestral roots and long-held Roman citizenship. Belonging to such a tribe distinguished them from freedmen, who were confined to the less prestigious urban tribes. It was Scaurus' great-grandfather who had first moved south, during Sulla's colonisation of Pompeii in the late Republic, when new opportunities opened along the Bay of Naples. There the family had built its fortune on the production of fish sauce, a trade both lucrative and stigmatised. And the Empire, it turned out, loved fish sauce.

When his great-grandfather first settled in the town, he established *garum* workshops along the Via Stabiana in the south-eastern quarter. Scaurus had sold these around 50 years ago when he had inherited the family business, and moved operations to the vast fish-sauce plants on the Iberian Peninsula, retaining only seven in the town for processing. Before long, his *garum* was being traded as far as southern Gaul. Now, Scaurus commanded a third of the *garum* trade in Campania, and the best fish sauce in Italy.* Even the general of the Roman military fleet at Misenum, Gaius Plinius Secundus,† had written about it 2 years ago in his *Natural Histories*, his ambitious work cataloguing everything from trees and wine to animals and earthquakes.‡ Umbricii *garum* really was

---

* It is generally accepted, based on the available evidence, that Scaurus the Elder became active in Pompeii between 25 and 35 CE. In total, Scaurus and his associates (mostly freedpeople) are named on around 30 per cent of the inscribed fish-sauce containers discovered in Pompeii and Herculaneum. Recent excavations in Pompeii have found that fish-sauce vats in workshops on the Via Stabiana were installed around the time of Pompeii's colonisation (80 BCE) and removed in the first third of the first century CE.
† Better known as Pliny the Elder.
‡ Pliny finished his *Natural Histories* in 77 CE. He mentions that Pompeii was famed for *garum* production (31.43.8).

the best. And this success had paved the way for his son to build on it further.

Scaurus had felt such pride the day his son took office as *duumvir*. The campaign had been nothing short of triumphant, with lavish gladiator games and beast hunts in the amphitheatre, the kind of spectacle Pompeii never forgot. He had funded them gladly.

That pride had long since curdled into sorrow.

After his boy's sudden death, Scaurus had sought the only tribute that felt worthy: a tomb just outside the city gates, grand and enduring, and deserving of *fama*. Carved friezes wrapped around the sarcophagus showing gladiators mid-clash, horses rearing, shields braced against flying spears. Every plume-topped helmet and sharpened blade seemed ready to move, to come alive. Just for a moment. The way he wished his son would.

Beneath the fighters, the scenes of wild animal hunts, *venationes*, that had once thrilled the amphitheatre crowds played out in marble. In the final panel, a lone gladiator faced a snarling wolf with only a short *gladius*, his stance defiant. Scaurus had insisted

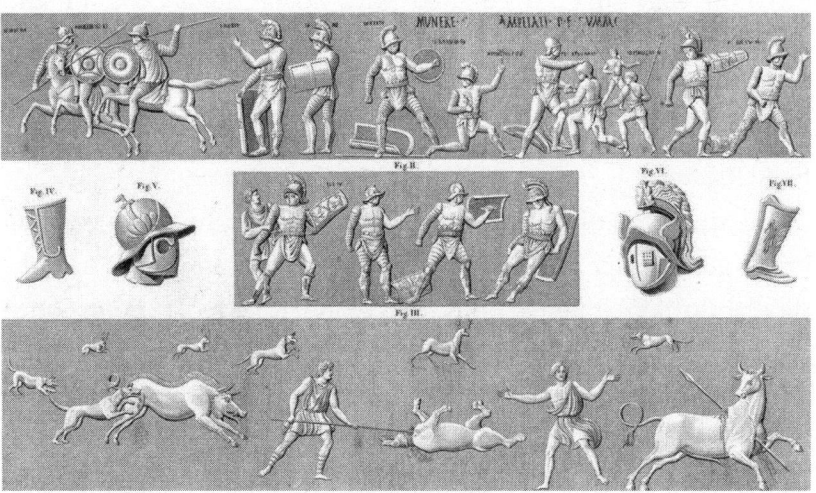

Figure 23: Decorative friezes on the tomb of the Younger Scaurus

on that image, because to him, the wolf was the Fate Atropos, a silent, watching beast, ready to cut the thread of life when least expected. On his last visit, he'd noticed new names painted beside the figures. Written in bold red graffiti, the names of the gladiators and their trainer, Numerius Festus Ampliatus, had been added to the scene. When someone had told him of the impromptu additions, Scaurus hadn't minded. His son had always taken pride in the people's voice; he wouldn't have wanted the names removed. And so he honoured that spirit by letting Pompeii speak to his son's memory.

* * *

Though Scaurus' family was from one of the ancient and original rural tribes of Rome, their role as merchants still carried a shadow of prejudice, no matter how profitable the trade. Scaurus understood that lineage and wealth alone were not enough: he had to make his mark. Inspired by the grandeur of the city's elite, and the villas running along the cliffs of the Bay of Naples, he had realised early on that survival equated with social advancement, and advancement was not achieved by blending in, but by standing out. Because of this he had, for years, been shaping a home worthy of drawing envious whispers throughout the halls of Pompeii's finest estates.

The traditions of spectacle and self-promotion, first set in motion by his grandfather and sustained by his father, were woven into the very fabric of their family home. His grandfather had commissioned the mosaic which now decorated the main atrium of their grand *domus*, its four corners around the central *impluvium* pool bearing proud declarations of the family's success. Tiny *tesserae* tiles, painstakingly cut on site, formed the intricate mosaic designs of their signature *garum* jars, with each one paired with bold white inscriptions celebrating their finest products: '*The flower of* Liquamen', '*The flower of* garum, *made from mackerel, a product of Scaurus*', and twice over, '*The best* Liquamen, *from the shop of Scaurus*'.

Because there was *liquamen*, and then there was *garum*. The untrained palate might think them all the same, just varying shades of brine and decay, but to Scaurus, the difference was glaring. The *true garum*, his *garum*, was a thing of perfection. Whole small fish, mostly mackerel, sardines and anchovies, were layered with sea salt in vast ceramic vats and left to ferment beneath the sun.

Over months, flesh would dissolve into liquid gold, the first pressing yielding the 'flower of *garum*', called *flos gari*. This was a rich and glossy sauce, coloured a deep brown or near black, with an intense, yet complex, flavour. Only the finest was decanted into *urcei* and stamped with his name, before being sent to Rome, Africa and Gaul where wealthy tables demanded nothing but the best. Those who could afford it drizzled it over roasted dormice, blended it with honey on oysters, or stirred it into spiced sauces.

Garos, the Greek version, had its own long pedigree. The Phoenicians traded it, the Carthaginians adapted it, and each region created its own twist, adding herbs, vinegar and honey. Scaurus had thought of making it himself, but it was niche. His fortune was in volume, and *liquamen* had always been a staple earner for the business. Because, unlike *garum*, *liquamen* was made from scraps: the blood, guts and shattered spines of mackerel, all tossed into *dolia* and left to break down. It was harsher and saltier but much more affordable, and it was always in demand. Tavern cooks bought the light-golden condiment by the *amphora* and the plebeian poured it over everything. In Pompeii, *liquamen* was a necessity, not a luxury.

Then came *allec*, the thick sludge left behind after *garum* was drained off. Pungent and unrefined, it fed the poor, the pigs and

Figure 24: Mosaic motifs depicting the different fish sauce products of Aulus Umbricius Scaurus

the eels that needed fattening. Even that turned a profit. But *garum sociorum* was Scaurus' masterpiece; a black *garum* made from fresh mackerel blood, pulped the moment it left the water. The result was a dark, potent and brutally salty sauce that burned the throat. Not everyone could stomach it, but that was the point. A man's ability to endure *garum sociorum* was as much a test of status as it was of palate.

Standing now in the atrium, Scaurus' eyes lingered on the mosaics, long since laid. He thought of how many visitors had paused to absorb the craftsmanship and the message beneath it all: the brand of the Umbricii, Scaurus' fish sauce. Turning, he beckoned the decorators trailing behind to follow him, their arms laden with scrolls, pigments and tools. The sound of their hurried steps echoed across the polished floors as they followed the imposing, but old, figure of Scaurus towards the *triclinium*.

Scaurus had envisioned future guests reclining for hours in a newer, grander dining room, their bellies full of extravagant dishes, their laughter and conversation punctuated by the powerful flavours of his finest *garum*, proudly displayed on the table at the centre. This was the room where his vision would find its fullest expression. He had spent weeks planning its frescoes with the painters, drawing inspiration from the harbours and seas that sustained his trade, and that he gazed upon every day from the terrace in his vast home. He envisioned grand nautical scenes, full of movement and energy: ships arriving at busy docks, sailors unloading *amphorae*, merchants haggling over goods. In large, framed panels in the centre of the walls, strung fish would be painted in vibrant detail, while in smaller, landscape panels, he had requested images of the sea life found in the Bay of Naples and the River Sarno: crabs, fish, molluscs. The colours, he insisted, must evoke the deep, rich blues of the Mediterranean, the golden light of Pompeii's sunlit shores, and the earthy reds of Campania's soil.*

The head decorator began to explain the process. 'We'll grind the pigments into fine powders and mix them with lime. Then we'll apply them directly while the plaster is still wet so that the colours fuse into the wall. For the murals, we'll work in grids, taking a panel each.'

'Good. I want this to last.'

'It will. What you paint here, people will see for generations.'†

Soon the panels would be slotted into the gaps left for them in the walls, merging with the larger frescoes to create an unbroken vision of the life that had shaped his family's fortune.‡ The paintings would tell the story of their rise and their empire.

The painter gestured to the far wall. 'So, just to go over it once more … this is where the gods will go: Neptune, Salacia at his side, a centaur with serpent-like coils, and Amphitrite with her robes caught in a wind.'

'And here,' he crossed the room, 'the Tritons with conch shells at their lips, Nereids trailing behind them with garlands of coral and

---

* Although Scaurus' house has been excavated, little is known about it. This is largely due to the damage it sustained during bombing on 13 September 1943, which left the structure in a derelict and hazardous state. Unusually, no formal records of the house's frescoes survive. However, it's likely they were self-promotional in nature and referenced his trade, which was a common decorative choice (particularly among freedmen).

† Sadly, Scaurus' grand home is now in bad repair, and these designs are instead based on nautical frescoes found elsewhere in the town. Painters generally appear to have worked to the same or similar designs, repeating them in varying qualities.

‡ There are remnants of frescoes from Campania, housed in the Archaeological Museum of Naples, which are square in shape and painted onto plaster. They were found propped to the side, waiting to be inserted into the square space made for them in the wall.

pearls. Then in the water we'll have fish darting between reeds, and an octopus opening its arms.'

They turned to the final wall, where they had planned a more personal scene.

'And here we'll have Glaucus, the Boeotian fisherman.'

Scaurus nodded, seeing it clearly: the surge of water, seaweed curling in the current, Glaucus tasting the enchanted herb that granted him immortality, shaping him into something more than human. As they talked, two painters began laying sheets on the floor and marking out the grid directly onto the wall, while a third began mixing slaked lime with fine marble dust and water to create the plaster base.

'Shall I tell you more about the process?'

Without taking his eyes off the walls, Scaurus inclined his head.

'The colours have to sink into the wall itself,' the painter explained. 'We start with two layers of plaster: first the *arriccio*, which is rough and thick, then the smoother and finer *intonaco*, which he's doing down there. Then we'll paint on top while it's wet.'*

Scaurus finally turned, his hands clasped behind him. 'And the colours?'

'Ochres for warmth, cinnabar for a rich, deep red, malachite for the greens, and azurite for the sea. We can also use *orpiment*, a beautiful orange-yellow pigment, and Egyptian blue, but we'd need to prepare this. We'd have to sift it to a fine grain, but it would mean you'd get a lovely, luminous quality. The *orpiment* and Egyptian blue are very rare, so they'd come at an extra cost. Worth it though. You don't want to scrimp on a display like this.'

'Use both. I want it to be of the highest quality possible,' Scaurus said.

---

* These are modern, Italian names for the materials.

'Done.' The painter tried to hide his glee at his successful upsell. 'We should be done in a couple of days, barring mishaps. But there shouldn't be any of those.'

Scaurus finally turned to the painter. 'Let's give them something worth looking at.'

* * *

Scaurus braced himself as the *strigil* scraped across his oiled skin, the tool's curved bronze blade cleaning the sweat and dirt from his body. It was now mid-afternoon and having left the painters to their work, he had made his way through the busy streets to the largest bathing complex in the city.

His own private baths were perfectly serviceable. More than that, they were designed for comfort, privacy and indulgence. The steam rooms were scented with laurel and the plunge pool tiled in polished *cipollino* marble, its swirling green veins a delicate touch to the overall display of opulence. He could have spent the morning there

Figure 25: A bronze toilet set, including a strigil

and reclined in quiet luxury, but he had always liked the public baths. He liked being among men who talked of trade, politics and business deals, where whispers carried faster than water down the sloped Pompeian streets on a rainy day. A man in his position could not simply sit in his house, waiting for news to come to him. He had built his fortune by knowing the right things at the right time, and for that, the baths remained invaluable. It was also, he admitted to himself, a matter of pride. Here, among the merchants and the shopkeepers, he was one of the people, a part of Pompeii.

Scaurus allowed himself to relax on the table in the warm, dry space of the *tepidarium* as the young female slave continued to drag the blade across his back. It left a deep, lingering ache where his muscles resisted the treatment. The *strigil* was a necessary discomfort, a ritual purification of sorts, that he had long since stopped seeing as an indulgence. It was essential to keep the body balanced and in working order.

As a young man he had once left these chambers feeling invigorated, with a sense of sharpened purpose. But age had settled into him slowly, like sediment sinking to the bottom of an *amphora*, inevitable and irreversible. He sat up with a groan. This was how life was meant to be, unhurried days like this, without the pull of business. That burden should belong to his son now, not to him.

The lamps burned low in the *apodyterium* changing room, filled with the smell of damp wool, scented oil and worn sandals drying by the brazier. Around him, men moved unhurriedly, rubbing their hair with cloths, draping themselves in tunics and conversing as slaves fetched their belongings. Scaurus spotted one of his slaves waiting just inside.

'I want to stop by the workshop near the amphitheatre,' he said, pulling his tunic over his head. 'Is there anything else I'm meant to deal with today?'

As he shook out the folds, a familiar figure stepped into view: Euxinus. He had been expecting to see him at some point this week. The younger man had lingered just long enough in the baths to make their meeting seem unplanned, yet not so long that it might appear he had been waiting. Clever and calculated. Scaurus recognised the manoeuvre because he had once played the same game.

Euxinus' tunic, though fine, showed wear at the seams, a sign that success, real and permanent success, had yet to settle upon him. News of the popularity of his inn garden had reached Scaurus' ears and he had even heard about the innkeeper's participation in the *Vinalia* harvest, gathering grapes from his own vines. Euxinus was a man on the cusp, it seemed, teetering between ambition and opportunities yet unclaimed. After cursory greetings, they both dressed in silence, Scaurus fastening his cloak with the ease of habit, the cold pin pressing against his fingers. Euxinus did the same, his movements slower and watchful. He was waiting for the right moment, for the older man to set the pace. Scaurus let the silence stretch.

Scaurus left the warmth of the *apodyterium* behind and stepped into the cooler air of the public latrine attached to the baths. A long stone bench lined one wall, each seat carved with a smooth, rounded opening. Beneath, a steady flow of water ran through a channel, part of a system designed to carry waste away and keep the space clean. As Scaurus settled onto the cool stone, he observed the scene around him.

Men of various standings occupied the latrine, their conversations a blend of casual banter and serious discourse. He recognised most of the faces around him; Pompeii was a small city. The atmosphere was always social, the absence of partitions fostering a sense of camaraderie, where the usual boundaries of status and decorum

THE EVERYMAN

were set aside. To his right, the laughter of a group of young men sharing a joke about a barmaid echoed off the tiled walls. To his left, two merchants discussed the work of the current *aediles*, eagerly predicting the successes and failures of two of the four for the next year: Gaius Cuspius Pansa and Lucius Popidius Secundus. Perhaps they would be more proactive in fixing the earthquake damage, the men said, though there was very little point these days. In the last week alone, they had experienced several small quakes. Scaurus made a mental note to feed this back to Pansa at the feast tonight.

A slave moved discreetly along the row of men, offering small sponges on sticks, *tersoria*, dipped in vinegar water, the standard tool for personal hygiene. Scaurus accepted one with a nod, appreciating the efficiency of the bathhouse's attendants. Beside him, Euxinus lowered himself onto the bench. With a few measured remarks on the city's affairs and the uncertain months ahead, Scaurus brought the visit to a close. Euxinus followed suit, offering to walk with him to the end of the main street, his slaves trailing behind. As they passed a busy tavern where laughter spilled onto the street, Euxinus seized his moment, beginning his petition by framing his inn as a business opportunity. He talked of the improvements he'd made and the people who now visited.

'See it as a bonus,' Euxinus implored eagerly, leaning in slightly. 'A way to tighten your grip on Pompeii's appetites. Your flower of *garum*, the finest in the city, should be in every top establishment.'

He glanced around, then lowered his voice. 'My inn is already making a name for itself. Merchants, ships' captains, men who understand where the city's heading, they're all gathering there. They talk trade over dinner, and the real business comes when the wine flows.' He gave Scaurus a cheeky grin.

Scaurus paused at a shop counter, letting the idea sink in. Pointing to a mix of nuts held in a *dolium* set into the counter, the shopkeeper poured a handful into Scaurus' hand before taking his coin. They carried on walking.

'I might know a supplier,' Scaurus replied with a wry, knowing smile.

'Exactly what I was thinking!' Euxinus grew louder, feeling encouraged. 'The flower of *garum* shouldn't just be for villas. Money in Pompeii is now in the hands of the many, and the right men already visit my place, men with real coin to spend. They don't need a senator's invitation to crave the taste of wealth.'

Scaurus mulled the idea over as he chewed the almonds and walnuts, the warmth of the afternoon sun gracing his cheek. Euxinus wanted to stock Scaurus' finest, most refined sauce, the kind normally reserved for the wealthy households, which they poured into small *urcei* and sent directly to patrician kitchens. It was not something typically sold in taverns or inns, but clearly Euxinus could see the potential profit to be made. Tradesmen generally made do with *liquamen* or the standard grades of *garum*. The innkeeper's request was bold, but not unreasonable.

'Pompeii's growing fat on men like us,' Euxinus pressed. 'Why not let them have a taste of the same *garum* that graces the tables on the Bay? Let them feel they're part of it, and they'll come back, again and again.'

They passed a brazier in the street where a slave stirred the embers, sending up a thin curl of smoke, the scent of olive wood spiralling into the air. The clatter of carts was starting to slow as the afternoon wore on, and the aroma of meat stew drifted from a nearby shop.

Euxinus lowered his voice a little: 'Besides, Scaurus … to serve jars bearing your noble Roman name in my inn; it would do more for me than just fill a few pouches. It would raise up my business. And increase your customer base. Another line of income.'

Next to them, a butcher tipped out a bucket of blood and offcuts into the street for the stray dogs to fight over, their scrabbling paws kicking up dust. Scaurus glanced at the younger man as he weighed the risks. He was shrewd, that much was clear, and eager. If anything, this sale could serve as a test. On the one hand, it could lower the exclusivity of his finest product and put some of his more refined customers off. But on the other hand, if Euxinus could make men come to his inn not just for wine and stew but for a taste of something finer, then perhaps there was a new market to be tapped.

A deep, booming laugh broke from Scaurus' chest, rich and unrestrained, rolling through the street. He clapped Euxinus on the back, the force of it nearly knocking the man off balance. Creases fanned at the corners of the old businessman's eyes as he grinned, the momentary air of calculation giving way to instinct and pleasure. Nothing made him happier than ambition in a tradesman. 'Why not?' His voice carried the warmth of a man who had built his fortune not just on shrewd deals but on knowing when to take a chance and enjoy it. This was how the best business was done. Not in stiff formalities, but in moments like this, between men chasing the same thing: money.

Though no written contracts were drawn up for such modest transactions, the gravity of a verbal agreement, made in the bustling streets of Pompeii, was not to be underestimated. In agreeing to Euxinus' proposal, Scaurus was not only conducting business but affirming his role as a steadfast participant in the age-old tradition of Roman commerce, where a spoken commitment carried the weight of one's entire legacy. They both understood that failing to honour this pact would lead to consequences far more damaging than any legal reprimand; it would erode the trust that was the currency of their trade. In Pompeii, where social standing was as critical as wealth, a man's integrity was his most valuable asset. As the mule-driven carts rumbled past, the deal was sealed with a few solemn words:

'Do you pledge your flower of *garum* will be given for a 3-month trial?'

'I pledge.'

This was the essence of *stipulatio*, a formal, spoken contract in which one party posed a clear question and the other gave a matching reply. No scribes or seals, only the presence of the gods as silent witnesses. Content he had achieved what he had wanted, Euxinus said his farewells and peeled away down a side alley, vanishing into the tangle of backstreets.

A savoury smell wound its way through the air from a nearby *taberna* and caught Scaurus' attention. It was one he had visited many times before. At the back of the counter, clay bowls were stacked, and inside, hot meals steamed from the *dolia*. A large bronze pot, blackened at the edges from years of use, sat bubbling over a hearth. The weary-looking female shopkeeper in a plain tunic stirred the mixture with a ladle, lifting chunks of pork that glistened in a heavy broth infused with herbs and spices. Beside it, a tray of stuffed *lucanicae* sausages sizzled, their skins crisping as they oozed juices onto the hot surface. Scaurus' stomach clenched in sudden hunger. He had eaten earlier, but this – this was something else entirely.

Vetutius Placidus, the broad-shouldered owner whose tunic bore the telltale stains of years spent behind a counter, caught sight of Scaurus and smiled, gesturing to a wooden table in the corner of the front of the shop, along the wall to the right of the counter. Scaurus took a seat and stretched his legs across the slab of worn

THE EVERYMAN

Figure 26: Shop front with counter and shrine in the Thermopolium of Vetutius Placidus (I.8.8)

stone. Before him, a slave placed a bowl of peppered lentil and pork-belly stew, dashed with his own *liquamen* and some red wine, alongside a small *urceus* of Scaurus' flower of *garum*, kept aside just for him. The stew clung to the sides of the dish, its surface rippling with heat. It came with a chunk of bread from a fresh *panis quadratus* loaf, baked to a perfect golden brown and dusted with a light scattering of poppy seeds. A cup of watered-down Falernian, an esteemed, potent white 'wine of the Caesars' from the slopes of Mount Falernus, north of the Bay of Naples, had just enough sharpness to cut through the richness of the meal.

He ate slowly and methodically, tearing off pieces of bread to soak in the stew, and savouring the way the salt and spices settled on his tongue. Around him, the shop buzzed with the low hum of conversation and movement. A pair of artisans argued over the outcome of a bet placed on the upcoming gladiatorial games, their voices rising. A rat darted along the floor, keeping close to the counter, and snatched up a stray piece of bread before vanishing from sight. The female shopkeeper who had been ladling the stew counted coins into her palm before passing a full bowl to an elderly gentleman of humble origins, judging by his clothes.

Behind him, two dice players were hunched over their throws, mumbling under their breath as each roll determined their fate. At the counter, a man in a slightly finer tunic than the rest leant on the marble speaking to the owner in the low, measured tones of negotiation. Business never ceased in Pompeii. Scaurus took another sip of his Falernian and leaned back as he watched the world move around him in the shop and on the street outside. You would never catch a politician in here, he thought. It was a shame. The city lived in places like this: not in the marble of the forum or the grandeur of politicians' entrance hallways, but in the worn counters of the hot food shops, and in the smell of freshly baked bread blending with the sweat of men who had worked hard that day.

* * *

The sun hung low over the horizon, but the smaller of Pompeii's two harbours still pulsed with life.* As Scaurus stepped onto the stone-paved quay, he was aware of his full belly pressing against the wool of his tunic. So much for a healthy balance, he thought. The sea breeze carried a cacophony of sounds: the creak of ships strain-

---

* Scaurus was at the Marine Port, the smaller of two ports in Pompeii, and the one closest to the mouth of the River Sarno, opening out into the Mediterranean Sea. The other port was Moregine, further up the river. It could be accessed via the Porta Stabia, one of the main gates out of the city.

ing against their moorings, the bark of traders hawking their wares, the gruff commands of sailors unloading cargo and the raucous cries of circling seagulls. Scaurus breathed in the pungent tang of fish, salt and tar, the lifeblood of his family's fortune.

He exhaled slowly, rolling the tension from his shoulders, and observed the workers in front of him. Slender slaves, their skin burnished gold from years in the sun, were hauling crates of fish sauce from a newly docked vessel. He had spent the last hour overseeing the latest shipment, ensuring that the precious *garum sociorum* had arrived unspoiled with its resin-sealed jars intact. The usual back pain was starting to creep in again. He pushed his hand into the small of his back as he watched the final *amphora* being unloaded and turned away from the bustle of the harbour, his mind shifting towards the comforts of home. One of his dock slaves, Eutychus, drew near carrying a writing tablet and stylus in his hand, the fresh marks of the day's import counts pressed deep into the wax.

'Your freedman, Umbricius Agathopus, collected his batch before noon,' Eutychus said. 'Deliveries are already underway for your other freedman, Umbricius Abascantus …'

Scaurus' mind drifted to the slave's countenance as he spoke: the furrowed brow, the flat voice. For a man whose name meant 'happy', he rarely looked it. Just as well he kept tallies and figures. No customer would buy *garum* from that expression.

'I believe that tomorrow Lucius Aelius is picking up the kosher shipments from your workshop near the amphitheatre for Umbricia Fortunata to sell in their shop.'

Scaurus inclined his head. 'Excellent. When you're next at the workshops, see that the *urcei* are properly marked.'

Like many *garum* traders, he had found the small, one-handed *urcei* perfect for selling sauce in ready measures. Some customers even brought their own, returning time and again to refill them at one of his seven remaining workshops scattered around the city. 'Each vessel must name the product, its quality and the workshop,' he reminded him. 'It must be clear that every drop comes from my hands, *ex officina Scauri*.' To him, details mattered. His brand held his family's reputation, and their name stood for quality.

Satisfied with the day's operations at the port, Scaurus strode up the slight incline leading to his sprawling villa. Around him, the city exhaled as it reached the ninth hour, the frenetic energy of the forum ahead beginning to ease as the last stall owners packed away their goods and slaves hauled home the day's purchases. Across Pompeii, taverns began to swell with hungry, early evening customers.

Arriving home, Scaurus made his way through his vast property, slaves darting into shadows as he passed through the *atria*, along the corridors, past many a side room, until he emerged into the rear colonnaded garden overlooking the Bay of Naples. A cool breeze carried the salt of the sea, mixing with the faint aromas of oil lamps. From this spot, he had a direct view of the sea which had made his family's name, and as the day gave way to the soft embrace of twilight, Scaurus sat in serene quiet, watching the sun's last light shimmer over gentle waves on the horizon. His wife, ever a pillar of strength and insight, joined him with a gentle smile.

'We'll need extra cushions for the *triclinium*,' she said. 'And I'll have one of the slaves check the lamps. We can't have them smoking again.'

Scaurus folded his hands in his lap. 'And the wine? I assume it's handled.'

'It is. I've arranged for two *amphorae* from the Caecuban estate. You know how your cousin always complains if it's anything else.'

THE EVERYMAN

Caecuban wine had once been favoured by emperors: rich, potent and costly. Though the estate's best days were behind it, its name still carried weight, especially among those who liked to be seen drinking the right vintage. Scaurus watched his wife with fondness, almost able to see the wheels turning in her mind as she moved through each detail with ease. As *domina*, she oversaw every room, every servant, every schedule. But still, she asked, as she always did, to ensure nothing had slipped: 'And the household? You're happy with it?'

He reached for her hand. 'I am. As ever, because of you.'

A great noise broke their serenity.

Their grandchildren, nieces and nephews burst onto the terrace, all laughter and flying limbs, shattering the calm with their joyful chaos. The boys became quickly immersed in a lively game of *harpastum*, chasing a leather ball with a mix of disarray and coordination that reminded Scaurus of the military drills of his own youth. The game was a preparation for the roles they might one day assume in society, whether on the battlefield or in civic duty.

Nearby, among the fragrant boughs of flowering shrubs, his granddaughters staged scenes of domestic life, imitating the duties of Roman matrons with an earnestness that belied their age. Their dolls, crafted from clay and wax, would one day be offered up in a rite of passage to the household gods, as a symbolic relinquishment of childhood. Under the shade of a young olive tree, two of the older children strategised over a game of *tabula*, their brows furrowed in concentration as they learned the virtues of foresight and planning.*

From his comfortable vantage point, Scaurus felt a profound sense of comfort in the *familia* he had built. His son's widow and

---

* *Tabula* is an ancient Greco-Roman version of backgammon.

their children still lived beneath his roof. They, the next generation of his household, were under Scaurus' enduring authority as *paterfamilias*. It was the way of Rome's elite, and he took pride in continuing the tradition. His daughter had moved, as expected, to her husband's estate, though she visited often with her children, just as she had today. His family was the bearer of his legacy, and of Rome itself. Every careful move in a game of *tabula*, every make-believe scene of domestic life, became rehearsal: the boys learning strategy and command, the girls the art of patience, grace and keeping the peace, each absorbing the roles Rome would soon demand of them. Here, beneath his olive trees, the world of Rome played out in miniature: each generation learning from the last, preparing to carry the familial legacy forward.

A cool sea breeze blew through the columns. The grandchildren were called in from play but, not eager to go inside, they darted once more across the garden. Surrounded by the warm embrace of family, Scaurus' gaze drifted back to the horizon. Each wave that broke upon the shore spoke of cycles and seasons, of challenges endured and weathered together, bound by tradition, and by love, in the heart of Pompeii.

Soon, he would make his way to the amphitheatre to attend the games as an honoured guest of Pansa, before the incoming politician's feast. It was the role he had played for years, supporting younger men as they climbed the treacherous ladder of Pompeian politics, lending his support. That was how things worked in Pompeii. But for now, he allowed himself to remain here, still and rooted, among his *familia*.

* * *

Pompeii was quiet, wrapped in the stillness of night, as Scaurus leaned back against the cushioned bench in his private room, the taste of spiced wine lingering on his tongue. Like many couples of their standing, he slept separately from his wife. The feast had not long ended, and the memory of it clung to his senses. Pansa had spared no expense. The atrium had been bathed in the golden glow of lanterns and torches, their light catching on the polished marble of the *impluvium*, where rose petals floated on water perfumed with myrrh. The guests had been greeted with *mulsum* served in delicate glass cups, the rich, honeyed wine that gripped the senses. At the entrance, slaves had passed around bowls of salted almonds and fried chickpeas, their crunch a welcome bite to whet the appetite. Fine touches designed to impress.

Once they had reclined in the dining room, the *gustatio*, the first course began, light but extravagant. Platters of oysters were arranged in shimmering half-shells and drizzled with Scaurus' own *garum sociorum*. Honeyed dormice followed, their bodies fat and stuffed with minced pork and pine nuts, and their skins rolled with honey and poppy seeds. The scent of freshly baked *libum*, a soft cheese bread still warm from Pansa's personal bakery on site, mixed with the sharp tang of *moretum*, a garlic and herb spread that burned pleasantly at the throat.

With appetites sharpened, the *prima mensa* was brought in with great ceremony. A magnificent local roast boar was placed at the centre of the room, its belly filled with sausages and figs and the crackled skin under a honey glaze. Close behind a roast peacock, its iridescent feathers painstakingly reattached for display, was paraded through the room before being carved and served on elegant platters. The meat, tender and gamey, was complemented by a sauce of dates and spiced *garum*. Lentils, slow-stewed with coriander and *muria*, the intensely salty brine left over from *garum* production, offered an earthy contrast. Scaurus told the group with pride: 'It might be a by-product, but *muria* still holds a depth of flavour. Notice the savoury richness of the taste.'

The lentils were paired with generous slabs of *panis siligineus*, the finest white bread. Then came braised sow's udder, its buttery softness melting on the tongue, considered among the most refined delicacies of the Roman table. Crayfish, cuttlefish and octopus followed, bathed in a glossy *oenogarum*, a sauce of wine and herbs boiled with the fish, providing a briny, luxurious counterpoint to the heavier dishes. Scaurus, tasting it, paused. There might be a market for this, he had thought: *oenogarum*, ready-made. He would speak to the workshop in the morning.

By the time the *secunda mensa*, the dessert course, had arrived, Scaurus was ready to leave, though he pushed himself to stay. It was worth it. Dishes of pears stewed in honey and cinnamon, their syrup thick and clinging, were set beside towering plates of *dulcia piperata*, honey cakes dusted with black pepper for a sharp contrast of flavour. A fine *patina de piris*, a baked pear custard, was served in bowls, its creamy texture infused with sweet spices from the East. Pansa's culminating gesture, however, had been a final flourish of indulgence: a dish of imported dates from Parthia, stuffed with almonds and rolled in honey, accompanied by aged Falernian wine poured from chilled jugs. Pansa had spared nothing in his bid to impress.

He had watched young Erotis drink himself into disgrace, and Pansa, flushed with pride, stage the grand gesture of freeing a slave before his guests. To the uninitiated it had looked like pure benevolence, a master's sudden magnanimity. Such spectacles were the oldest trick in a Roman man's book: manumission at a feast bought not only applause but a lifetime of obligation. A Junian Latin freedman remained bound to his patron by ties as enduring as any chain. His vote, his labour, his loyalty, even his possessions at death.

Scaurus had never cared for Pansa, nor the familiar breed of men he represented. Too vain, too eager to be seen as virtuous. He was reminded of the wise words of the philosopher Plato: those who take office should not be lovers of rule. Rome's new men seemed not to be aware of this quality.

Safe in the comfort of his home, Scaurus reclined deeper into his cushions, the dreaded pain in his back impossible to ignore. Already feeling the effects of a hangover – no denying he was an old man now – Scaurus remembered the look on the slave's face, that trembling disbelief as his freedom was announced. The theatre may have been hollow, the moment for the man had been real.

Yet Scaurus knew better than the young men who puffed out their chests. True wealth was not measured in the dishes served, nor in the Falernian poured into golden cups. It lay in the names spoken between mouthfuls, and in the weight of alliances forged over honeyed dormice. And in the *garum*, always the *garum*, that lubricated the conversation as surely as it seasoned the food. Scaurus had seen it in that very house years before, at Pansa's father's feasts, when Pompeii still felt close to the heartbeat of Rome itself, swelling as it had been with the early Roman colonisers mixing with the established Samnite families. Those evenings, swollen with rhetoric and ambition, seemed now like the waning flame of what the older circle, himself included, called the last flicker of the Golden Age.

It was a time even before Scaurus, when men like his father and grandfather had lived leaner, worked harder, and spoke of service before self. Rome had not yet drowned itself in luxuries from every corner of the Empire, nor trained its sons to measure honour by the weight of silver. Back then, most people got their food from their humble kitchen gardens, making do with what they had. How harmless their fare had been then. But now even vegetables bore the marks of ambition; cabbages were now too large to fit onto a pauper's table, and asparagus, once freely gathered in the wild, was now cultivated for size and spectacle. He'd heard that in a nearby town they bred asparagus spears so heavy it took only three to the pound, when once a dozen had met the same weight. Even Nature herself had bent to vanity.*

Female modesty, too, wasn't merely an ornament, and they certainly weren't engaging in business. They didn't negotiate in the *tablinum*, nor press their husbands into politics. It was Augustus who had loosened the threads. He had made a spectacle of his sister Octavia and wife Livia, setting them up as examples of Roman matronly virtue, in contrast to Cleopatra, that foreign queen whose will was sharper than the swords of Antony's legions. From then on, the balance had tilted. Octavia, Livia and those who followed were women of steely purpose, while the soft emperors by their side proved malleable, distracted and content to let their wives rule in all but name.

Scaurus' grandfather used to sigh over such things, muttering that it was the beginning of the end. And perhaps the old man had been right. Looking back now, across the long drift of years, Scaurus felt it. Every age told itself that the past had been sturdier, more virtuous, more deserving of respect; yet he felt that something had indeed shifted. Rome, which once seemed built upon iron and oak, appeared softened into wax and silk, luxurious, pliant, less worthy of the name that had once made nations trem-

---

* I have paraphrased a rant taken from Pliny the Elder's *Natural Histories*, in which he is scorning the vices of early imperial Roman citizens.

THE EVERYMAN

ble. Gazing around sleepily at the luxuries of his *cubiculum* bedroom, the irony of his reminiscing wasn't lost on him. Scaurus closed his eyes, his breathing growing heavy, and clung to the memory of those golden days as Somnus, gentle god of sleep, drew him into darkness.

* * *

The next morning, Scaurus rose early, as he always did. The air inside his *domus* was cool and, beyond the shutters, the city was shaking itself awake. He could hear footsteps on stone and the occasional bray of a mule hitched outside a shop nearby. The distant roar of the sea carried on the breeze. The sound was so familiar to him that he only really noticed it in moments like this, in the quiet of dawn. One of his slaves, a quick-footed Greek, had already laid out a simple breakfast of watered-down wine, dried figs and a handful of olives, enough to settle the stomach without weighing him down. He'd never bought into the elite ideal of skipping breakfast; he was a working man, always had been, and he

Figure 27: Scene of the forum in Pompeii seen in a fresco from the Estate of Julia Felix (II.4.2-3)

needed his sustenance. He chewed slowly as sleep left his head, rolling a fig between his fingers and watching its wrinkled skin give way to the sticky flesh beneath.

After a brief, salubrious walk around his vast house, Scaurus dressed against the morning cold and stepped out into the streets of Pompeii. He decided to take a slow morning, the wine from the evening of revelry pressing heavy on his forehead. He would visit one of his newer workshops to observe operations before seeing some friends, then pick up business again in the afternoon. He walked with the unhurried yet confident gait of a man of his age, moving through streets still damp from the morning sweep, where household slaves flung buckets of water across the raised pavement onto the lower level of the street below. The scent of wet stone and fresh bread cooked during the night blended with the sharp tang of urine, the remnants of the night's chamber pots left on street corners for collection by the town's fullers.

The forum opened up before him, its great marble columns catching the first slant of sunlight. The names of great emperors, etched in bronze, glinted on their façades. He cut across the vast space where shopkeepers were in the process of erecting pop-up stalls and walked down the step to the pedestrianised stretch of the Via dell'Abbondanza. Passing the sloped entrance to the slave market, built by the woman called Eumachia, wicked feminine ambition made flesh, he turned right after the main crossroads to avoid the busiest shopping street. Shutters creaked open above him, revealing masses of dark, curly hair, the hallmark of strong Campanian women. As they peered out, they leaned on wooden sills, arms folded, calling to neighbours and exchanging the first gossip of the day. Some had decorated their windowsills with flowers, others had hung washing out, the October air still dry enough to do so. At ground level, a shoemaker crouched outside his shop, restringing a worn sandal with strips of softened leather, his head bowed close to the lantern at his side.

The walls, as ever, were plastered with the names of politicians and unknown people who wished to make their mark on the city, though down this street, the support for one of this year's four *aediles*, Lucius Popidius Secundus, a fellow diner at last night's feast, was especially prevalent. Scaurus passed a trio of men lolling about outside a house, waiting to be admitted to begin construction work and filling their bellies with bread. A beggar sat slumped against a column, hands outstretched, called for a kindness that would not come. He looked down his long nose at the figure on the floor: he was no better than a slave. Lazy with no ambition.

The traffic trundled in the opposite direction as he turned onto the street of one of his workshops. This part of the city was mercifully quieter, with vineyards and orchards spread over the plots of houses demolished after the great quake. He passed Euxinus' *caupona* and glanced inside, but he could only see a broad woman with a kind, rosy-cheeked face setting up for the day. Just a few steps further on rose the workshop. The pavement here was low; a ramp up to the workshop would be helpful, he noted, as he watched his men load jars of fish sauce onto a cart, the mule tied to one of the many holes in the pavement made for this purpose. They worked quickly, for while the cart spanned the width of the one-way street, no other cart could get by. He would speak to Pansa about getting permission to install a ramp the next time he saw him.

The driver was Lucius Aelius, husband of his freedwoman, Umbricia Fortunata. Just inside the doorway, he spotted a young worker wrestling with a precarious stack of small jars, one tilting dangerously out of place. Lurching forward, he caught it just in time before it could shatter.

'Nearly had a fish sauce bath there! Get some straw between them next time, it'll keep the jars steady.' His comment earned a wide grin from the boy, who darted inside, *amphora* in hand.

'Ah! Hard at work, I see,' he beamed, delivering a jovial slap to Lucius' back.

Never missing an opportunity to get his hands dirty, Scaurus helped load the remaining terracotta bottles onto the cart, before stepping inside the bustling workshop, where slaves and paid workers weaved in and out of one another. Over his shoulder, he called to Lucius: 'Tell Fortunata I said *salve*.'

Walking through the front rooms of the property, Scaurus moved past baskets piled high with the morning's catch of mackerel, their silvery scales still slick with seawater. In the kitchen to his left, a pot of water bubbled steadily on the hearth, ready to clean the *amphorae* for reuse. Near a low corner basin, a slave bent over a pile of *urcei*, scrubbing the insides with a stiff brush, his knuckles raw from the work. Another carried a stack of freshly scoured *amphorae*, heading for the rear garden where they would be placed upside down in the sun to dry.

Passing through a narrow doorway, Scaurus stepped into the heart of the workshop, an area open to the elements that had once been a luxurious peristyle garden. Shaded colonnades had enclosed a retreat of greenery and sculpted fountains, peaceful and healthful, before he had transformed it into a place of industry after the former owners, weary of the quakes, had sold it off. Now, it was a place of labour, dust and noise. Along one side of the portico, a tiled roof rested on two sturdy columns, providing shelter for unsealed containers. In the central garden, two great fig trees stood, their broad leaves offering shade to the workers below. One of them had stood for at least three decades; the other Scaurus himself had helped to plant 10 years earlier, in what felt like another lifetime.* His son had been alive then, full of promise. He exhaled softly, pushing the thought aside.

His gaze lingered on the walls of the peristyle, where yellow frescoes remained remarkably vivid despite the years of wear. Painted laurel and delicate greenery unfurled with striking realism, curling between songbirds that darted through imaginary fig trees. Before the scenes stood a small altar with a carved floral pattern, a relic of the long-faded devotions of the house's former residents. In the far corner, a slave stepped out from the modest latrine recently added for the workers, its low roof now used to store tools. Even there, the walls bore decoration, sharp green leaves twisting across a deep red background.

To Scaurus' left, a secondary kitchen had been installed, larger than the one at the front of the house. A great hearth blazed at its heart, flames licking at the pots suspended above, their contents bubbling and thick with spice. Above it, the ever-watchful serpent fresco curled protectively around an altar strewn with pinecones, promising prosperity and warding off misfortune. Atop the hearth, a small tripod supported a simmering concoction. Scaurus leaned in, catching the unmistakable scent of *garum* laced with wine and herbs. His overseer, trailing close behind, noted his interest.

'*Oenogarum?*' asked Scaurus, his eyebrow raised. 'This is what I had last night at the feast. I've been wondering whether it was worth bottling.'

---

* Two fig trees were indeed found here by excavators, their root cavities having been preserved as plaster casts in the same manner as the victims of Pompeii. During the eruption, the trees were surrounded by pumice and ash and, in the years following, had decayed, leaving a gap in the volcanic matter. This was then filled with plaster of Paris by the excavators. They dated the trees based on the size of their trunks and roots.

Figure 28: The courtyard in the Garum *Workshop (I.12.8) with the original embedded* dolia. *The door leads to the rear garden*

'Just our thoughts, too,' the overseer said. 'Right now, we're reducing it over a low heat; a little bit of *garum*, some wine, a few herbs and a smidge of honey. I've been experimenting with ways to quicken the fermentation process as well, keeping some of our pots in the hottest rooms.'

He hesitated before adding, 'I also heard of another method: boiling the *garum* with oregano to speed up the fermentation process.'

The very thought of speeding up the process perfected by his forefathers made Scaurus' nose wrinkle, but he nodded his approval. Innovation always had its place when there were new products to be sold and more money to be made. Feeling suddenly oppressed by the heat and throng of bodies around him, Scaurus stepped back out into the open air.

In the nearest corner of the peristyle, six massive *dolia* were embedded in the ground. Five brimmed with fish sauce decanted from *amphorae*, kept cool and stable until required, while the sixth was being siphoned off into freshly washed *urcei* for sealing

THE EVERYMAN

Figure 29: Hearth in the kitchen at the Garum Workshop *(I.12.8) with tripod found here*

and distribution.* Scaurus lifted the lid of one of the full *dolia* and inhaled. The pungent scent filled his nostrils: the unmistakable perfume of profit. He watched as his workers sealed the *urcei* with fresh pitch, spreading the sticky black resin around the stoppers to keep air and moisture out. An illiterate slave completed

---

* When excavators opened these pots, they found the small bones and vertebrae of anchovies in five of the pots. The excavator, Amadeo Maiuri, stated that when these vessels were excavated and opened in 1960, the smell of fish was still fresh, and remained so for some time after exposure to the air.

the process, labelling each jar with a bold inscription that he didn't understand:

'*The best* liquamen, *from the shop of Scaurus.*'

With business at the workshop settled for the day, Scaurus' mind turned elsewhere. It had been some time since he had visited the gladiator barracks, and as a friend of the *lanista*, the gladiator trainer and owner, it was only proper to show his face now and then. The timing felt right: last night's games had gone in his favour. The fighter he had backed had emerged victorious, earning Scaurus a gratifying sum, much to the irritation of the overly confident Paquius Proculus who had wagered against him. The memory amused him. A visit today would allow him to pass on his congratulations and enjoy his success all over again.

* * *

The sounds reached him first: the perpetual thud of wooden swords, the sharp commands of the *lanista*, the grunt of exertion as two fighters became locked in a mock struggle. The passageways leading to the barracks were dim, their walls painted in deep reds and ochres. Stepping through the colonnade, Scaurus emerged into the training ground where, around its perimeter, he could see the wooden doors which punctuated the walls. Some were ajar, revealing glimpses of the sparse living quarters beyond, while others were closed against the cool morning air. The training arena stretched before him, a rectangle of well-worn sand bearing the scars of countless drills. The scent of sweat, oiled leather and damp earth was overwhelming. He barely registered when he passed a room with shackles attached to the walls.

After the great quake, the gladiatorial training school had been forced to relocate to the portico of the Greek Theatre and its courtyard had become the heart of the new barracks. Within those walls,

THE EVERYMAN

Figure 30: Iron slave shackle found in the Gladiator Barracks at Pompeii

the daily pulse of discipline and survival carried on without pause, day in, day out, feeding the city's insatiable hunger for gladiator blood. The sheer scale of the operation was impressive. There was the kitchen which fed the many gladiators their vegetarian diet of beans, barley and legumes in the mess hall three times a day. Then there were the stables where the horses and mules were kept, and the armoury where equipment was stored between training and fights.* On the east side, a narrow staircase led to the *lanista's* quarters and a balcony, where other trainers and off-duty gladiators now stood watching the men training in the yard.

The courtyard was alive with motion. The *lanista* barked commands, his voice sharp as a drawn blade. The steady clash of *rudis* against *rudis* bounced off the walls and dust rose in faint clouds beneath shifting feet. The dull crack of their wooden training swords was a faint echo of the steel these men would later wield

---

* Many items of gladiatorial use were found here, including armour, weapons and even shackles. The bodies of a number of people were discovered, too, including a high-status woman wearing beautiful jewellery.

in the amphitheatre. Scaurus lingered at the edge of the training ground, surveying the scene. He had placed bets on many of these men over the years, watched them bleed and triumph to the roar of the crowds, and seen more still die for the sport. Here, stripped of spectacle, they were simply men, sweating and shaping themselves into instruments of survival.

The mix of enslaved and free men before him were a varied lot, from raw recruits with uncertain stances to veterans whose bodies bore the brutal script of past battles. Most had been captured in faraway lands and sold as gladiators due to their physique or skill or spirit. Others had chosen the path, either out of their desperation for money, or the draw of fame. The *hoplomachus* gladiator, armed to resemble a Greek *hoplite* soldier, moved fast. Lean yet muscly, like a hunting dog, his bare feet scuffed the gritty dirt as he thrust his spear. His movements were quick and aggressive, designed to wear down a slower opponent. In the arena, he would be more heavily armoured: a *manica* iron-laminated guard on his right arm, his legs protected by tall shinpad greaves, and in his hands, a small, circular shield, a spear and a sword. His helmet would be high crested with a wide brim, but for now, his face was bare.

The *murmillo* was an Imperial adaptation of the earlier Gaul-type gladiator, once portraying the enemies of Rome who, by now, were so well-integrated into Roman society that it was out of fashion to depict them as villains. In contrast to the *hoplomachus*, the *murmillo* stood solid as an ox, waiting rather than striking. He was heavier, built for power rather than speed, and he had the look of a man who could take any beating. He would ordinarily wear a large, rounded helmet with a high crest, designed to evoke the image of a sea monster, its broad shape making it harder for his opponent to land a clean strike. In his hand he would carry a massive rectangu-

THE EVERYMAN

lar *scutum* shield, large enough to cover most of his body while fighting with his *gladius* sword.

Scaurus knew better than anyone the true origin of this Roman gladiator, and why his helmet usually contained images of a special type of fish: the Greek *mormyrus*. This creature glided with effortless grace, conserving its strength until the moment it unleashed a sudden, electric strike. This was no mindless predator, nor a reck-

Figure 31: Murmillo *helmet found in the Gladiator Barracks at Pompeii*

less hunter. It was a master of calculation, adapting to currents and threats with precision. The *murmillo* fought the same way. Burdened with a heavy shield and helmet, he was not the fastest in the arena, nor the most agile, but his size was intimidating. He held his ground, biding his time, absorbing the wild, frenzied attacks of lighter-armed opponents before delivering the decisive blow.

Scaurus turned his attention to another pair of fighters in the far corner of the courtyard: a *retiarius* and a *secutor*. The fisherman and the hunter. Scaurus had always found this type of match compelling: not just for the spectacle, but because he understood it in his bones. Watching the *retiarius* cast his net, the movement was so familiar it pulled him back in time, to the long, quiet mornings at the shore with his father. The wet sand had clung to his feet, the net in his hands slick with seawater and brine. The salt had stung his nostrils and the tide had lapped at his ankles. He had been no more than 10, standing beside his father as the man crouched and pulled a rope through his teeth, a hole worn into his molars from the repetitive motion.* They need not have been there, there were plenty of men to do the hard labour for them, but his father, and his father before him, believed a true Roman's hands should not remain soft but must at least bear the memory of labour.

'It's not strength that fills the baskets, boy,' his father had told him. 'It's knowing when to throw and when to wait.'

Patience. That was what made a fisherman. The ability to read the water, to see the subtle flicker of silver beneath the surface, to understand the movement of the tide. The net had to fall at exactly

---

* The back tooth of one of the victims of the eruption in Herculaneum was found to have a hole in it, formed from the continuous movement of a rope through it. This led excavators to believe that he was a fisherman, as the movement matches those made by net makers and fishermen even today.

the right moment. No sooner, no later. He had learned that lesson well, in business and in life. Now, in the sunlit courtyard of the barracks, the *retiarius* flicked his wrist, and the net unfurled in a perfect arc. The *secutor* twisted sharply, dodging left, but not fast enough. The weighted edge of the net caught against his arm, dragging across his side. Not a clean throw, but a warning. A second chance.

Figure 32: Graffiti showing gladiator match records from Pompeii, including victories by the popular fighters Hilarus (14 victories) and Marcus Attilius (a novice gladiator; 'tiro vicit')

The *secutor* surged forward, tearing free of the net's edge and pressing the attack before the *retiarius* could gather it again. That was the risk, always. If you mistimed the cast or let the moment slip, you left yourself wide open. The *lanista* barked an order, and the *retiarius* and *secutor* reset, their bodies coiling with fresh anticipation. The game began again.

Scaurus exhaled, rubbing his hands over his head where once there had been thick hair. He thought back to last night's fight, the din of the crowd at an ear-ringing level. He had sat close enough to see the blood spatter. The *murmillo*, Marcus Attilius, the latest celebrity in the Campanian gladiatorial circuit, had fought the *thraex* Lucius Raecius Felix, a veteran gladiator modelled after the soldiers of Thrace known for their agility and precision. Felix was nearing the end of his career, with 12 victories to his name. Both had fought hard, matching each other stroke for stroke, their footwork sharp and their shields battered with the force of each blocked strike.

Felix had been quicker and more agile, at least at the start. He had fought with a smaller, rectangular shield called a *parmula*, made for swift, calculated deflections, and a curved *sica* blade, angled for slicing under an opponent's guard. On his head he wore a helmet with the distinctive high crest, a full-face guard with small eye holes, and plume holders for added display. His speed had almost turned the tide of the fight more than once.

Almost.

His helmet and shield lost behind him, Felix had knelt with his chest heaving after Attilius had delivered a blow to his thigh in one swift moment. His ruby red blood soaked the sand of the arena beneath him.

The bleeding Felix had turned his sweaty face in the direction of the premium seats, where the town's most important people sat, in

THE EVERYMAN

Figure 33: Fresco of two gladiators, a Murmillo *and a* Thracian, *fighting. Found in a* thermopolium *(hot food shop) in Region V*

a final appeal, wordlessly asking whether his life still held value to them. Scaurus had watched, his own fingers clenching at his knee. The crowd had screamed for blood, but in the end, only one man's choice mattered. The veteran gladiator was granted clemency. The fight ended and, as the sand was raked smooth and fresh sawdust scattered, the injured trudged into the *sanitarium*, the room dedicated to treating their wounds. The next match had been announced with all the pomp and revelry of a festival procession.

A hand landed on Scaurus' shoulder, bringing him back to the present. It was his friend, Numerius Festus Ampliatus, the *lanista* of the barracks, and the subject of the graffiti on his son's tomb.

'Fancy a warm wine, Scaurus?' he said with a grin, already steering him towards one of the side rooms.

* * *

By late morning, the sky had softened into a golden haze when Scaurus arrived at the house of the Vettii brothers on the other side of town. Pausing in the vestibule of the side entrance to the house, reserved for members of the household and close friends, Scaurus eyed the fresco of Priapus that loomed to his right. The god of prosperity stood grotesquely well-endowed, his phallus carefully balanced against a bag of gold, a crude but effective symbol of what mattered in this household. No subtle metaphors here. Money equalled power, virility and success.

The slave, who recognised Scaurus, permitted him into the atrium. It was a grand space, larger than most in Pompeii, designed to impress and intimidate guests the moment they entered. The rainwater in the *impluvium* rippled with the vibration of people moving about the house.

Figure 34: Prostitution graffito *on the left wall of the entrance hall of the House of the Vettii (VI.15.1). It says: EUTYHIS GRECA ASSIBUS II MORIBUS BELLIS, 'Eutychis, Greek, nice mannered, for two asses'*

THE EVERYMAN

Scaurus had known Aulus Vettius Conviva and Aulus Vettius Restitutus for years.* Most had. They were former slaves who, through trade and shrewd investments, had risen to join the ranks of the wealthiest men in the city. They had made their fortunes as wine merchants, moneylenders and landlords, and they were proud of it. Scaurus had seen their gold rings flash over silk-draped couches at banquets, extending invitations only to those who would be useful to them. They threw lavish, wild feasts that blurred the line between decadence and vulgarity, all to remind the world who they were and where they had come from. And in their relentless climb towards the heights of the elite, Scaurus understood them. Money was the only path open to men like them, a substitute for the political engagements and hereditary privileges reserved for people like himself, the *ingenui*, or those born free.

As he stepped into the atrium, he took in the extravagant frescoes that surrounded him. There was no place for restraint here either, and certainly no attempt at modesty. The Vettii had adorned their home with the finest, most fashionable decorations Pompeii had to offer. At the base of a pillar, a painted slave balanced a tray with exaggerated precision; even the lowest in the household were commemorated. No space had been left untouched. Birds perched on painted shelves, garlands curled around illusionistic columns, and figures danced along the panels in a riot of colour.

While he waited for his friends to receive him, his eye caught on a new piece of graffiti on the wall: 'Eutychis, Greek, nice mannered, for two *asses*'. A good deal. Perhaps he could use her before returning home. It might release some of the tension he had been feeling.

* As with most of the relationships in this book, this one is imagined, but highly possible. Scaurus and the Vettii brothers were living in Pompeii at the same time and had a lot in common. They would almost certainly have known about each other, if not as acquaintances or friends.

Scaurus had made use of the Vettii brothers' discrete arrangement before, tucked away in the far corner of the house, beyond the great household shrine and kitchen. They had even adorned the walls with the familiar erotic scenes of the town's brothels. He didn't like to risk the public houses himself; the chamber here provided all the privacy he required.

As he recalled his previous visits to the room, a slave bearing a striking resemblance to the one in the painting at the bottom of the pillar appeared around the corner and told Scaurus his masters would meet him in one of the dining rooms. He was led beyond the atrium, into quarters where most visitors would never be admitted. This was confirmation of his status as a trusted friend of the masters of the house. Passing through the verdant peristyle, planted with all manner of greenery, and dotted with gleaming statues, Scaurus stepped through the latticework doors into a world of red and black revelry.

Figure 35: Wall frescoes in the House of the Vettii (VI.15.1)

THE EVERYMAN

Here was the brothers' societal rise laid out in paint, a story of labour turned to profit, and industry transformed into luxury. It wasn't something to be ashamed of, as the elite in Rome thought of mercantile trades, but something to advertise freely, especially in Pompeii. The deep crimson of the walls, richer than spilled red wine, glowed in the soft light filtering from the peristyle, while a black lower register edged in delicate gold anchored the space. Miniature scenes of industry played out in exquisite detail all around the room. Around the perimeter, plump, winged cupids danced along the walls. But these were no idle cherubic figures, lazily drifting through the heavens. These cupids pressed wine, made perfumes, crafted jewellery and traded goods in an echo of the labour that had built this home.

Scaurus was once again drawn to his favourite scenes. In the far corner, a winged cupid tugged at a bright yellow cloth, stretching it taut on a frame, his tiny hands straining with effort. Around him, others stomped on fabric submerged in dye vats, their little feet churning the colours into the cloth. Nearby, a merchant cupid displayed finished bolts of fabric, their colours bold and bright, enticing passing customers with the promise of quality.

Though not Scaurus' trade, he had always felt a connection to the perfumers' panel. It captured true industry: cupids mixing fragrant oils with crushed petals, their fingers deft as they poured the concoctions into glass bottles. Some handled the fragile vials with care, while others stood before wooden cabinets lined with miniature idols of the gods. Off to the side, glass-blowing cupids worked in unison, their cheeks puffed as they blew molten glass into perfume flasks, small but exquisite, each in a swirl of colours.

Beyond them, a chariot race was in full, chaotic motion. A cupid had taken a spill, his legs flailing as his noble deer-drawn chariot collapsed in a tangled heap. Others skidded to a halt, wings flapping, while the victor, palm frond raised high, basked in his moment of triumph. In the next panel, a group of goldsmith cupids worked in quiet concentration. One hunched over his handiwork, his tiny brow furrowed with focus. Another weighed precious metal on a miniature set of scales, while behind him, a cupid added his latest creation to a glowing furnace. Two further cupids worked at an anvil, the hammer of one suspended in the air, ready to fall.

Scaurus stood in thought; he had never noticed this detail before. The hammer, frozen mid-swing, held a moment of inevitability. The scales, finely balanced, measured more than just goods; they weighed choices and fate, the fragile line between fortune and failure. How many times had he stood like that cupid, not only weighing fish or *garum*, but the decisions that would shape his life? Trade was never just about profit: it was about knowing when to take a risk, when to hold back, and when to tip the balance in your

Figure 36: Cupid goldsmiths from the House of the Vettii (VI.15.1)

favour. A fraction too much, and the balance would shift. In an instant, the hammer could fall.

Then, a crack, deep and hollow in sound.

The silence that followed stretched thin and taut, as though the walls were bracing themselves for what might come next.

Then another sound, louder this time; a groan rising from beneath, vast and ancient, as though the earth was awakening from a slumber. The groan turned into a tremor, violent and unrelenting.

Scaurus' fingers tightened into a fist. The hammer on the wall remained poised in the air, its blow yet to land.

The slave appeared in the doorway, his face pale and voice uncertain. Scaurus barely heard him. His eyes were still on the cupids.

And then the room lurched, a ferocious jolt that sent a fine spray of plaster dust cascading from the ceiling and made the walls quiver like the surface of disturbed water. This was not just another tremor.

The Fates were bringing the hammer down.

CHAPTER FOUR

THE WORKING POOR FAMILY

ONE DAY IN NOVEMBER 79 CE

Umbricia Fortunata was sure this was the spot.

The city was gone, smothered beneath a vast, unyielding sea of stone. No walls, no doorways, no garden. No home. Only this desolation, endless and silent, stretching as far as the eye could see, the tops of pillars poking from the ground like gravestones.

Around her, others searched, their grief raw and unrelenting. A man dug at the hardened earth with bare hands until his nails split, a strangled sob catching in his throat. A woman fell to her knees, clutching at nothing, keening for children she would never hold again. Some wandered around aimlessly, dazed and hollow-eyed, while others stood motionless, swallowed by the weight of what they had lost. What they could never get back.

The land beneath them was thick with the dead, but few bodies remained to be mourned. They were encased in the stone itself, sealed in the moment they had been overtaken, their lives swallowed by the roar of the mountain.

Fortunata did not weep.

She simply stood, hands curled at her sides, nails digging into her palms as she willed herself to feel something beyond the cold, suffocating numbness creeping through her limbs.

She was standing above him. She knew it in her gut.

'Take the children,' he had said, hands firm on her shoulders, the heat of his palms pressing through her tunic. 'Go ahead. I'll find you. I promise.'

There had been no time to argue, no time to fight. The sky had been falling, the air thick and unbreathable, the darkness clawing towards them like some great beast unfurling its wings. So, she had taken their children and ran, fighting through the crush of bodies, breathless and stumbling as the earth had shaken.

On the back of a cart, she'd looked back often, seeing only darkness and the menacing orange glow of Vesuvius. But in the early hours of the next morning, as they reached a high ridge many miles beyond the city walls, she turned once more. That was when she had seen it.

The cloud.

A roiling wall of black and fire, thundering down the slopes of the mountain, devouring everything in its path.

She had known in that moment she would never hear his voice again, never see his face, never feel his arms wrap around her.

He was here, below her feet, locked in the stone.

Her breath caught in her throat as she crouched, pressing her palm to the hardened earth as if she could reach through it, as if the warmth of his skin might rise to meet her touch. But there was nothing.

Nothing but the wind, skimming cold over the ruined land.

Nothing but the weight of time ahead of her, pressing her down.

Nothing but absence.

THE WORKING POOR FAMILY

THE SEVENTH HOUR (12 NOON), 23 OCTOBER 79 CE

Umbricia Fortunata lingered in the threshold of her shop, watching as the day carried on with its usual unhurried flow. Across the street, the *thermopolium* of Equitius was in full swing, the sizzle of hot oil and the bright chatter of customers drifting across the street. She breathed in the smell of roasting meat, which mixed with the earthier fragrances of figs, olives and vegetables piled high at her shopfront. The wide entrance of her shop was open to the street, an invitation to passing customers. Within, *amphorae* rested in tidy rows, filled to the brim with dark wine, golden olive oil and the prized *garum* of Scaurus that was a part of Fortunata's own legacy.

Fortunata had once been the property of Aulus Umbricius Scaurus. Now, as a freedwoman, she lived in his shop-house in the garden neighbourhood of Pompeii, cultivating the green sanctuary at the rear of the property under a *locatio conductio rei* agreement: instead of paying rent in coins, she paid in produce. She was also one of Scaurus' trusted purveyors of the Empire's most sought-after fish sauce.

Her husband Lucius Aelius worked alongside her, but it was Fortunata who had shaped their fortune. Throughout Pompeii and beyond, her name was stamped onto the slender *urcei* containing Scaurus' sauce. She catered to all tastes and customs, offering not just *garum* itself, the pure, unadulterated fish sauce favoured by connoisseurs, but also *garum castum*, a special variety prepared without certain fish species for those with dietary restrictions, such as Jewish communities. Her enterprise rested not only on the excellence of Scaurus' product but on her shrewd grasp of her customers' needs. Added to this was the weight of her former owner's name, which she had taken upon her manumission. In the Roman way, her name was the feminine form of his own. She lifted an *urceus* and though she couldn't read, the words painted on the side were so familiar to her:

'*Flower of* Garum *in pure form, from the distributor Umbricia Fortunata.*'

Fortunata often pondered on how long her name would endure after her death. How many seasons would pass before the last *urceus* bearing her mark was scrubbed clean, its inked letters dissolved beneath the hands of another merchant? After she had departed from this world, how much of her presence would remain?

Fortunata had bought her own freedom several years ago with the money saved from running parts of Scaurus' business for him.* Over time, she had earned his trust, until their relationship felt closer to partnership than obligation. For all his grumbling about the 'Golden Age', when women stayed at home, he had recognised the success she was bringing into his business and rewarded her with his consent to marry Lucius, a free-born *ingenui*. Though no longer bound to him in law by virtue of her marriage, Fortunata continued to manage contracts and trade for Scaurus as she always had.

She had come a long way since the day a merchant laughed in her face at an early attempt to close a deal for a *garum* shipment from the Iberian Peninsula. It had been raining for days, and that morning Fortunata had set out on the wet streets of Pompeii, anxious to secure her first deal as a freedwoman. A new merchant ship had just arrived at the dock and its crew were busy unloading

---

* We don't actually know how Fortunata earned her freedom, we only know that she was a freedwoman of the Scaurii.

THE WORKING POOR FAMILY

amphorae slick with water when she stepped forward to introduce herself.

'Look at this one!' one of them sneered. 'A whore who thinks she's Crassus himself.'*

The laughter soon turned coarse. A stocky dock worker, his mouth void of teeth, lunged forward and grabbed at her arm. She twisted free, but more hands closed around her tunic. Their jeers grew uglier, and for a moment she feared they meant to drag her down among the jars and ropes.

It was Eutychus, the dock slave, who had seen the start of the commotion and anticipated what was coming next, slipping away to fetch Scaurus from the other side of the dock where he was conducting his own business. He arrived just as the men began to push her towards the wall.

'Enough!' Scaurus barked, his voice carrying over the din of the dock. The hands fell away at once.

Fortunata, shaken but standing, waited for some word of defence now that she was a freedwoman, but Scaurus only scowled at the delay as the men returned to their work.

'Is the deal agreed?' he demanded.

'No, Scaurus,' she admitted, trying but failing to steady her shaking voice.

'Then next time, send for me sooner,' he said curtly, already turning to sign the tablets. A short while later, he pocketed the lion's share of the profit from the very deal she had fought to secure.

Being a former slave, and a mother and wife besides, only made an already difficult occupation more trying. She had been overlooked, second-guessed and spoken for more times than she could count.

---

* Marcus Licinius Crassus (115–53 BCE) was the richest man in Rome in the first century BCE, having earned his fortune through real estate, silver mining and loans.

Some semblance of respect had eventually come, though slowly and never without effort. Every marked jar, every satisfied customer, was not just a transaction but a rebuttal against a society built for freeborn men. Proof that she belonged. And it was here, in this humble corner of Pompeii, where her feeling of belonging took root.

Unlike the tumult of the adjoining great thoroughfare, where merchants jostled for space and travellers fresh from the River Sarno's docks pushed through the crowds, Fortunata had always loved how the street they lived on belonged to the locals. Here, life was steady and calm, a place where business was rooted in trust and familiarity. Above their shop, where her young daughter was napping, she had made the modest rooms overlooking the street homely, often keeping the wooden shutters drawn to shield against

Figure 37: Garum urcei. *The rear bottle bears the inscription* 'G.F. Scombri Scaurus'

the afternoon glare. At the rear, their storerooms lined the ground floor, where Lucius had embedded a *dolium* for storing *liquamen*, to be dispensed when needed. Heading back inside the shop, Fortunata walked through a narrow doorway to the right and into their garden, which stretched across the width of the *insula*. She was proud of this garden, an impressive yet peaceful retreat of vines, fruit trees and neat rows of vegetables. What they didn't sell, they ate.

Her enslaved past meant that Fortunata was familiar with the formal gardens of elite houses in the city, with their neat colonnades and sculpted symmetry. But theirs was different. This was a working space: practical and shaped by necessity rather than ornament, and created in place of buildings that were damaged in the great earthquake. There were no crisp sand paths or decorative fountains, just well-worn tracks carved out by habit and use. She and Lucius had raised the ground between the two main irrigation channels, forming a natural walkway between the house and their living area at the back of the garden. In the far corner by the cistern, they had half-buried six *dolia* into the earth, their broad clay mouths spilling over with herbs and late-blooming flowers.

Though the garden was pared back for winter, it still held on to its last flashes of colour, bearing the quiet traces of the year's labour, a cycle of effort and reward. Between the dormant vines, some propped against casually placed stakes and others curling around the 16 scattered trees, vegetables and herbs plugged the gaps. Garlic and onions stood in neat rows, while fat cabbage heads, their waxy leaves furled tight, dotted the earth in clusters. Lavender and rosemary stretched out their fragrant arms, and thyme crept low across the soil, its wiry stems weaving a sprawl of green.

Fortunata watched Lucius fondly as he entered the garden, the bronze bucket heavy with water from the public fountain down the

Figure 38: The garden of the working poor family at I.20.5

road. Usually, he spent little time with her in the garden. His world was structured by the routine deliveries of fish sauce and garden produce around the town. Trailing just behind him was their 10-year-old son. He had joined him for the morning rounds: first the usual delivery route through town, pulled by their mule, then down to the harbour to collect the shipment of *garum* that had just arrived from Hispania. Following his father, the boy carried a smaller *amphora* of his own filled with water and, without needing to be told, watered the beds closest to the house.

Fortunata examined the rows of crops with a practised eye. The grapevines had just shed their last leaves, their gnarled branches curling over the trellises, but the olive trees held on to their curled foliage, their fruit already picked, pressed off-site and sealed away in jars. The garden bore the mark of years of careful tending; each path and bed shaped with purpose. Lucius had laid out the irrigation channels with his usual patience, so that even during the hottest

THE WORKING POOR FAMILY

weeks of the summer, the soil remained watered. The longest of these ran straight along the wall from the cistern at the house to the far end of the plot; another traced a line between the trees at the garden's edge, carrying water to where it was needed. From these, smaller channels branched out across the soil. When the cistern was full, they could block the pipe's opening to slow the flow, enough to nourish the shoots but never enough to drown them. Around the base of their water cistern, the tools of daily life – a pair of tweezers for trimming lamp wicks, a cluster of eight small fishhooks for days by the river, or for hanging up fruits for preserving – lay scattered where they had been left after their last use.

For the next couple of hours, the family continued with their usual chores, tending to the garden and rearranging the shop, their world interrupted at intervals with the *tings* of customers ringing their bronze bell. Eventually, Fortunata placed a basket of lavender on a shelf, filled with the bunches she'd been tying together, and took a break, inhaling the stillness that had settled over their street.

On the adjoining main road, people were starting to filter towards the bathhouses before the peak hour of the day when the baths were at their noisiest and packed with bodies and chatter. The earlier din of carts had faded, replaced by the occasional creak of one passing by on the main street next to their home. Above, she heard the cooing sounds of her daughter stirring from her sleep and went upstairs to feed her before bringing her down to play freely in the garden while they worked.

There was no nursemaid, or *nutrix*, to help with childcare. As a freedwoman, she had, like many, lost contact with her family long ago, with any chance at reconnection impossible. Lucius' parents lived and worked across town, but, like them, they too did not have the luxury of time to help with the children. Instead,

Fortunata had sold *garum* with the baby tied to her chest and soothed a feverish child while haggling over *garum* by the *amphora*. She still remembered the birth; long and brutal, the midwife and local women present had been silent after the final push. And then, the cry. That thin, defiant cry. The men liked to talk of legacy, but it was women who bore it: bloodied, exhausted and without fanfare.

A few last customers drifted through the shop before closing. Among them was a young slave from Gaius Cuspius Pansa's household, a face she recognised. Fortunata reached for the finer produce set aside at the back and slipped it into his basket. It cost her a little, but she knew the gesture would keep Pansa's kitchens coming back, and that was worth far more.

Today, Fortunata moved through her closing tasks more quickly than usual. In just a few hours, the games would begin at the amphitheatre. Word had spread that Pansa, one of Pompeii's incoming *aediles*, had helped sponsor the spectacle, and many were eager to see whether he would take the opportunity to speak. Lucius had met him once, shortly before the election, when Pansa handed out free bread to the townsfolk, a gesture that had quietly tipped Lucius' voting tile into his box that July.

For a fleeting moment, Fortunata indulged a thought she had entertained before. What if, just for a day, the mischief of Saturnalia, the winter festival when societal roles were turned upside down, stretched further? What if women could cast their own votes, and hold office? She knew exactly who she would support in such a topsy-turvy world: Julia Felix, a businesswoman from her neighbourhood whose influence rivalled any man in the city. But that was not the world they lived in. With a small shake of her head, Fortunata returned to her work, gathering baskets from the display on the street outside.

THE WORKING POOR FAMILY

She lifted the figs and cherries first, then the grapes, cabbages and cucumbers, arranging the baskets neatly along the shelves inside the shop. Her son soon came in from the garden and joined her, mimicking her movements, his brow furrowed as he concentrated. At her feet, her daughter clung to the hem of her skirt, small fingers reaching for the crinkled surface of a cabbage or to stuff a cherry in her mouth, only for her mother to whisk it away at the last moment, before she could swallow the stone.

Fortunata glanced down the street one more time to make sure there weren't any last-minute shoppers. There had been talk from other local towns of new laws designed to keep merchants within their thresholds, to clear the clutter and make more space for pedestrians on pavements. She could not imagine such a thing happening here. If there was one thing that Pompeians did not do, it was keep to thresholds. Life in this city spilled outwards, its streets an extension of homes and businesses and its rhythm dictated by the ebb and flow of trade. Though long colonised, the city still clung to the independence it had always sought to protect. She had seen many a barber's chair perched on a pavement's edge, shorn curls catching in the breeze. All over the city, cookshops leaked onto footpaths, and blacksmiths and potters' workshops sprawled out beyond their shop fronts, the items hanging there a tempting invitation to come inside and spend. Butchers, too, hung their cuts near the doorways, the slabs of meat swaying so close to passers-by that one could reach out and trace the marbled lines of fat with a finger.

The warm dusk air turned cool as the low sun slipped behind a cloud. She pulled the shutters across, the wooden slats groaning as they folded into place along the groove in the wall and threshold. Lucius would lock them later. Passing back into the garden, her gaze drifted to the top of the boundary wall, where Lucius and a

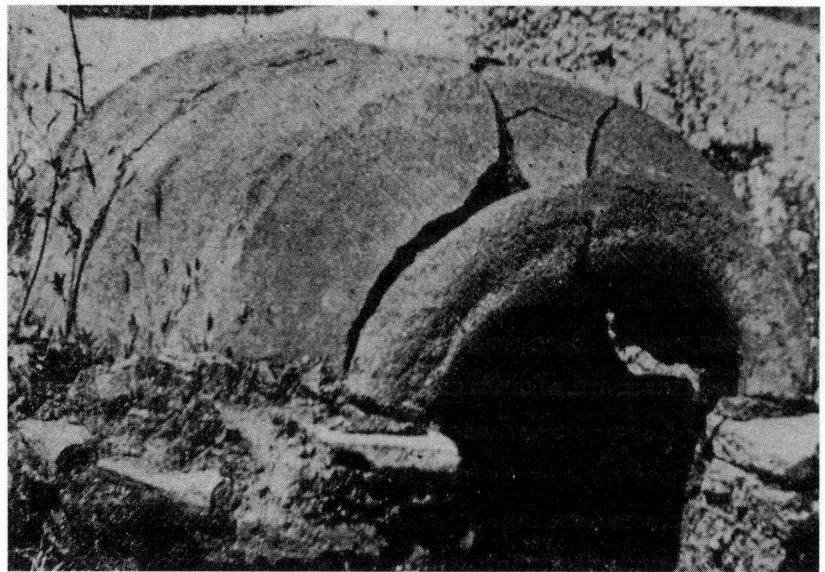

Figure 39: A dog kennel, made from an old terracotta pot, found in the House of the Garden of Hercules (II.8.6)

few neighbours had cemented shards of broken *amphorae* along the edge, a makeshift solution to the problem of local children climbing over at night to steal fruit from their trees. For now, it seemed to be doing the trick, but in time, they would likely follow their neighbours' lead and get a dog to keep watch. Many gardens in the district had one, nestled inside an old pot that had been cut in half and partly buried in the soil, its den warmed through by the day's sun.

The family who would be joining them for dinner in the garden that evening had two dogs in their orchard. The larger one, supposedly the guard dog, was all soft eyes and a wagging tail, more interested in coaxing scraps from visitors than she was in standing sentry. But the smaller one, fierce, fearless and utterly devoted to his duty, was the true protector. He had the heart of a beast twice his size and would bark at the first sign of an intruder, standing his ground against anyone he did not trust. He frequently caught rats, his tiny white-and-grey frame launching into action at speed. Fortunata had once visited to collect seeds and had been greeted by both dogs. The little one had circled her feet, eyes keen, sizing her up with the gravitas of a seasoned soldier. Only then had the bigger one lumbered over, knocking against her legs and nearly licking her to death in greeting. She had laughed at the contrast then, charmed by the pair.* The neighbours, a Jewish family to whom she sent orders of her kosher *garum castum*, spoke of their little dog with fondness, calling him Oz, which they told her meant 'strength' or 'courage' in Hebrew. Perhaps, she thought, her family would find a dog like that for their own garden one day.

Smiling at the thought, she moved along the garden's edge, pausing to tend to the fruit and nut trees. Their branches stretched skywards, skeletal against the dimming sky. Following the advice of her neighbours, that trees should be freed of useless wood, Fortunata inspected each branch along the wall, searching for any dead or overgrown areas. She placed the curved blade of her knife against a brittle, leafless limb, applying a gentle pressure to cut it cleanly off. The branch snapped with a soft crack, falling to the ground. Later she would gather it for kindling, for cooking at the back of the garden or for the brazier kept inside their stuffy, upstairs apartment. She worked methodically, the pruning knife slicing through the wood as she progressed from tree to tree, trimming away only what was necessary.

Kneeling, she reached for one of the larger cabbage plants, twisting its stem with a firm motion. The roots gave way with a satisfying snap, the weight of the vegetable solid in her hands. One by one,

---

* The bones of two dogs, one large and one small, were found in the Large Orchard at I.22, alongside the bones of many other animals. They may have been kept in the garden, or otherwise were the remains of meals.

she harvested a few more, brushing the loose dirt from their bases before setting them in her basket. This land, this soil; it gave so freely and so richly. Campania had always been generous, its earth yielding more than the farmers could ask for, sometimes even three or four harvests a year. Their cabbages and onions grew large and full-flavoured, a staple on every table, while figs and Pompeii's famous cherries filled the markets, their sweetness praised across the Empire. The vineyards and olive groves that sprawled across the countryside fed not just Pompeii, but even Rome itself, their oils and wines sought after in distant cities.

Straightening up, Fortunata lifted the heavy basket and made her way to the far end of the garden where the family had their outdoor living space. Over the years, she had shaped it into a simple but functional retreat for her family. Three trees nearby offered shade in the height of summer, and, by mid-afternoon, the garden wall cast a long, cooling shadow. She stooped to prepare the cooking area, setting out her pots and pans in the corner. Nearby, her loom weights sat untouched, waiting for the next time she needed to weave a cloak or tunic. Their trusty bronze tripod, a portable stand for cooking and warmth, would soon hold the pot for their evening meal. She arranged the other cooking utensils around it, shaping a makeshift kitchen beneath the open sky.

Above her, Lucius and some fellow gardeners had stretched an awning from the wall, a makeshift canopy that softened the blaze of hotter days. Within the stone of the back wall, Lucius had hollowed out a small triangular niche to create a modest household shrine, where they placed offerings before their evening meals. Soon, the colder weather would push them inside, but for now, they dined here most nights, their lanterns flickering in the night air and their cooking fire lending its warmth. She paused, adjusting the basket on her hip, and glanced up at the painted plaster cling-

THE WORKING POOR FAMILY

Figure 40: Cooking utensils found at the rear of the working-poor garden at I.20.5

ing to the far wall: faint remnants of another life, when houses once stood where their garden now was.

When the great quake had hit 17 years ago, the damage to the buildings had been too great, and the structures too unstable, and so they had been torn down and cleared away to make room for something new. Scaurus, the property owner, had seen no reason to rebuild, at least for now.* Others had done the same, turning houses into workshops, warehouses and rental spaces. It was easier that way. There was no stopping the tremors, no guarantee that a newly built home would not suffer the same fate. Besides, gardens

---

* We do not know who owned this property, but here I am making an example of the links that may have existed between freed people and their patrons. A lot of the properties in this part of the town were repurposed in this manner after the earthquake of 62 CE, including this one.

had their own value, especially these days when demand for local produce was on the rise. And so here they were, among the greenery, the cooling air, the lingering scent of damp earth and cut rosemary. The garden would sleep soon, the harvests thinning as winter crept closer. But in the months to come, the cycle would begin again. The soil would soften and, gods willing, new shoots would push through, allowing the land to give back once more.

Fortunata called out to her children as she passed through the rows of their garden, her voice carrying over the vines. Her son dashed up to her, his face bright with excitement as he held out a small coin he had found between the roots. Fortunata smiled and closed her hand gently around his. 'Keep it for your *peculium*,' she said, 'and ask your father if you might spend it at the *palaestra* later.'* Lucius encouraged their son to manage his savings, eager for him to learn the value of money, something he himself had lacked in his youth. Both he and Fortunata dreamed of more for the boy, a life built on the understanding, security and independence that came from knowing how to stand on one's own feet.

Her daughter toddled alongside clutching her mother's tunic with a small but determined grip. As Lucius slid the doors shut across the shopfront, they clicked into the groove along the stone threshold. He locked them with a click and slipped the key into the pouch at his waist as they joined the growing throng surging in the direction of the amphitheatre only one block away. The streets hummed with excitement and feverish anticipation for the games ahead. As they neared the amphitheatre, the sounds of the gathering crowd grew.

Beneath the spreading branches of tall evergreens and plane trees, merchants and hawkers had set up their stalls, their displays

---

* The *palaestra* was the exercise and social hub of the city.

THE WORKING POOR FAMILY

overflowing with wares. Everywhere, the senses were overwhelmed by colour, scent and the shifting energy of the city. Fruit sellers arranged their baskets in careful heaps, the jewel-bright skins glistening in the slanting light and their earthy fragrance folding into the perfume and oil drifting behind bodies who had bathed for the games. Fortunata noticed a peddler selling garlands of flowers, their bright colours standing out against the dusty ground. A nut-seller wove through the crowd, his voice rising over the hum, while a butcher held up skewers of grilled meat which enticed many a passing man. Children darted between the stalls, eyes wide as they watched performers juggle and musicians play.

At a nearby stall, a spice merchant called out, his skin darkened from years beneath the sun. Before him, trays of the fragrant treasures were displayed; cumin the colour of burnished gold, coriander seeds pale and round like tiny pearls and black pepper as dark as ink, its heat prized by those wealthy enough to use it to season their meals. Fortunata was lucky to have a small supply at home; she would use it tonight, she thought. The day seemed worthy of it.

Fortunata's son tugged on her elbow, his gaze caught by a stall where rows of small terracotta figurines were on display. Clutching the coin he had found that day, he pointed eagerly at a gladiator with a shield, propped up next to a small Jupiter and a tiny horse. These simple, unglazed figures, crafted by local potters, were popular among children and sold for an *as*, an affordable souvenir for the masses.

'I want this one,' he said, snatching it up before anyone else could claim it.

Fortunata smiled. 'You're sure? Not the horse?'

He shook his head with certainty. 'The gladiator.'

With a small nod, she gave her permission. He handed over the coin, almost bursting with happiness, and clutched the figure to his chest, eyes shining. 'I'm going to show Papa,' he said, already running off into the crowd.

Fortunata lingered, her eyes caught by the rounded bodies of terracotta lanterns decorated with simple designs of swans and maenads, the female followers of the god of wine and revelry, Bacchus. Undecorated, practical and mass-produced using moulds, the lamps were inexpensive, priced between 1 and 2 *asses*. Fortunata traced the delicate features of Cupid etched into the surface of one of the lamps, his hair pulled up into a topknot. It was a little more expensive than the others, but she so seldom treated herself.

Passing it to the stall keeper, he added a coil of string for the wick and poured a small vial of olive oil into the hole. Striking a flame from another lamp, he gave it back to Fortunata as the wick caught with a soft hiss.

'There you go,' he said. 'Good flame on that one. Should last you a lifetime.'

'A long night will do,' she replied, cupping it carefully as she handed him the coins. The little flame danced in the oil, casting a soft, steady glow, and filled the air with the familiar scent of warm oil and smoke. The little lamp would light their way to their seats in the amphitheatre, and would later offer what comfort it could in the hours to come.

Fortunata and her family arrived at the amphitheatre, passing through the towering stone arches filled with more stalls. After handing their *tesserae* to the porters, entry tokens Lucius had collected for free in the forum days earlier,* the family moved

---

* *Tesserae*, tokens made most often of small pieces of bone, ivory or lead, granted entry to the games and were distributed in advance by magistrates or their agents, often in the forum or other civic spaces. This was part of public benefaction or electioneering. The tokens sometimes bore numbers or inscriptions indicating seating or areas within the amphitheatre, according to status and/or gender.

THE WORKING POOR FAMILY

through into the long, shadowed corridors. The air grew cooler and the hum of voices echoed off the stone. Climbing the worn steps, they emerged into the glare of the amphitheatre and found some seats among the ordinary townsfolk. They were apart from the wealthier patrons but still had a clear view of the arena below. They passed a local fishmonger, still smelling of his wares, who gave them a toothy grin. A few spectators down, a nearby baker nodded in recognition, his arms devoid of their usual dusting of flour. He had a few of his best products to share with his seat neighbours, his legendary *spira*, thin, spiral-crusted pastries sometimes filled with fruit, and *globi*, small fried balls of cheesy dough dipped in honey. He was a regular sight in the mornings, but now, like everyone else, he joined his fellow citizens for the games.

Lucius and Fortunata's friends and neighbours were already gathered in the stands. Grey-haired men and women leaned close in quiet conversation, their faces lined with years of watching the same spectacles side-by-side. A young couple nearby exchanged greetings, the mother rocking her infant in a sling, the child's eyes roving across the sea of strangers. Others from their neighbourhood offered nods and waves, their faces alight with anticipation. The place buzzed with excitement. Around them, Pompeii's tightly knit community pressed together, each life woven into the fabric of the others. Fortunata felt the thrill of shared expectation as all eyes turned towards the arena, waiting for the spectacle to begin.

After one of the current *aediles* had spoken, Gaius Cuspius Pansa stepped forward. Fortunata watched him closely, noting his commanding tone and the way he addressed the crowd as if speaking directly to each family in turn. His gestures were broad and his words chosen to inspire unity and pride in their shared heritage, a most skilful way of securing the people's loyalty. She glanced at Lucius beside her, quiet as always, his expression unreadable. He was not one for grand words or gestures, but his steadiness carried more weight in her eyes than all of Pansa's polished phrases. Men like the *aedile* would always take the credit, but it was those like Lucius, and women like herself, who kept the city turning, unseen and unacknowledged.

When the first clash of iron rang through the amphitheatre, the crowd erupted: roars of encouragement, gasps of shock, the collective intake of breath as blades found flesh. Fortunata's son sat transfixed, his mouth agape as he drank in every movement below. Fortunata stifled a laugh and nudged Lucius, who followed her gaze. The boy's wide-eyed wonder drew a few quiet chuckles from those nearby, a brief, shared amusement that softened the brutality of the scene below. To Fortunata's other side, her daughter's cheek pressed warm against her arm, less interested in the violence unfolding before her as she played with her small terracotta doll, moving the joints so that it appeared to be dancing.

Metal flashed. A gladiator faltered, stumbled. His victorious opponent lifted his sword high, waiting for the signal that would seal the defeated man's fate. The amphitheatre thundered with shouts of cruelty and pleas of mercy. Even the children grasped the brutal truth: gladiators who fell and did not rise would be dragged from the sand, their fate sealed by the will of the crowd and the judgment of the *editor*. Only one thing was ever certain – life is fragile. Today's hero might be nothing more than a memory tomorrow, removed from the world of the living by forces far greater than himself.

When the games ended, the energy of the spectacle still crackling in the air, the amphitheatre emptied in a slow tide through the *vomitoria*, the grand vaulted passageways leading to the concourse outside. Lanterns bobbed through the dusk as excited retellings of the battles poured from the lips of the young and old alike.

THE WORKING POOR FAMILY

Children turned sticks into swords and relived the clash of titans they had just witnessed, their excited voices bouncing off the stone walls of the city.

When they reached the shop-house, Lucius and their neighbour Salvius carried on together towards Salvius' nearby garden to fetch the piglet intended for their feast. Salvius' wife Lusoria joined Fortunata and the children as they went on inside, their little lanterns creating shadows as they moved through the dark house and out into the garden. One by one they pressed the flames of their handheld lanterns to those in the living area at the rear until the area was bathed in a warm orange glow. From over the wall came the unmistakable sounds of a couple enjoying each other, which made Lusoria and Fortunata exchange a giggle. By the time the men returned, the women had settled in the garden and the children were chasing one another between the trees and vines. The smoke of smouldering wood curled into the night as the embers glowed and warmed the cool air. Around it, the neighbours settled in easy companionship.

The piglet for the feast rested in Fortunata's arms, small and plump, its destiny fixed the moment it was chosen at the market. Tradition demanded an acknowledgment of its sacrifice, a gesture of respect before the meal could begin. As she held the small creature, Fortunata poured a few drops of wine onto the earth, saying a quiet invocation. A laurel leaf, plucked fresh from the garden, was pressed to the piglet's brow as a token offering to the household gods. In the triangular niche of the *lararium* shrine, a small flame burned, its glow illuminating the figures of the household *lares*, silent protectors of their family and home. Fortunata held the animal steady as Lucius made a clean and swift cut across its neck. The blood spilled in a dark ribbon into a shallow dish, which Fortunata set aside to enrich the sauce.

She lay the piglet's body before her on a woven mat and worked swiftly; speed was essential. Using a pot of hot water that had been boiling on the tripod, she scalded the bristles and scraped them away until the skin was smooth beneath her hands. Then, before the flesh could stiffen, she made another careful incision at the throat, her fingers deft as she reached inside to draw out the entrails. The womb was discarded without ceremony, but the other organs were kept, their warmth steaming as they were set aside. Standing, she made an offering of the piglet's liver to the household gods, sprinkling perfume from a small glass bottle, one of a few she kept for regular offerings at the back of the garden.

The piglet's small body was lowered into the bubbling bronze pot and the sharp scent of blanching flesh weaved into the smoky air. While the piglet parboiled, Fortunata crouched beside the tripod and spooned a blend of lovage and oregano from a small bronze container into a dish. She then added a splash of broth to bind the herbs into a paste to make *moretum*, the quintessential dish of the ancestral Roman gardener. Beside her, her friend leaned in with approval as Fortunata cracked two eggs and beat them in gently, thickening the mixture to just the right consistency.*

By now, the skin of the piglet had softened. As it cooled enough to handle, Fortunata scooped handfuls of prepared forcemeat and pressed it into the hollowed cavity, filling every space, before trussing the piglet's legs with twine. Like many, she had no grand roasting spit and no fine metal stand, only the simplest of methods and tools, time-tested and reliable. Placing the piglet in a woven basket, it was lowered once more into the pot.

The broth roiled, and around the fire, their voices quieted for a

---

* The recipe that Fortunata is following is inspired by the collection of recipes written by Apicius in the fifth century CE.

THE WORKING POOR FAMILY

moment as the piglet disappeared beneath the surface once more. Now, they would wait. Time passed easily; the warmth of the fire, the low murmur of voices and the scent of cooking meat filled the night air. Occasionally, Lucius or Fortunata would pull the basket out to test the tenderness of the meat. When at last the piglet was ready and pulled from the pot, its skin glowed pale and supple, glistening with broth. Fortunata wiped it clean and with a careful hand scattered a pinch of precious black pepper over the pig from her coveted stash.

The knife parted the flesh with ease. With each share she spooned a side of cumin lentils onto each *terra sigillata* plate with ceremony, a small luxury in their humble world. On the bottom of one, the name of the freedman potter, Nicostratus, was written in small letters. Fortunata reached for a clay flask of *garum* and eased out the stopper. The briny tang of Scaurus' sauce, bottled only one street away, reached their nostrils and made their stomachs rumble. The bottle went from hand to hand, each guest adding a trickle of *garum* to their meat. Wine from the nearby hills was poured and watered down, terracotta cups were filled and refilled in the glow of the fire, and plates knocked softly together as the quiet laughter of the friends carried through the garden. Between mouthfuls, the men and Salvius' son grew ever more animated, reliving the day's games until the *murmillo's* sudden comeback was played out in voices loud and theatrical, as though the arena itself had followed them home.

'That *murmillo* was solid.' Salvius laughed as he reached for more bread. 'Didn't waste a single move. Just kept pressing him back.'

Lucius gave a low chuckle. 'He knew exactly what he was doing. Let the *thraex* dance around for the first few passes, then started leaning into it. I thought he was going to flatten him with that shield alone.'

'That slice under the arm, did you see it?' Salvius' teenage son piped up. 'The *thraex* had real skill.' He mimicked the move in the air with enthusiasm, provoking a laugh from the group.

'The *thraex* was too fast for his own good,' Salvius said, refilling his cup. 'All flash, no finish. You can't win on footwork alone.'

'He was holding on at the end,' Lucius said. 'Didn't fall, even with the blood pouring out of his leg. It took guts, that.'

Across the table, the women had been listening with quiet smiles. Fortunata spoke first.

'I thought he was beautiful to watch,' she said quietly to her friend, wiping her hands on a cloth. 'Like a dancer with a blade.'

Lusoria giggled. 'If he'd taken that helmet off a bit sooner, I might have been cheering for him a bit louder.'

The men laughed, Lucius speaking over the group in jest. 'He'd have tripped over his own ego if he knew how many women were watching him that closely!'

His young son, half-listening, held up his little clay figure. 'Is this the one who won?'

Lucius put his arm around his son and smiled. 'That's him. Marcus Attilius, the rising star *murmillo*.'

A calmness blanketed the night as the younger children, tired but content, played near the adults, safe within their humble sanctuary. When the last pieces of food had been consumed, and the conversations had grown slower and softer, Fortunata felt the familiar sense of comfort and gratitude for her family and their community settle over her. Lusoria made to help Fortunata with the cleaning, but Fortunata urged her to leave it. When their guests had finally departed, Fortunata lifted the bronze *amphora* from the cistern propped against the shop wall and, by the glow of her new Cupid lamp, rinsed the long-handled pan and bronze funnel, tilting them gently to wash away the fine residue inside. Water

THE WORKING POOR FAMILY

splashed over the dulled metal, pooling on the grass around her feet. She carried the utensils to the living area at the back of the garden, then bent to lift her daughter, who had fallen asleep by the fire. Moving quietly along the path, her sleeping child in her arms, something slipped free from her hair. A small bronze hairpin, its tip adorned with a finely cast bird, lost among the shadows.

DAWN, 24 OCTOBER 79 CE

Morning light filtered through their small window and, beyond it, the city was waking: shopkeepers pulling back their shutters, farmers travelling out of the city to their fields on carts, and early risers making their way through the streets. Their modest apartment upstairs, with only two rooms and low ceilings, held just what was necessary: two low-slung beds in the *cubiculum* bedroom, one shared by Lucius and Fortunata, the other shared by the children, alongside a wooden chest for their belongings and an oil lamp on a simple bronze stand. In the other, longer room, a table was placed in front of storage cupboards, and the stairs led to their shop below.

Lucius Aelius removed his rough woollen cloak from a nail on the wall, careful not to wake his children as he wrapped it tightly around him. The narrow stairs creaked as he descended to find Fortunata sitting outside mending a tunic by the light of a lamp. He greeted her with a gentle kiss on the head. Nursing a wine headache, Lucius crossed the road to the *hospitium* inn for travellers to collect his mule, just as he did every morning.

Lucius had long followed the wisdom of Roman agriculturalists, knowledge passed down through generations of his family. By lodging his mule in purpose-built stables near his house, he ensured proper ventilation and a comfortable stall, sparing the animal the windowless back rooms of his own home where the stagnant air would have encouraged the respiratory ailments to which mules were particularly prone. Anyway, it was good to get a permanent spot while he could. Lucius had heard rumours from fellow traders about the way things were run in Puteoli, the major port town not too far away. Over there, merchants were required to stable their animals in specific public areas, keeping the streets clear for trade and transport. It made sense in a place as busy as Puteoli, with ships and carts constantly coming in and out; the streets would be chaotic without such regulations.

Though Pompeii wasn't as large or as frantic, Lucius sometimes wondered if things would change here too. The streets had grown busier in recent years: more carts, more animals, more people passing through. The town felt like it was expanding, stretching to accommodate more than it once had. But for now, Pompeii's quieter lanes, like the one where his shop stood, managed well enough without the need for such rules.

The terracotta window with its arched openings let in the cool morning air, carrying with it the rustling sound of October leaves. Lucius greeted the stable hands with a nod. Inside, the scent of fresh hay mixed with the lingering smell of the horses and mules. Once a grand home, the building now served as a functional stable, its original elegance barely visible and its floors worn from years of service, now covered with straw. His mule was stalled in what had been a place of gathering, perhaps a dining room or a family's shared space.

A sturdy and reliable creature, his mule was one of the few permanent residents at the stable; the other animals mainly belonged to transient lodgers of the *hospitium*. He found it tethered to one of the iron rings set into the wall: enough to keep the animals steady and prevent them from crowding one another in the

THE WORKING POOR FAMILY

tight space. At the mule's feet, the owner's guard dog lay curled up in the straw. The creature wandered the stables and nearby streets at will, lying wherever it pleased, a silent observer of the daily comings and goings. Nearby, a wooden trough built against the north wall held a fresh measure of hay.

Despite these tight quarters, the space was orderly: voids in the walls served as makeshift feeding stations, and narrow windows, fitted with terracotta slats, cast soft beams of light through the otherwise dim interior. His mule stood patiently as Lucius approached and patted the animal's broad neck, feeling the warmth of its coat. It had been a good, though expensive, purchase: strong and steady, he was perfect for hauling a cart of produce or the many jars of *garum* they sold for Scaurus. Lucius led the mule out into the street and over the road to his own entrance, its hooves

Figure 41: Early Byzantine mosaic of a man feeding his mule, from Istanbul (modern Turkey)

clacking against the stone. The sun was rising higher now as he tied the mule up to the cart with a length of durable rope, looping it through the wooden yoke crafted to fit securely over the animal's shoulders. The yoke was essential, distributing the weight of the loaded cart evenly. Lucius checked the leather harness, making sure it wouldn't chafe or strain the animal on the day's journey ahead.

The cart was a strong, two-wheeled design common in towns like Pompeii, and built from thick planks, its frame designed to bear a heavy cargo. Metal bands reinforced the wheels, allowing them to endure the relentless wear of rough stone streets without splintering. From the storage rooms at the back of the shop, Lucius carried out small jars of *garum*, layering straw between them to absorb the jolts of the uneven roads. Satisfied with the arrangement, he gave the mule an encouraging pat. The animal flicked an ear, steady and untroubled, long accustomed to early starts and long days. As Lucius climbed onto the cart, Fortunata caught his arm, pressing a brief kiss to his cheek, her fingers lingering against the sleeve of his hooded cloak. He met her gaze for a moment, then smiled.

'I'll see you at the *palaestra* early afternoon.'

'See you,' she said. 'I'll be hawking our produce somewhere around there.'

With a final wave, he set off into the waking streets of Pompeii.

* * *

Lucius' first stop of the day was one of Scaurus' bustling workshops, located in the same neighbourhood as his own home, just one block north. As he neared the establishment, the air carried the unmistakable tang of fermenting fish, a scent that seemed to cling to the very walls it touched. Unlike the grand *domus* of its wealthy owner across town, this space was purely functional, repurposed from what had once been a modest private residence. The former peristyle garden had long since been transformed into the beating heart of the operation, its shaded colonnade now serving a more practical purpose. Beneath the simple tiled roof, large *dolia* stood in orderly rows, their coarse surfaces now streaked with brine and fish oils.

The courtyard buzzed with controlled efficiency, its workers made up of both paid workers and slaves, their tunics marked with the telltale signs of their trade. With the help of two slaves, he stacked the jars of *liquamen* onto his cart first, followed by the *muria* and, lastly, the smaller jars of *hallex*, the thick, gritty dregs left behind in *garum* production. Lucius heard the familiar boom of Scaurus' voice before he saw him. Around the businessman, the air always seemed to shift in a way that Lucius had always admired. He turned just in time to feel the man's palm clap against his back. Unlike other wealthy merchants who kept their distance from the labour that fuelled their fortunes, Scaurus seemed to thrive in the bustle of industry.

'Ah! Hard at work, I see.'

Lucius made to reply, but Scaurus was already striding into the workshop, exchanging a few words as he passed, his broad frame exuding the easy confidence of a man at home among the people.

'Tell Fortunata I said *salve*,' came the parting call. Lucius gave a half-wave as he climbed onto the cart and gathered the reins.

As the mule started forward, he glanced back at the workshop. Scaurus was gone from view, but his voice still carried. Lucius straightened a little in his seat. Perhaps one day he and his wife would be in a similar position, successful business owners, well known and respected in Pompeii. A man could dream.

* * *

Lucius' route took him past the crowded forum, where vendors called out to early customers and artisans set up their wares. Their counters overflowed with goods: bright baskets of apples and figs, clusters of grapes and heaps of beans, alongside household items, like terracotta cups, delicate glass bowls, freshly waxed tablets for writing and lanterns. He manoeuvred the cart through the one-way streets, each marked out by stepping stones or public fountains. He had a total of five further shops to visit today, one as far away as the public baths in the north-western corner of the city. The morning air was fresh, carrying scents of bread baking from nearby *pistrinae*, where slaves worked at long tables and hot wood ovens.

His first delivery was to a *taberna*, a simple wine shop marked by its wide, open entrance and modest counter, designed to be accessible to those passing on foot. The owner, a broad-shouldered man called Veturinus Iulianus, was standing cross-armed beside a slave sweeping the front step. Inside, Lucius found a dim space lined with specially made wooden shelves, with grooves to hold *amphorae*. Together they unloaded a batch of *garum* bottles, each marked in red. This one carried the specific order and address of the recipient: '*Flower of* garum *in its pure form, from Umbricia Fortunata for Veturinus Iulianus*'.

Next, navigating his cart down one of Pompeii's narrower streets, Lucius passed tall, multi-storey apartment blocks that loomed over the road. The upper storeys, accessed by steep, narrow staircases, housed Pompeii's poorer residents, their rooms cramped and dark. A blacksmith's workshop loomed ahead, its furnace casting an eerie glow as hammers struck iron in an unrelenting rhythm. Sparks flared and died, the odour of scorched metal and the unrelenting heat of the forge radiating in waves onto the street outside. Lucius reined in his mule, watching as molten ore was drawn from the fire and reshaped under the brutal weight of the hammer. Tools, weapons, household idols, all things forged to endure. It evoked the image of Vulcan, the god of fire and forge, who toiled in a cavernous workshop far below the earth, his hammer blows echoing through stone and stirring the mountain from within.

Lucius next paid a visit to the fullers, where clothes were cleaned and dyed. The shop was a riot of colour; bolts of fabric spilling from their stacks in shades of ochre, indigo and deep russet, and lines of clothes drying in the sun. The fabrics fluttered in the breeze as the fuller and his slaves worked, long since immune to the strong smell of ammonia that they used to clean the clothes. In the corner, a purple-lined toga, its rich colour reserved for the elite, lay carefully folded, a mark of status few could afford. Such garments, woven and dyed in workshops across the city, were symbols of wealth, identity and ambition, their worth measured in their colour.

The owner barely looked up at Lucius, too busy unfurling a bolt of deep crimson wool for an eager buyer and giving orders to the slaves working at the nearby vats. Without ceremony, Lucius set the deliveries down by a wall as a slave hurried to pay him, and he left for his next stop. He found the front of the counter of the *thermopolium* adorned with frescoes of ripened fruit and curling vines, the shopkeeper's promise of abundance to hungry customers. Above, *tintinnabula* wind chimes tinkled in the breeze, their large phallic shapes designed to keep the evil eye away from the shop, alongside strings of garlic and various pots and pans. Behind the counter, shelves were stacked high with *amphorae* of wine, *urcei* of *garum*, plates, bowls and cups, and various items of food. The owner and his slaves moved swiftly as they served customers, lifting the lids of the large *dolia* to ladle food into their waiting bowls. As Lucius unloaded the last of the vendor's order of *liquamen*, the shopkeeper nodded his thanks, too occupied with counting coins for small talk.

By late morning, the streets were thick with a tide of merchants, artisans and spectators moving to and from their places of work. Rounding the corner, Lucius followed the smell of fresh bread and arrived at the bakery of Popidius Priscus. Tethering his mule to one of the holes carved into the pavement, he swung down from the cart and pulled a large *urceus* onto his shoulder. Pompeii's bakeries never rested. Priscus' grinding mills were on full display here, each one powered by a donkey or a slave. They worked endlessly, churning through grain in a haze of flour and sweat. Both beast and man lived a brutal existence, their lungs thick with dust and their bodies driven by the relentless demands of the ovens. In other bakeries, the slaves were locked away and chained to their work, their only source of light filtering through the bars of windows set high into the walls.

Figure 42: Bakery of Popidius Priscus (VII.2.22) in Pompeii with oven and mills

THE WORKING POOR FAMILY

Near the entrance, the baker pulled another round of bread from the deep oven, his long-handled paddle moving with precision, stacking the loaves onto a nearby wooden table. Each bore his own personal stamp. Seeing Lucius, he waved him over and Lucius dropped off four *urcei* of *liquamen*, plus a couple of small bottles of *garum*. He accepted his usual tip of a crusty loaf.

As Lucius rolled on, he only half-registered the city from his vantage point atop his cart. Small shrines nestled into street corners gave off faint curls of fragrant incense, left as offerings to the *lares* of each neighbourhood. In the distance, the sharp clang of hammers echoed from a workshop, met with the booming bark of a large dog. Peals of children's laughter echoed through the streets as they wove dangerously between the moving carts.

Through open doorways, glimpses of other worlds slid by. In the *atria* of the wealthy, women sat weaving in the cool shade, while porters nodded off in doorways and guard dogs lay chained at thresholds. Beyond them lay rich rooms and lush gardens of a type Lucius could only dream of stepping into.

He nodded to other cart drivers with the easy familiarity of shared routines. As the cart rattled on, a teenager's voice cut through the noise of the street.

'Lucius!' he jeered, grinning at his friends. 'It's Fortunata who wears the toga in your house!'

The boys doubled over with mirth, shoving each other before vanishing around a corner. Lucius swallowed the flush of shame and flicked the reins, glad to be rid of his deliveries for the day. He guided the mule and cart through the streets to his final stop on the other side of town, the *palaestra*, where his wife would be hawking her wares in the shadow of the amphitheatre.

* * *

Fortunata had left a friend to mind the shop for the afternoon. The *palaestra*, built at great expense to honour Pompeii's devotion to health, strength and civic pride thrummed with energy. Encircled by a magnificent portico, its tall columns cast long shadows across the open expanse. Beneath the colonnades, people rested on chilled floors and chatted with friends and family, untouched by the warm sun. Nearby, men with corded muscles stretched and exercised, while others stood back, nodding in approval or offering critiques. At intervals, men and women lolled around braziers on which they cooked meat and vegetables. A surgeon had set up his clinic, instruments laid out in front of him as he inspected the broken finger of a construction worker.

In one corner, a painter was completing a notice in large red letters as two elderly men stood watching in approving silence, their hands clasped behind their backs. Every so often, a shout split the air, followed by the splash of someone leaping into the great rectangular swimming pool that dominated the heart of the space. Fed by Pompeii's aqueducts, its clear water shimmered in the autumn light. On the plaster walls of the portico, graffiti captured the city's pulse in playful boasts, crude jests and earnest declarations of love. Some scratched names were simply an attempt at permanence in an impermanent world, while others mocked politicians, their barbs cutting. The personal and the political overlapped effortlessly in Pompeii. Fortunata paid these words no mind as she wove through the crowd, a wicker basket, brimming with fresh garden produce, balanced on her hip.

Her voice rose clear above the bustle, warm and melodic:

'Fresh figs! Sweet as honey! Grapes straight from the vine!'

The scent of herbs followed her, drifting from the bundles of rosemary, thyme and sage in her basket. She knew exactly where to place herself, where the passing crowd would be busiest and where the pull of appetite worked most in her favour. Nearby, beneath the portico running around three sides of the large *palaestra*, a cluster of dust-streaked boys sat cross-legged on the smooth stone, their tunics rumpled from play. Their teacher, an elderly Greek man with a white wisp of a beard, stood before them. The morning had been filled with copying words onto wax tablets, repeating lines aloud and learning simple sums, but now he regaled them with tales of great battles and of heroes long dead. The boys leaned forward, enthralled and wide-eyed, their small hands cupping their chins. Among them, her son, sitting utterly still, was absorbing every word.

For a moment, Fortunata paused, her heart swelling with pride. Scaurus himself had sponsored the boy's education, an extraordinary gift for a child of their means. She thanked the gods for his generosity, remembering the merchant's voice, firm with conviction: 'The direction in which education starts a man will determine his future in life.'*

Fortunata watched as the tutor concluded his tale, gesturing for the boys to begin their final task of the day. With the sharp tips of their styluses, they scratched letters of the alphabet into the plaster of the wall, their movements careful and hesitant, some more practised than others. She lingered to watch her son a moment longer before turning to check on her daughter, who was being bounced up and down in a group of women and children in one corner of the *palaestra*. Her voice lifted once more into the air.

At that moment, Lucius and his cart rolled to a halt along a quieter back alley, where one of the *palaestra*'s many entrances opened out onto the street. As he stepped down onto the stones, Lucius caught sight of Fortunata through the archway and was

---

* A quote from Plato.

struck by her beauty. Her curly dark hair was tousled into a mound on her head, and the soft glow of her red cheeks in the afternoon sun was made even more beautiful by her melodic voice, which rang out over the noise of the crowd. As he stood mesmerised, a sudden rush of movement caught his eye. A flock of birds burst from a rooftop, their wings cutting through the air in a frantic, jarring flight, as if startled by something unseen.

For a moment, the street seemed to halt, a brief, unnatural hush settling like the heavy silence before a storm.

A shudder rippled through the ground, a deep, gut-wrenching pulse that sent a jolt up Lucius' legs. Overhead, the *palaestra* trembled, and with a sharp crack a roof tile wrenched itself loose, tumbling down in a sudden, violent descent. It shattered against the stone with a piercing clang, its fragments skittering across the pavement.

An almighty boom split the air.

The mule reared, its eyes rolling and ears flattened against its skull. Its hooves clattered against the cobbles in panic. The cart lurched. Lucius snatched at the reins, muscles straining to steady the animal before it could bolt.

The air itself seemed to recoil, the echo of the explosion rolling over the city in a wave of dread.

His head jerked towards the sound. Above the city, an impenetrable plume of darkness was rising, unfurling like the breath of some monstrous creature stirring from its slumber.

Beneath him, the ground gave another restless groan. Something was wrong. Terribly and irreversibly wrong.

CHAPTER FIVE
THE INNKEEPER

AROUND THE EIGHTH HOUR (1 P.M.), 24 OCTOBER 79 CE

The world was ending.

The deafening roar, drowning out every other sound, was deeper than thunder and heavier than anything Euxinus had ever heard in his life. It came from everywhere all at once, rolling through the earth, through the sky, through his very bones.

The ground heaved and tombs collapsed in a deafening cascade, stone shattering like glass in the City of the Dead where he stood. A fissure raced across the street, swallowing stones and sending whole walls crashing down in clouds of dust.

Euxinus barely kept his footing, staggering backwards as another loud boom pulsed through the air. He turned, his eyes meeting a sight that stole his breath.

A black column, twisting and seething, rose into the heavens. It billowed higher, churning in furious currents that stretched impossibly far into the sky.

For a brief, terrible moment, time fractured.

His mind wrenched backwards, pulled into the stillness of the morning, when the sky had been blue and the air soft with the scent of stew and wine.

He had watched the new freedman, Petrinus, step into his *caupona* at dawn, the red *pileus* perched atop his head. Though his expression was uncertain, Euxinus had detected a fragile hope, the kind that came only when a man saw the world as his own for the first time.

He had poured the boy a drink and watched him hold the cup in both hands. A first act of liberty, something so simple and so ordinary, yet to him it had seemed to mean everything. The ground beneath you isn't always as solid as it seems, he had said, watching the words settle over Petrinus.

Now, the earth beneath him convulsed, and dust choked the air, thick and suffocating.

Another memory, one that was older and deeper, lodged in the marrow of his bones.

Her laughter. The way she used to scold him for working too late. Her smile in the quiet of the morning, when the world had not yet stirred, when it was just the two of them, just the warmth of their bodies and the knowledge that she was there. In those moments, she was at her most beautiful.

Just moments ago, he had whispered a prayer to her memory in the necropolis, his fingers gently tracing the letters of her name carved into the stone.

Until we meet again.

The ground shook again, harder this time, sending his body lurching to the ground.

THE INNKEEPER

THE EIGHTH HOUR (1 P.M.), 23 OCTOBER 79 CE

Euxinus stood on the edge of the raised pavement, the dust swirling around him as he peered down the bustling street towards the amphitheatre. The midday sun glinted on the terracotta roofs and the crowd surged like a living river, the games-goers jostling and shouting, their excitement palpable. In the distance he could see laden carts crossing one of the main streets in and out of the city, the Via di Nocera. Some came from the direction of the centre of town, while others flowed from outside the city gates, having gathered fresh produce from the farms outside the walls. The stones, judiciously positioned, guided the chaotic flow of traffic in one- and two-way systems around the city.

Figure 43: The Caupona of Euxinus (I.11.11)

Euxinus impatiently scanned the crowd for the delivery he was waiting for: a shipment from a new supplier. '*At Pompeii, near the Amphitheatre, to the* copo *of Euxinus*', he'd instructed the delivery slave.* And still, they were late. Typical. It had to be today, games day no less, when the inn would be busier than normal. The beast hunts were about to start in the amphitheatre, a precursor to tonight's main event of the gladiatorial games, and yet he was here waiting for a cart. He wanted to catch a close-up glimpse of the incoming *aedile* elects for the next year. Apparently one of them, Gaius Cuspius Pansa, was already caught up in the event organisation, despite not yet being sworn into office. Imagine doing work for nothing, he thought wryly.

Euxinus stood beneath the painted sign he'd commissioned a few months ago, placed on full display by his inn's entrance. His inspiration had come one morning in early summer, when the flowers in his inn garden were in bloom and garlands from a recent festival were hanging about the place. His wife was there then; how she had loved the small songbirds nestled in the trees. 'Look, the sparrow is catching ants on that wall,' she had exclaimed, the child in her seeming most apparent at moments like this. 'The jackdaws have become bolder; I think they are starting to recognise me as a friend.' It struck him then, looking at her young, rosy face, how lucky he was. And that was when he had decided; a phoenix wishing his customers the same luck would be the perfect choice for his inn sign.

Though his wife was gone now, Euxinus was not alone. He had hired Biria to help him with the day-to-day running of the inn after his wife passed, and she was everything he needed in a second-in-command: earthy, ruddy-cheeked and quick-witted. In every

---

* This inscription was found on a terracotta *amphora* inside Euxinus' *caupona*.

THE INNKEEPER

way, she was Campanian in spirit. There was also Iustus, the head gardener across the road, whose orchard and vineyard bordered the same stretch of street. A friend of many years, he had stood by Euxinus through the hardest days. It was he who had joined Euxinus in pooling funds for the electoral notice painted on the wall beside the phoenix. Together, they had paid for a notice endorsing Quintus Postumius and Marcus Cerrinius in their bid for the joint *aedileship*. Even after 2 years, the red letters still held their colour. Hinnulus, the painter, had said it would last. He had been right.

The inn still held reminders of his wife. Between the dining room and the garden door, a *lararium* shrine was nestled in the wall behind the great stone counter, where *dolia* were sunk deep into the masonry. Painted there, a coiling serpent, the *genius loci*, or guardian spirit, promised protection for the inn and all who lived or dined beneath its roof. Each morning, his wife had made an offering, whispering prayers as she lit the lamp, her ritual gentle and familiar. Now Biria tended the shrine. She didn't say the words in quite the same way, but the intention was there, and that was enough.

But there had barely been enough time for prayers lately. Within the brightly painted walls, the inn was fit to bursting. The walls throughout had been painted in bright colours, even upstairs: clean lines and cheerful tones chosen to lift the spirits of weary merchants and games-goers, who today would tumble into bed, aching and content. Every room had been full this week, the warm October days drawing travellers eager to savour the last of the garden sun before the cooler days to come. People had come from every direction: Nuceria, Nola, Stabiae, Surrentum, Neapolis, Puteoli, even the elite from Herculaneum, their crisp tunics and scented oils trailing over the threshold like they belonged to another world.

Figure 44: Inside the Caupona of Euxinus (I.11.11), with the counter in the foreground, the dining room and lararium shrine to the rear, and the garden to the right

Euxinus grinned to himself. The more the merrier. At times like this, he was especially grateful for Biria's extra pair of hands. She moved between tables with ease, stirred pots without missing a beat and poured wine with the kind of attentiveness that made even the gruffest of customers soften. And when the mood soured, as it sometimes did, she handled the situation in her firm, uncompromising way.

He stepped inside his inn where the hum of conversation combined with the clatter of dishes, and the scent of roasted meat and spiced wine laced the air. By the doorway, two Jews, part of a small growing population in Pompeii, stood talking to one another intently. At the end of the L-shaped counter, a Syrian merchant stumbled through an order in halting Latin to Biria, who was attempting to piece together the odd word with difficulty. Behind

THE INNKEEPER

the counter, Scybale, Euxinus' old female slave, long since part of the furniture and the family, was busy ladling a broad bean and vegetable stew from a large iron pot. It bubbled atop a roof-tile fire bed, the heat from the hearth flames licking the sides. Behind her, his two younger slaves hustled, refilling the large terracotta pots embedded in the shop counter, one with honeyed figs and apricots, another with boar stew.

Although the dish included only a scant quantity of meat, Euxinus stretched the flavour with pulses and herbs. It was a matter of balance. Guests left full and satisfied, and no one asked too many questions. He peered into the pot and took the ladle from Scybale's hands. 'Careful,' he said. 'We don't want to be throwing in coins with the boar.' Biria gave Scybale a sly, reassuring smile. The old slave tipped more lentils into the pot, wiped her hands on her tunic and moved on to serve a local shoemaker at the bar. Steam clung to the rafters as bowls and cups were filled to the brim. Some patrons gulped their food standing; others ambled into the vine-draped garden or through the door into the back room, where meals frequently stretched long into the night.

Euxinus edged past the mass of customers and leaned into the square window cut into the dining room wall. Inside, the room pressed with warmth and noise. The easy hum of chatter at Euxinus' inn was broken only by the clink of dice on wood and the shuffle of gaming counters across worn tables, their coin bets piling at the centre. In the far corner, three North African traders, having moored their boat in the main port of Pompeii that morning, argued over the price of oil as they picked at their plates with calloused hands. The language that was leaving their wine-stained lips was entirely foreign to most ears in the room.

Regular patrons filled the rest of the space, absorbed in a lively game of *alea*, the dice-throwing favourite that kept wagers high and tensions higher still. Euxinus moved to stand over the group, his near-permanent fixtures in his inn, and rested a hand on each shoulder as he leaned in to watch the next throw. The thrill was in the simplicity: a single roll of the dice determined the victor, and fortunes could change in an instant. At other times, more strategy-minded players opted for the Game of Twelve Markings, which was played on a board by moving tiles in clever sequences. The aim was simple: race your pieces around the track before your opponent, knocking theirs off along the way.

Across the room, two women in the corner started waving, trying to flag down Biria, who was topping off cups at the next table. 'Over here!' one yelled. Biria turned towards the women. Seeing there was only enough wine left for one cup, one of them laughed and pulled the jug towards herself. 'It's mine!' she joked. Biria, ever unflappable, shook her head with a grin, her curls bouncing around her round face. 'Whoever wants it should take it,' she laughed.

An imposing figure appeared in the doorway, and the two women lit up at once: 'Oceanus! Come and drink with us!'

Cheers rang out through the room as the imposing figure of Oceanus, the famed gladiator of Pompeii, now a *libertus*, stepped inside. A plain tunic clung to his broad shoulders, his every movement carrying the easy confidence of a man born to be watched. The women pushed the cup towards him, giggling and teasing each other as though they'd caught a prize. Oceanus took the cup with a grin and raised it high to the roar of the crowd. 'You've no idea how good it feels to be on this side of the games,' he laughed.

As the day neared the ninth hour, Euxinus greeted yet more customers as they entered through the large shop front and went straight into the garden, trying to put the delay of the cart to the back of his mind. What had once been a modest patch of herbs and a few nut trees had flourished into a lush vineyard, his newest –

THE INNKEEPER

Figure 45: Fresco of a bar scene from Pompeii showing two female customers interacting with the bar maid, and calling Oceanus, the gladiator, over to drink

and certainly smartest – venture. He had harvested the grapes during the Vinalia back in August and sent them off for pressing, wisely avoiding the costly investment of presses himself. Even Cato the Elder, the revered Republican expert on Roman agriculture, knew better than to fall for the trap of spending more than necessary. Or so Iustus had told him, anyway. Now, the pressed juice was fermenting in two large *dolia* jars at the back of the garden, their lids shut and sealed with resin. Unlike others, he'd chosen not to bury them in the ground, knowing that keeping them in the open would strengthen the wine. It would go much further with his customers that way. Besides, they liked the kind of wine that gave them a headache the next day.

Though his plot wasn't big, it was certainly larger than most, and he was determined to turn every inch into gold. There was a grow-

Figure 46: The dining garden in the Caupona of Euxinus (I.11.11), with a private dining area to the right

ing trend, all the way from Rome, for outdoor dining, but Euxinus had gone a step further by adding a private dining room to the garden, perfect for those who wanted to impress friends or enjoy their meal in peace, away from the rowdy groups. He had even installed a pair of garden latrines, an uncommon indulgence that offered far superior privacy to the public facilities scattered around town. As inside, the garden was rammed with games-goers. At one table, a group of elderly local men were hunched over a board of *latrunculi*, their eyes narrowed and each move well considered, as if commanding real armies, while throughout the rest of the garden, groups of people from Pompeii and far beyond drank side-by-side, united by their thirst for wine and blood.

Euxinus peered down the street one last time, scanning for the delivery cart. By Jupiter, where was it? But just as he was completing a transaction with a small slave from Pansa's household, one of his own slaves dashed over to announce the arrival of the delivery. Euxinus elbowed his way through the sea of customers to the front of his shop. Both of the sturdy horses hitched to the cart, one

THE INNKEEPER

brown, the other white, were utterly unphased by the noise and chaos of the Roman street. Two lively young men hopped down from the wagon and swiftly tied up the horses to the loop in the pavement. The brown horse bent over the edge of the public fountain outside the inn and took a drink. Euxinus' slaves stood ready on the pavement, storage jars in hand, still bearing the faded markings from the last delivery. This refill system was a far cheaper alternative to buying fresh *amphorae*, though whether his customers would notice any difference in the wine remained to be seen. He'd sweeten a few with honey and spice to make *mulsum*, then send them on to Pansa, adding a generous margin for the effort, of course.

One of the men lifted away a heavy cloth from the back of the cart, revealing a large pigskin sack filled with wine from one of the villas in Pompeii's hinterland. He pulled out the spout and began to fill the terracotta jars, chatting with his companion as the dark liquid gushed out, never wasting a drop. Once each *amphora* was filled, the second man sealed it with sticky black resin and passed it

Figure 47: Painting of an original fresco from Pompei showing a wine cart, by Giuseppe Marsigli (18 January 1828)

to Euxinus' slaves, who hurried inside with the weighty jars. *Amphora* after *amphora* was filled, sealed and stored until the transaction was complete. The young men pocketed their payment, 20 *asses* per amphora, before untying the horses.* Euxinus at once set Scybale to preparing the *mulsum* for Pansa's feast, and ordered the *amphorae* to be carried to the politician's house on the backs of his slaves as soon as they were ready.

The order finally complete, Euxinus couldn't resist the pull of the amphitheatre any longer. Before he joined the swelling crowd, he made one last round of his *caupona*, making conversation with the customers and bantering with regulars and serving wine. The light from the glistening oil lamps inside spilled over into the garden, where others had been placed on tables, and the vines' shadows danced on the walls. Inside, the activity had slowed to a comfortable lull.

Biria was at the shrine in the corner, her face illuminated by the dim light of the fire as she made another offering. The serpent painted on the wall, winding its way towards the altar, seemed to come alive in the light. Her quiet prayers asked the gods to watch over the inn and its guests. To the side, a slave on his hands and knees was scrubbing away the vomit of a customer who had clearly overindulged in wine, while another was sweeping crisp, autumn leaves which had blown in and settled around the counter.

'I'm leaving, Biria,' Euxinus called to her. 'Keep an eye on that rowdy lot in the garden.' He smirked. 'I don't want any trouble while I'm away.'

'Just go!' she urged, her attention already returning to the altar. Satisfied that everything was in order, Euxinus stepped out into the

---

* Martial, a famous Roman satirist living in Rome during the mid-first century CE, records the cost of an amphora of wine as 20 *asses*, which would be a little more than a day's wage for a labourer.

THE INNKEEPER

street, pulling his woollen cloak around him. The sound of the crowds drifted on the warm breeze – not yet thunderous, but loud enough to tell him he was running late. From the right, people streamed in groups from the forum, laughing and joking, shouting out to one another and placing children on shoulders. As he made the short walk towards the venue, he passed the usual scene of prostitutes leaning against the columns of the *palaestra*, casting glances at passing men. In the corners, families gathered in huddles, chatting as they cooked meals over small braziers. They should come to my inn and save themselves the trouble, he thought.

This crowd was calm and jovial today, nothing like the one in 59, when the infamous riot broke out. Euxinus had been there. What had started as a heated argument between the Pompeians and visitors from the nearby town of Nuceria had spiralled into a violent

Figure 48: Fresco depicting the Riot of Pompeii in 59 CE, from the House of Anicetus (I.3.23)

brawl. The crowd had surged like a herd of wild deer, pushing and pulling in every direction. First stones were hurled, then weapons were drawn. Those who fell were trampled underfoot, and even women were caught up in the mayhem. The screams of the wounded had mixed with the furious roars of the fighters. The Nucerians had fared far worse than the Pompeians; many of them had been carried off to Rome having lost limbs, and others still were bereaved of parents and children. Pompeii was punished with a 10-year ban on games and trade guilds, a harsh sentence from Nero and the Senate in Rome, though one the town had paid little heed to.

Euxinus entered the amphitheatre, moving through the crowd to his seat midway up the rows. The seating was bathed in a dim, shifting light, the braziers and oil lamps of the people creating an uneven glow. As a freeborn man, he technically had the right to sit in the seats below women and slaves, and above the wealthiest citizens whose status earned them seats closest to the arena floor. In practice, though, things were more fluid, especially in Pompeii. Here, most of the townsfolk packed into the mid-tier rows together, regardless of precise rank.

He found a seat beside a few fellow innkeepers, men he knew through the informal local trade group, each bearing the rough hands and easy humour of those used to long days and longer nights. As the crowd settled, all eyes turned to the *pulvinar*, the raised box reserved for dignitaries, where Gaius Cuspius Pansa rose to speak. Draped in finery and framed by torchlight, he looked every inch the embodiment of *Romanitas*, that noble ideal of what it meant to be Roman, as he raised his hand in solemn address. A few words to the gods, a few more to the people of Pompeii, and with that, the evening's games began.

The crowd exploded into cheers as the gates swung open and the first gladiators stepped into the ring. The opening match was

THE INNKEEPER

between Julian gladiators trained in the imperial gladiatorial school at Capua, once owned by Julius Caesar. The *ludus* was said to be so vast that the great Republican orator and politician, Cicero, had once claimed that it held 5,000 shields. A novice *murmillo*, Marcus Attilius, was to fight the second match of his career. Everyone in Pompeii by now knew that Marcus, being neither a slave nor a freedman, had signed up for life in the arena of his own accord, due to having major debts. At first, everyone thought he was mad, but he had surprised them all, defeating his first opponent, the previously unbeaten veteran Hilarius.

Tonight, the rising star was to take on Lucius Raecius Felix, a *thraex* gladiator with 12 matches and 12 victories to his name. The two bodies clashed, sand kicking up around them, the sound of blade on shield ringing out through the amphitheatre. For long minutes, they traded blows: Felix with deft, flicking attacks, Attilius with punishing thrusts. Then, with a sudden opening, the younger fighter struck hard and Felix staggered. A gasp rippled through the arena as Felix fell to his knees, his bright blood staining the sand around him. The young victor played to the crowd, his arms raised as he coaxed the stands into a frenzy, their raised voices baying for Felix's life.

Euxinus watched with bated breath as the *editor* stood, his arm extended in front of him and his thumb pointing to the side. The crowd grew louder as Felix, his helmet lost, looked up to the *pulvinar* in a plea for mercy. The *editor's* thumb pointed down and the crowd groaned, their support for Felix through his 12 victories not enough to outweigh their thirst for blood.* Euxinus breathed a sigh of relief as he watched Marcus help Felix to his feet, the pair walk-

---

* In truth, fighting to the death wasn't a common outcome for gladiatorial fights, due to the cost of training and keeping a gladiator. Instead they would commonly fight for first blood.

ing into the *sanitarium* together to have their wounds tended. They had both survived another night. The other door, the *spoliarium*, where the corpses of fallen gladiators were dragged, was waiting for those less fortunate.

As the sand was cleared for the next spectacle, Euxinus leaned back, sharing snacks with his companions and tossing dice on a small tile between them. A swell of pride rose in his chest; this was what he loved about Pompeii. The games, the heat of the crowd, the collective life of a city united, breathing as one. His inn would be filled with stories tonight, the wine would flow and Pompeii would celebrate until the early hours.

It felt, in that moment, as though this kind of joy could last forever.

* * *

The next morning at dawn, Euxinus lay in the dark thinking of his day ahead, before eventually dragging his body from his bed. Eyes sticky with sleep, he watched as a mouse scuttled across the room, hugging the wall before disappearing below the wooden door. In Pompeii, the first activities of the day began within the first 2 hours of sunrise. Slaves rose early to prepare the household for their masters, and farmers rose even earlier, in time to reach the fields in the hinterland by dawn, determined to make the most of the daylight hours and, in the summer, to avoid the heat of the day. Though the carts stayed their noise in the night, the bakeries were often in full swing, the misery of the slaves and mules as relentless as their toil.

From his room, Euxinus could hear the ever-dutiful Biria arriving and drawing back the shutters. He marvelled at her stamina. Only a couple of hours ago she had pulled the sturdy wooden shutters closed for security, yet here she was, preparing the inn for the

THE INNKEEPER

early customers. Euxinus was sitting on the edge of his bed when Scybale entered, ready to assist with the morning tasks. His thoughts briefly turned to the new bed he had commissioned from the carpenter, Tullius. He would need to go to see it today, before its delivery. He could picture the beautiful curves at each end, and the sturdy slats beneath the mattress, made from timber collected in the ancient woods near the town.

Unlike many innkeepers, Euxinus had the funds to invest in a decent mattress. His was filled with soft grasses and wrapped in a thick, red-striped woollen cover. It wasn't as luxurious as the fine linen or feather-stuffed mattresses used by Pompeii's wealthiest, but it was far more comfortable than the lumpy straw beds most common folk endured. Last night's chill had made him grateful for the warm woollen tunic he'd worn to bed. It wouldn't be long before the heavy wool blankets came out to keep the guests warm.

Euxinus walked over to the small table in the corner of his apartment as Scybale handed him a terracotta bowl filled with warm *puls*, a working-man's grain porridge made from spelt and water. On the table she had already placed a small platter of hard cheese as well as a few walnuts and dried apricots. Euxinus thought through his day as he ate.

He pulled on a simple daytime tunic and fastened a pouch of money at his belt, then bent over to tug on his woollen socks. His iron-studded *caligae* came next, sturdy sandals favoured by soldiers and working men for their resilience. Made of thick leather, they left the toes exposed, with heavy soles and straps that laced firmly across the foot and tied at the ankle.

He stepped down into the garden, his sandals slapping against the stone. A lizard skittered across the path and vanished beneath a cluster of vines. On the far wall, the painted serpents coiled in silence, their tongues frozen mid-flick. From somewhere beyond his property, a rooster pierced the morning with a ragged crow. In the late winter and early spring, he would come out at this hour to prune the vines, cutting back the old growth to give strength to new shoots. He had always done this himself; in the spirit of his ancestors, there was nothing more virtuous, nothing more Pompeian, than turning the soil with your own hands.

The inn was already filling with customers. The first to arrive were the farmers and gardeners, followed closely by local artisans: carpenters, stonemasons and blacksmiths who spent their lives waking before first light. As they shuffled in, their leather aprons still dusted with yesterday's work, they would often order the cheapest breakfast option, the *puls*. Not long after, small-time merchants and traders began to wander in. They tended to have more coins and more time to spare, given they had help opening up their shops. Their *ientaculum* breakfast reflected this more leisurely approach: bread, perhaps with cheese or some locally grown fruit. Nothing fancy, but a step above the gruel of the labourers. They lingered by the counter, some sipping watered-down wine, most drinking water, chatting about business and exchanging the latest gossip from the forum.

By mid-morning, the town's wealthier patrons and small business owners often passed through on their way back from visiting their patrons at the morning meeting, the *salutatio*. They came for their *prandium*, the midday meal eaten at the sixth hour. Some opted for cold meat or fish, others had honey-smeared bread or fresh produce, like fruit and nuts, sourced from nearby gardens. Most of them didn't rush; instead, they took their time, sharing a few words with Euxinus about local politics or last night's gladiator matches. And then came the slaves, on their way to fetch supplies for their masters, slipping in and out of the inn with barely a word.

THE INNKEEPER

Collecting the required items, they blended into the noise of the streets as discretely as they came.

Amidst the familiar shuffle of regulars, a figure stepped inside. Euxinus' eye caught the flash of red atop his head, his *pileus* bright and unmistakable. Just yesterday, the slave had entered the *caupona* as a nobody, purchasing supplies for his master. Today, he entered as his own man. Euxinus wiped his hands on a cloth and took in the sight of him. The shift in posture, the subtle weightlessness in his step, albeit with the touch of uncertainty and awkward awareness of his own body; they were all signs of a man no longer carrying the burden of ownership. Euxinus welcomed him in and poured him a drink.

* * *

Like most Romans, Euxinus took regular baths at the local establishment, often once or twice per week, opting for a bucket the rest of the time. He usually upped his visits in the winter to stave off the cold and today he felt like warming up. His favourite happened to be the closest to his inn. Hopefully he would catch a familiar face while he was there too.

'You're not headed towards the Stabian Baths, are you?' Euxinus asked a familiar cart driver parked across the street, who had just finished unloading old *amphorae* for filling inside Iustus' vineyard workshop.

'The forum's our next stop. Hop on.'

Euxinus climbed aboard, and they set off through the street leading from the nearest gate northbound and left onto the Via dell'Abbondanza. Passing through the busiest area of the city was unavoidable given the one-way system in place on Euxinus' road. Agricultural gardens that had sprung up after the great quake could be seen alongside, with many more buildings still undergoing repair. The memory of that day still lingered in Euxinus' heart. Gods, it had been terrifying: the ground buckling beneath his feet, the sudden cracks ripping through walls, the chaos that had swallowed the streets. Half the city had been in ruins, and for a while, he wasn't sure if his inn would survive.

But resilient Pompeii had rebuilt itself, with enterprising farmers transforming empty plots into fertile patches of vineyards and orchards. As they passed by these green spaces, the scent of tilled earth and the sound of songbirds filled the air. Still, the sight of the gardens stirred something deep within him. They were a reminder that life in Pompeii could shift in an instant. He glanced at the horizon where Mount Vesuvius loomed. He'd heard some things about the mountain from others around town, people more well-read than him.

Strabo, a historian long since passed, had written that Vesuvius looked scorched, like it had once burned from within. He described the summit as barren and full of blackened hollows, and the stones as though they'd been through fire. He believed it used to be full of live craters, burned out many years ago. But he also thought this was the reason why the land around the mountain was so fertile.

Another writer, the architect Vitruvius, popular with builders who frequented his inn, had written about the mountain too, saying that fires once raged beneath it. That's what Vitruvius thought had caused the Pompeian sponge-stone: it had been changed by fire until it took on an airy, brittle form, something builders had to be wary of.

Euxinus shook off his drifting thoughts as the cart lurched to a halt near the forum. Climbing down, he made his way towards the imposing entrance of the Stabian Baths, where the magnificent doorway opened onto the vast area of the inner exercise courtyard. Lined with towering columns, the open-air gymnasium pulsed with movement. Men of all ages wrestled, boxed and lifted hand weights at a steady pace, their grunts rising over the monotonous thud of fists wrapped in cloth meeting bare flesh. Some sparred in pairs, others stretched, their skin shining with oil in the morning light. Before heading into the changing rooms, Euxinus paused a moment to take it all in. He remembered the vanity of his younger days, eager to prove himself in this very courtyard, before the years, and grief, had begun to trace their lines upon him.

The rectangular *apodyterium*, or changing room, was lined with stone benches and the walls filled with niches, each one carefully numbered for bathers to store their belongings. Frescoes of nymphs, gods and mythological heroes adorned the upper walls, casting a sense of opulence over what was otherwise a functional space. Euxinus handed over his tunic and sandals to a young slave, who quickly stowed them in a nearby niche. He gave the boy a coin to keep them safe.

He headed first into the *frigidarium*, a small, round room taken up mostly by a circular cold plunge pool at the centre, and surrounded by small annexes holding statues around the edge. A few oil lamps set into the walls glowed faintly as other bathers took the plunge into the icy pool, their sharp intakes of breath audible as the water hit their skin.

Passing back through the changing room, Euxinus stepped into the *tepidarium*, the warm room designed to ease the transition between the cool air of the *frigidarium* and *apodyterium*, and the intense heat of the baths. The heat radiated up from the floor beneath his feet, carried through the hollow spaces by the *hypocaust* system, a network of raised tiles and brick stacks that circulated hot air from a nearby furnace. The walls here, too, were adorned with frescoes, their bright colours muted by the steamy air. One man winced as a *strigil* passed over a particularly tender spot, while another accepted a small terracotta bowl of dried figs and nuts. Further along, a man reclined with his mouth wide open as a dentist tended to his teeth, the tools of his trade laid out on the bench beside him.*

Euxinus headed next into the *caldarium*, the hot room and the heart of the Roman bathing experience. This room was closest to the furnace where the slaves sweated below, doomed to feed the fires from dawn to dusk. The heat hit him like a wave, the temperature far more intense than the *tepidarium*, as steam rose from the large rectangular hot-water pool, the *alveus*, at the far end. Some men reclined by the pool, dipping their feet into the hot water before sliding in to soak, or cooled their head or hands using the *labrum*, a large, raised marble basin. Others simply sat talking on the marble benches. As he reclined, Euxinus could hear the gurgle of water being poured into the *alveus* by a slave, and he allowed the warmth to seep into his muscles, loosening the stiffness in his tired back and shoulders.

At last, he pushed himself up from the bench, sweat slick on his body, and made for the *tepidarium*. There, through the mist, Euxinus spotted a familiar figure: Scaurus. Just the man he was looking for. The old businessman lay basking in the soft light filtering in from a small window high above, his back shining under a fresh layer of oil. Scaurus had always been meticulous about his health. He lounged with the effortless confidence of a wealthy man, his belly softened by years of indulgent banquets. Despite this, his sharp gaze still carried the instincts of someone who had once fought to get ahead. Euxinus wouldn't pounce on him just yet; the man was enjoying a good scrape down from a pretty slave. He would have to choose his time well.

* Teeth and medical instruments have been found in the baths of Pompeii, leading archaeologists to believe that dental procedures were carried out inside them.

THE INNKEEPER

Once the old man's ablutions were finally complete, Scaurus hauled himself up with a grunt and vanished into the changing room where a slave waited, his tunic ready in his hands. Euxinus greeted the older man with the sort of crisp formality reserved for those who held more power, and trailed him, casually enough, into the adjoining public latrine. There, as was custom, they exchanged the usual niceties over the soft echo of trickling water and the less than pleasant scents rising from the channel of water beneath them. As Scaurus made for the exit, Euxinus fell into step beside him, shadowing the older man through the colonnade and back out into the afternoon sun.

As they walked, Euxinus began to outline the improvements he'd made to the inn. He spoke of steady trade, a growing crowd of regulars and the new additions that gave his inn just enough polish to stand apart. He delivered it all with the studied mix of deference and subdued confidence that men like Scaurus expected: enough humility to show he knew his place coupled with enough ambition to make himself worth backing. Scaurus gave nothing away as he listened, his eyes always focused ahead. A faint grunt, perhaps, or the twitch of an eyebrow. He was so difficult to read. Euxinus pressed on, undeterred.

It wasn't until a shopkeeper leaned across a counter with a ladle of nuts that the older man's face softened. That was all Euxinus needed. Guiding the conversation towards what he really wanted, he talked of the latest changes in Pompeii, how it swelled with men who had coin in their pockets and ideas above their station. Let them believe they were dining like the elite, and they'd come back, again and again, just for the illusion. Especially if the jar bore a name like Scaurus'.

They came to a halt on the Via dell'Abbondanza, the usual chaos of street life swirling around them. Still, Scaurus said nothing and, for a moment, Euxinus thought he'd overreached himself. But then the old man, laughing, boomed, 'Why not?' With a hearty slap to Euxinus' back, and in the usual process of *stipulatio*, they sealed the deal. Euxinus exhaled, relieved. Thank the gods he went for it.

'I started with nothing,' Scaurus said, 'and I've sat at tables with men who once wouldn't have given me a second glance. But the only difference between men like them and men like us: we remember where we came from. And most importantly …' He leaned in. 'We know when to seize an opportunity.'

Grinning from ear to ear, Euxinus watched Scaurus pad away down the street. The deal secured, he turned his mind to the next task of the day: a visit to the furniture maker to ensure everything was in order for tomorrow's delivery. Tullius' carpentry workshop was just a few blocks north of the forum. Passing beneath the great arch beyond the Temple of Jupiter, Euxinus stepped onto the broad, bustling street that led towards the town's outer walls and one of its watchtowers.

* * *

The bold fresco of the carpenters' procession marked the place, painted proudly on the pillar between the shopfront and the main door. In it, three men carried a heavy wooden platform draped in garlands, their muscles tensed as they marched with purpose. Above them, a group of slaves worked away, two sawing through a thick beam, another hauling a fresh piece of timber into place. Euxinus paused, taking in the striking scene. The craftsmen who worked here were respected for their skill, but it was the painter who had brought the space to life. Another painting showed festive garlands draped across the platform, a sign of celebration, in honour of Minerva, goddess of wisdom and craftsmanship. Her image adorned the pillars alongside Mercury and Fortuna, bringers

THE INNKEEPER

of prosperity and protection. To the right of the door, an electoral notice urged support for Siricus as *quinquennalis*, the magistrate elected every 5 years to oversee the town's administration.

One painting stood out to Euxinus above the rest: a vivid scene of Daedalus and Pasiphaë. The story was strange, unsettling even, but perfectly suited to a carpentry workshop. Daedalus, the master craftsman, had built the hollow wooden cow that allowed Pasiphaë to deceive the bull she had failed to sacrifice to Neptune. Angered by her actions, Neptune cursed her with an unbridled desire for the animal, and from that union she conceived the Minotaur. Next to this was a grand procession in honour of Minerva and Daedalus, captured in a rich colour. A tribute to the goddess of handicrafts

Figure 49: Fresco of the carpenter's procession found outside the Workshop of Tullius (VI.7.9)

and the legendary craftsman she favoured, it seemed to shimmer with motion, as though the figures might step forward at any moment.

As he walked through the wide entrance, wood shavings crackled underfoot and the warm, earthy scent of raw timber enveloped him. The steady rhythm of saws and chisels echoed through the space. Slaves and apprentices moved with urgency, some treating wood, others sawing or carving, while a few more added decorative flourishes to freshly carved pieces. Every inch of the workshop was in use: planks stacked against the walls; tools scattered across benches; and half-finished furniture occupying every available surface. There was no sign of living quarters on the ground floor. Perhaps, Euxinus thought, Tullius and his family slept upstairs.

Tullius, a broad-shouldered man with a streak of resin smeared across his tunic, looked up from the chair legs that he was modelling as Euxinus approached. Like many craftsmen in Pompeii, he came from modest stock, the son of a landless plebeian, but he had since carved out a respectable position for himself. While his world was rooted in the practical, in the chisels, hammers and carpentry squares, Tullius also saw his work as an art, the result of years dedicated to learning and perfecting his craft.

Tullius' shop flourished as part of Pompeii's collegial system, trade associations that supported and organised the city's craftsmen. Like many other craftsmen, he had honed his abilities over long years of apprenticeship. Sent out as a boy to learn a trade by his parents, he quickly discovered an instinct for the kinds of pieces that would appeal to the town's wealthier families. Most of his work focused on functional items: sturdy chairs, stools and fittings for homes and businesses. But it was in the more intricate commissions, like the greyhound-legged table Euxinus had ordered, that his true craftsmanship revealed itself.

THE INNKEEPER

'Euxinus! I was expecting you,' he called out, wiping his hands on a cloth as he walked over to greet him.

Euxinus glanced around, eyeing the raw wood stacked high in the corner. 'Busy day?' he asked, nodding towards the half-finished tables and chairs.

'Always is,' Tullius replied, grinning. 'Your pieces are ready.'

His hands, broad and roughened from years of labour, swept towards the corner where newly fashioned pieces stood. Among them, a wooden table with a circular top immediately drew Euxinus' eye. Its three curved legs, carved in the shape of lion's legs, ended in broad sculpted paws, with a finely detailed lion's head halfway up each leg. The craftsmanship was superb. It would be perfect for his new private dining room. Running his hand over the polished surface, Euxinus nodded in approval. This was a table that would leave an impression.

Figure 50: (left) Carbonised table from Herculaneum; (right) matching table from a painted fresco in Herculaneum

Beside it stood a simple wooden cabinet with a single shelf, unadorned and practical, and polished to a sleek finish with olive oil, like the rest of the furniture. Euxinus had ordered it for storing extra plates, utensils and jugs, knowing that storage space in the kitchen and dining area was always in short supply. Tullius had understood Euxinus' brief for utility; though plain, the cabinet was solidly built, its sturdy frame designed to endure years of use. For the main bar area of the inn, Tullius had put together a set of unembellished square tables, and alongside them were simple chairs and stools. They were made to last and strong enough to survive even the roughest of customers.

Finally, Tullius led him to two new wooden beds, one destined for a guestroom, the other for Euxinus himself. Three simple wooden panels enclosed the sides, with the base made of evenly spaced slats. Euxinus could already picture his weary guests falling onto the guest bed after a long day at the amphitheatre, or working at the market, grateful for whatever comfort his inn could offer. At a nearby workbench, Tullius grabbed a piece of charcoal and began tallying up the prices on a scrap of wood. Once the deal was struck, he clapped Euxinus on the back with a gratified grin. The furniture would be delivered the next day. Euxinus let the air fill his lungs as he stepped outside; with these new additions, and Scaurus' product, his *caupona* was shaping up to be a real gem in Pompeii's flourishing entertainment district.

* * *

After returning from the workshop, Euxinus took a moment to check on the *caupona*, ensuring everything was running as smoothly as it could. With the afternoon rush approaching, he would soon need to be back behind the counter, but for now, there was another

THE INNKEEPER

task to complete, one he preferred to handle in peace. Making his way back up the main high street, he took a right into the garden district and arrived at one of the houses that had been converted into a horticultural business. He breathed in the sweet smell of perfumes drifting through the open door. The new owner had seized the opportunity to profit from the growing demand for perfume, a luxury that had filtered down from the elite circles of Rome and the grand villas along the coast. To supply their own ingredients, they had planted a large flower garden, ensuring a steady source of blossoms, as well as olive trees for the oil needed in the perfume-making process.

Passing through the threshold, he was enveloped with the heady fragrances of crushed flowers, musky olive oil and sweet earth. Sunlight filtered through the doorway onto the mosaic threshold, where the words '*Cras Credo*' warned of the proprietor's policy: 'I will give credit tomorrow'. He knew how they felt. The walls of the atrium were faded but riddled with rough scratches, marks of the shopkeeper's accounts and transactions over the years. Against one wall, a small display shelf held glass perfume bottles of varying sizes and colours, their iridescent surfaces glistening.

The shop was small, intimate even, and void of the usual industry found in other shops. Much of the activity happened in the back rooms and in the garden, out of sight. On a low counter, garlands of vibrant flowers, roses and violets were laid out, their colours vivid against the backdrop of the dim interior. Euxinus marvelled at their delicate arrangements.

'*Salve*, Euxinus!' called a familiar voice from within. The shopkeeper, an old man with kind eyes, gestured towards a doorway leading to the garden. 'Come. In all this time you've been our customer, I don't think you've ever seen our centre of industry in bloom.'

He opened a back door onto the most extraordinary sight. The garden stretched out, wide and orderly, a canvas of brilliant colour framed by the humble walls of the property. At its heart stood a grand *lararium* shrine to Hercules, the marble statue weathered but still magnificent. A stone altar in front bore faint traces of recent offerings, the scent of charred herbs lingering as Euxinus and the gardener passed by on a small path. To the left, an elegant outdoor dining *triclinium* had been arranged beneath a lattice of vines for the guild of flower growers and other tradesmen who gathered here, offering an elegant space to meet for meals and business. Clusters of dark grapes, their skins taut with ripeness, hung within reach above the cushion-covered couches, left for diners to pluck as they pleased.

Just beyond, a masonry cistern shimmered with reflected light, its surface occasionally rippled by the slow drip of water from a

Figure 51: The Garden of Hercules (II.8.6) during excavations in 1972, showing the triclinium *and dog kennel to the left, the* lararium *shrine with Hercules in the centre, and root cavities throughout the garden*

THE INNKEEPER

carved channel in the wall. On the street outside, a slave poured water from a public fountain into a spout built into the wall. It fed directly through to the garden inside, where a channel carried the flow into a large storage jar. At the rear of the garden, next to the shrine to Hercules, Euxinus noticed the dog kennel, the usual occupant of which was now sleeping in a warm patch of sun near some borders. The garden was alive with movement: the buzz of bees as they darted between the flower beds, the rustling of leaves in the gentle breeze, the murmur of the slaves' voices drifting up from where they worked.

The garden beds themselves were a marvel of precision. Rows of soil, framed by narrow irrigation channels, cradled neatly spaced blooms of roses, chamomiles, violets and geraniums. Small terracotta pots stood along the walls, spilling over with greenery having been repurposed as garden containers. It was a thoughtfully cultivated space, not just for purpose and profit, but for beauty.

The shopkeeper's wife appeared behind him, her eyes soft as she handed Euxinus a small vial of his late wife's favourite perfume: jasmine and lily, delicate but strong, just as Fausta had been. Euxinus' eye lingered on the pure-white petals of a line of lilies nearby, their fragrance familiar as the scent she had once dabbed behind her ears each day. The shopkeeper's wife draped a garland, also made of jasmine and lily, over his shoulder. She tucked the small blue glass vial of perfume into his pouch, and when he placed a few coins into her hand as payment, he noticed for the first time two gold rings on her fingers.* By all appearances, their business was flourishing.

As he left, Euxinus looked up at the flower garlands swaying by the shop's entrance, their vibrant allure beckoning passers-by

---

* A skeleton (gender unspecified) was found in this garden wearing two gold rings.

headed towards the City of the Dead just beyond the gate. He smiled at the thought of how much his wife would have loved the garland around his neck, a small moment of beauty that they could no longer share.

Making his way down the steep slope and through one of the city's gates, he emerged into the *necropolis* on the other side of the city walls. The air was still, save for the faint hum of the city behind him. He had to walk some way to reach his wife's grave, set on the road outside the city, beyond the areas reserved for the elite. As he approached, the familiar ache in his chest returned. Euxinus knelt before the tomb, laying the garland gently on the stone. On his way to the perfume shop, he had purchased a small jar of wine stoppered with resin for the occasion. With slow movements, he poured a libation of wine and perfume, and draped the garland over her final resting place, picturing her face the whole time.

For a long moment, he sat in silence, letting the memories wash over him, eyes closed. He whispered a prayer, the words catching in his throat, and felt something rumble beneath him.

CHAPTER SIX

THE PRIEST OF ISIS

MIDWAY THROUGH THE EIGHTH HOUR (1.30 P.M.), 23 OCTOBER 79 CE

A warm breeze whispered through the columns of the temple's portico, brushing against Amisusius' skin as he took in the sight before him.* Devotees clad in crisp linen clothing moved in an incense-laden cloud, their voices rising in prayer or soft conversation. The heady, fragrant incense, a blend of frankincense and myrrh, curled in delicate spirals towards the open sky, giving the scene an otherworldly quality. Beneath that lingered the warm, slightly bitter scent of *kyphi*, the sacred Egyptian incense, a rich fusion of honey, wine, cinnamon and juniper that coated the throat and settled deep in the lungs.† At the centre of the walled complex

---

* Amisusius appears to be the name written under the portrait of a priest in the House of D. Octavius Quartio (II.2.2), though the actual translation of the name is debated.
† Today, we often think of incense as ready-made sticks. However, in the ancient world, incense referred to the offering of aromatic substances, such as resins or perfumes, which were burned on an altar or other sacrificial area.

stood the Temple of Isis, the sacred heart of the space, where the divine and the mortal worlds brushed fingers.

Amisusius' gaze lingered on the temple itself, its steep staircase rising majestically, flanked by tall columns that framed the grand entrance. To the right of the green-veined marble steps stood an ancient tablet mounted on a pillar, a relic brought generations ago from the motherland of Egypt. Its surface bore the carved symbols of that distant land, a script of enigmatic beauty. The intricate hieroglyphs, which he read with ease, recounted tales from the final two decades of Pharaonic rule, culminating in Egypt's conquest by Alexander the Great.

Amisusius had come from Rome to Pompeii 17 years ago, back when the cult of Isis was just beginning to take hold among the city's people. He had arrived in the year of the great quake, which

Figure 52: Reconstruction of the Temple of Isis, showing the purgatorium *and altar to the left*

THE PRIEST OF ISIS

had continued to plague the region in the years since. Just this week the city had been shaken by several more, each seeming stronger than the last. Quakes had always been a part of life in Campania, certainly, but not with the kind of devastation seen in the eighth year of Nero's reign.*

In the days that had followed, Amisusius, displaced and directionless like so many others, had found temporary shelter in a house converted into a communal sleeping space. The air had been stifling; the floors crowded with strangers who muttered in their sleep or stared blankly at the ceiling. It was there, in the darkness, that she came to him.

He could still feel the weight of the dream. The way it had unfolded so vividly and so real. Isis had appeared, her presence radiating a light that cut through the dark corners of his soul. Her voice had been commanding yet tender, and she had breathed forth the blessed fragrance of Arabia as she spoke.†

'I have seen your suffering,' she said, 'and I have chosen you to serve me. Rise, and let despair give way to purpose. You will rebuild, not just for yourself, but for all who seek refuge under my wings. I will teach you the magic of healing and renewal, and through you, my light will guide those who are lost.'

Her words carried the weight of destiny, wrapping around him like the folds of her shimmering garment. Then, the radiant figure had dissolved, giving way to a man with a shaved head, just like his own now, dressed in a bright white linen robe. He was the priest who would initiate him into her cult. When he woke, heart pounding and drenched in sweat, Amisusius knew he could no longer live

---

* 62 CE (Nero reigned between 54 and 68 CE).
† This is taken from Apuleius' *The Golden Ass*, Book 11, 20–30, where he describes initiation into the cult of Isis and confirms the importance of dreaming in the cult.

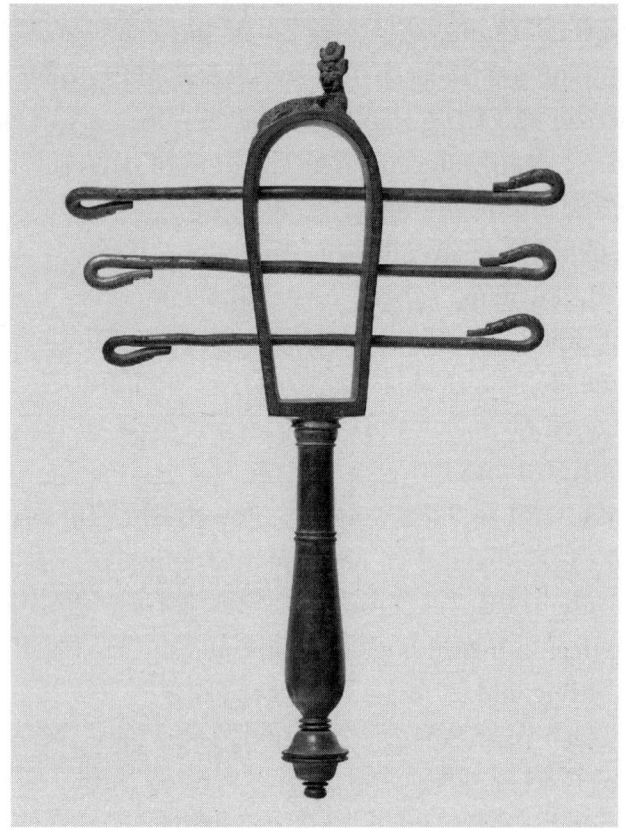

Figure 53: Sistrum *found in the Temple of Isis at Pompeii*

as he had before. He was to walk a different path, one where his life belonged to her.

Amisusius was dragged back to the present with the invigorating sound of Egyptian bronze *sistra* rattles being shaken by his fellow priests and priestesses. The heavy curtains, which usually veiled the idol from sight, had been drawn back at first light that morning. Sun poured into the *cella*, the sacred chamber at the temple's heart, illuminating the deific figures within. Against one wall stood Anubis, the jackal-headed guardian of the dead and guide through the afterlife. Opposite, the figure of Horus, son of Isis and Osiris,

THE PRIEST OF ISIS

embodied the triumph of life over death. But it was the pair at the centre, Isis and Osiris, on two 6-foot-high pedestals, who dominated the room. The figure of Isis was commanding and serene. Her golden crown rested on top of her head, adorned with the solar disc and *uraeus*, the sacred serpent worn on the headdresses of Egyptian deities and sovereigns. Her rainbow-coloured linen robes shimmered, the sacred Isiac knot firm across her chest as a symbol of eternity and power. She gleamed with a divine radiance. To the faithful, the idol was alive, a vessel infused with the presence of the goddess herself.

The courtyard was full now, the faithful pressing closer to the steps of the temple, all gazing in the direction of Isis' unveiled form. They prayed and chanted, their voices rising and falling in a divine chorus. The divinity of this sound often reminded Amisusius of why he had chosen this path, or rather, why Isis had chosen it for him. They could all feel it: her strength, her presence, projecting outwards like an unseen current, anchoring the courtyard of worshippers in her sacred energy. She was maternal, yet unyielding. The goddess who healed, guided, mourned and avenged. He bowed his head and felt her gaze upon him. No matter how many times he had stood before her, it never ceased to stir something deep within him, as if she could see into the very essence of his soul.

Isis was an Egyptian goddess with a chequered history. It was she who had tricked the mighty sun god Ra into revealing his secret name, granting her control over life and death. But above all, she was a widow destined to perpetually mourn the loss of her beloved husband Osiris, who had been murdered at the hands of his jealous brother, Seth. Osiris' body, ripped apart and scattered across the world, became the focus of Isis' devotion. She had searched ceaselessly, her determination unbroken, until at last she had recovered all his remains and breathed life into them again, piece by piece, through her magic and her love. Out of that love, sorrow became strength, and her loss became the foundation of renewal. She was the ultimate survivor, capable of defying death itself and wielding a power that even the other gods were compelled to respect.

It was little wonder, then, that her cult had taken root in Pompeii in the wake of Rome's conquest of Egypt under Augustus. By then the city was already a Roman colony, its ports welcoming goods from the farthest reaches of the Empire, with grain, luxuries and

Figure 54: Priests of Isis carry out a water ritual in a Temple of Isis. Found in Herculaneum, this fresco is dated to 62–79 CE

wealth from Egypt among them. In a town of merchants and travellers, Isis offered protection across the seas. To the poor, the enslaved and the marginalised, she was among the deities, like Bacchus, Mithras and Cybele, who provided a sanctuary and solace that Rome's traditional pantheon seldom offered. Women found in her a goddess who understood their lives: a mother, a mourner and a protector all at once. In her rites they were embraced, their prayers heard with the same weight as any free man's. The group of Isiaci standing before Amisusius was a mix of artisans and tradespeople, politicians and business people. From the wealthiest patrons to the humblest of freedmen, the worshippers stood beneath the gaze of the goddess, their piety uniting them.

Amisusius' eyes drifted to the smoking altar. In other temples, this altar would have been front and centre, but they had placed it slightly to the left to allow more room for the faithful to see the idol in all her glory. In the second of the two daily rituals, the first having been carried out at dawn, the worshippers gathered and placed offerings on the altar: crescent-shaped bread baked in the kitchen on site, ripe dates shipped in from Egypt, a scattering of pine-kernels and almonds, a cluster of the juiciest figs and the most fragrant oils, some imported from the motherland, others crafted in gardens just steps away from the temple. Nearby sat a low bronze brazier borrowed from the theatre next door, its sides adorned with tiny theatrical masks.

Lifting a gleaming gold vessel from the nearby table, Amisusius blessed the sacred water he had drawn from the temple's basement that morning. Carried all the way from the Nile, the lifeblood of his goddess's motherland, the sacred water felt cool and heavy in his hand, a tangible connection to a place he knew he was never likely to see. Amisusius' voice carried above the chants, his intonations met with fervent echoes from the crowd. As he looked over

Figure 55: Brazier found in the Temple of Isis at Pompeii

the gathered worshipers, a sea of bowed heads and raised hands, his eyes fell on one person in particular.

Julia Felix was a truly striking figure, resplendent in crisp white linen. Although unfettered by the desires of earthly beings, even Amisusius could appreciate her sheer beauty: her soft skin and jawline, strong Roman nose and cascading ringlets. Julia was one of the cult's most dedicated followers, her piety clear not only in her presence at every ritual but in the shrine she had built for Isis at her elaborate estate. She knelt beside her close friend Sutoria Primigenia as they followed the guidance of another of the priests on the temple steps, who now led the meditations and prayers.

The initiate for tomorrow, Octavius Quartio, was also present. He would not become one of the priests like Amisusius, who formed the temple hierarchy, led rites, administered the sanctuary and imparted sacred knowledge to both initiates and the wider community. Instead, he would undergo a ritual which would draw him closer to the goddess and bless him with the promise of a blissful afterlife. A gold seal ring gleamed on Quartio's finger, its imprint having been pressed into countless documents over the years as proof of his identity and status. His hair, neatly cut,

THE PRIEST OF ISIS

framed a clean-shaven face. He had the look of a man who was attentive to the grooming expected of his station. Having positioned himself slightly apart from the throng, his lips moved softly in prayer. To Amisusius, he embodied a rare balance of genuine piety and poise.

The temple timekeeper, the *horologos*, stepped forward to announce the arrival of the ninth hour, and the crowd turned their gaze towards the sanctuary doors. Amisusius, flanked by two priests and a priestess, the *stolists*, ascended the steps at the rear of the temple into the room at the top. The presence of the goddess's idol filled the space, even as Amisusius prepared to enact the sacred ritual that would conceal the statue from mortal eyes until dawn. With reverent precision, Amisusius lifted an intricately embroidered veil and, together with the *stolists*, climbed the wooden steps placed in front of the pedestals and draped the veil over the goddess's form. The fabric shimmered as it settled into place, marking the goddess's withdrawal into her divine realm. The sanctuary curtains were pulled across the *cella* opening before the *horologos* signalled the end of the ritual with the delicate clang of a pair of cymbals. The gathered worshippers bowed their heads in unison and the ritual concluded.

The worshippers began to drift apart, exchanging soft farewells. A few lingered, giving rise to little knots of conversation. The name of Pansa passed many of their lips, praising his part in the organisation of the games, and speculating as to whether he would give a speech. His electoral success was their triumph too, the Isiaci having offered their support to him during his campaign. Just across from the temple entrance, the show of their loyalty remained etched on the wall of a house nearby: '*Popidius Natalis, his client, with the worshippers of Isis, call for the election of Cuspius Pansa, aedile.*'

With the last of the faithful leaving through the temple's narrow doorway, a calm settled over the courtyard, broken only by the soft sounds of sweeping and brushing. Under the watchful guidance of Amisusius, the priests and priestesses began their chores. Just to the left of the temple entrance, at the larger of the two altars, a priestess swept the day's ash into a terracotta bowl and discarded it on the street outside. Another brushed the temple steps clean, while a young priest, initiated only that past spring, moved reverently between the perimeter statues, anointing each one with sacred water.

As the three of them replenished each lamp with oil for the evening, the creak of the temple door announced a new arrival. Marcus Popidius Natalis, client of Gaius Cuspius Pansa, stepped inside the temple complex.* He wore a fine linen tunic beneath a heavy woollen cloak, his wealth evident in the supple leather of his *calcei* and the gold signet ring set with a ruby Venus. He paused at one of the niches by the entrance, dipped his fingers into the cool sacred water and touched it to his brow in silent prayer. Then he straightened, composed, and turned to face Amisusius, who had paused in his duties to greet him.

Among the Isiaci, Natalis was a familiar and respected figure, a longtime devotee who had commissioned the electoral graffiti across from the temple. Amisusius knew this was no idle visit; Natalis had organised for Amisusius to visit the feast of Pansa today following the games, a calculated gesture on both sides. For Pansa, it was a chance to reinforce his bond with the most popular cult in the city, a faith embraced by the masses whose votes had carried

---

* There are no known references to Popidius Natalis' *praenomen* in Pompeii, but he may be the same Marcus Popidius Natalis mentioned in a late first-century CE funerary inscription, recording the burial of a homeborn slave girl named Hedone on an epitaph set up with Natalis' permission.

him into office. For Amisusius, it promised the continued goodwill of an incoming *aedile* whose influence would stretch to the maintenance of temples. With a respectful nod, Amisusius guided Natalis towards a shaded corner of the portico, where another statue of Isis kept a silent vigil.

'The Isiaci are pleased with Pansa's support,' Amisusius began, 'but expectations are growing.'

Natalis gave a short nod. 'He's aware,' he said. 'Pansa's not one to overpromise, but he understands what the Isiaci have done for him.'

'Faith thrives on promises fulfilled, and on the hope of more to come,' Amisusius offered softly. 'The people expect more processions worthy of the goddess, for the temple to be kept in honour, especially if it should suffer more damage should the quakes continue. This is what the Isiaci believe they have earned.'

The relationship between the temple and its supporters was delicate, a symbiotic bond built on trust, piety and civic ambition, and on reciprocal support. Upon entering the temple, Natalis had passed beneath a prominent reminder of his family's deep connection to this sacred place: a large marble inscription honouring Numerius Popidius Celsinus.*

In the aftermath of the great quake, Celsinus' freedman father, Numerius Popidius Ampliatus, and his wife, Corelia Celsa, had swiftly financed the restoration of the Temple of Isis in honour of their 6-year-old son, ensuring its survival before many others had even begun to rebuild their own properties. It was a fitting choice for the temple of a goddess who embodied resilience and rebirth, and a bold gesture which successfully propelled the boy into the ranks of Pompeii's elite. The council, eager to acknowledge such

---

* We do not know the relationship between Natalis and Numerius Popidius Celsinus, though they are from the same family, the Popidii. In 79 CE, Celsinus would have been 21 years old.

generosity had, in response, conferred on Celsinus an unprecedented honour: he was appointed as a *decurio*, a position of civic and religious authority, rarely, if ever, granted to one so young. Now in his twenties, Celsinus still held the role, contributing to civic, legal and religious affairs.

'The arrangements for this evening,' Natalis said, his voice low. 'They need to do more than impress. They need to suggest inevitability.'

Amisusius looked at him, unblinking. 'You want the gods to seem behind him.'

'The people already speak of omens. Now we need them to see confirmation. The ceremony must feel like something long foretold.'

Amisusius gave the barest nod. 'So, this isn't devotion. It's direction.'

'It's both,' Natalis replied. 'He honours the goddess. The goddess, in turn, has guided his rise. That is the message.'

Amisusius let the silence stretch a moment before answering. 'Then it will be done. With the gravity it deserves.'

Pansa and Natalis both understood that the words Amisusius spoke carried influence beyond the temple walls, and far beyond the cult itself. It was just as an inscription, written on a wall not far from the temple, read:

'*The worshippers of Isis are everywhere.*'

* * *

After Natalis had departed, Amisusius used the quieter hours to finish some essential bookkeeping in the small room beside the kitchen, working into the evening. A local merchant had offered to donate an Egyptian statue of Horus, Isis and Osiris' son, the god of kingship, healing, protection, and of the sun and sky, complete

THE PRIEST OF ISIS

with a formal dedication. While he welcomed sacred offerings, especially those imported from Egypt, Amisusius remained cautious. Too many and the temple risked becoming little more than a showcase for the wealthy, a place to parade generosity rather than to express true devotion. They already had a donated bust in the portico of a once-popular actor who had performed at the theatre next door. If this man wanted his statue placed within the sanctuary itself, he would need to prove his piety through regular attendance and rituals, not only treasures.

Rubbing his eyes with fatigue, he shut the sacred books and carried them out into the open temple complex, carefully placing them back in the hollow of one of the plinths in the *cella*. Tomorrow, he would initiate the new devotee. It had been 11 days since his dream; that night, the goddess had come to him as well as to Octavius Quartio. In his vision, Amisusius had been standing in the forecourt surrounding the large amphitheatre, looking into the garden of Octavius. Through the garden gate, Amisusius heard the voice of Isis, and he had followed the sound. Octavius' time had arrived, she had told him, and he had been chosen to lead him into the sacred mysteries as an initiate.*

Passing the main altar, Amisusius inclined his head to two priests emerging from the roofless *purgatorium*, their arms heavy with jars of sacred Nile water drawn from the chamber below. The stuccoed walls on its exterior stood out in raised relief: dolphins and serpents, priests mid-ritual, winged cupids and other divine figures drawn from myth and belief. It was the language of Rome, not Egypt; Isis wrapped in symbols that the Pompeians would know and trust. Here she was no longer the distant goddess of the Nile, but a pres-

---

* This also happens in Apuleius' *The Golden Ass*; a priest of Isis receives the calling in a dream to initiate a follower. The initiate sees the same priest in his own dream.

ence made familiar, her foreignness softened with Roman imagery into forms the city could claim as its own. Rome had long excelled at absorbing the faiths of the colonised, adopting and adapting them, rather than denying them. By weaving them into the Roman fabric, it created the illusion of the colonised maintaining their faiths, while it was in fact binding them closer to the growing Empire. None of the priests here had ever even seen Egypt, and likely never would.

As Amisusius stood at the entrance doorway to the temple precinct, he watched with amusement as a jubilant crowd spilled from the direction of the amphitheatre, their faces flushed with wine and the thrill of blood sport. A faint evening chill brushed his skin. This entire quarter of the city was ancient, first raised by the Greeks who had settled here many years ago and left their mark in stone. Drawn by the richness of the soil and the strategic sweep of the Bay of Naples, they had settled in the region centuries ago, marking the start of a long love affair between Greek culture and the Bay, and leaving their mark on Pompeii long before Rome.

The theatre they had built for telling tales of gods, heroes and fate in song and story now pressed against the temple complex, drawing the precinct into its orbit. Amisusius held a key to the theatre, a quiet privilege of the priesthood. From time to time, he would slip into the rows of stone seats, letting the plays wash over him; else, in quieter hours, he would tend to the sacred water features dotted throughout the temple complex.

To his right, the alleyway leading to the theatre's side entrance lay quiet for now. The priests and priestesses of Isis had once used it freely, but too many nights had been disturbed by rowdy drinkers who, chucked out from the nearby inns, had taken to using the secluded corner for anything but sacred acts. After enough disturbances, they had placed a heavy wooden door across the passage, keeping out the worst of the city's nocturnal revelry. Since then, things had been far more peaceful.

The temple's Egyptian slaves filed out from the temple doors, bearing the items needed for the ritual at the House of Pansa this evening. Amisusius watched in silence, the hypocrisy not lost on him. Those whose homeland had first worshipped the goddess now served her in bondage, while the priesthood was in Roman hands. He had long since learned to live with the contradiction, though it never sat easily with him. He adjusted his cloak as he stepped forward. He would have preferred to walk alone in quiet meditation, but the Isiaci, and Natalis above all, had insisted otherwise. The high priest of Isis was expected to carry himself with the dignity of Rome's other priests, a visible figure of authority. Ceremony had its place; the *Navigium Isidis*, with its spring procession and ship launched to sea, was proof enough of that, as were the torchlit rites of her birthday, the *Lychnapsia*.* In just 5 days there would be the *Isia* and the mourning and restoration of Osiris. Tonight, though, what they carried was simpler: tools and vessels for the rites, stored in boxes by the slaves who followed at his back.

The walk to Pansa's home on the Via dell'Abbondanza was short. To the right, the entrances to the house of the *gens Popidii* loomed in the dim lamplight, its corridors echoing with the music and revelry unfolding inside. Tonight, however, young Natalis would not be inside. He was expected at the feast of his patron, Pansa, the gathering that now drew Amisusius forward. As the group arrived at the Via dell'Abbondanza, the city's pulse grew louder. Despite the hour, the streets were stirring with life and revelry. Many were celebrating after the games, their laughter spilling from open door-

---

* The first, marking the start of the sailing season after winter, was held on 5 March, while the latter, thought to be held in honour of the goddess's birthday, was held on 12 August.

ways, while in the shadows, hushed negotiations unfolded, the city's undercurrent of night-time dealings undisturbed. To the east, revellers loitered outside a tavern, cups in hand, while a few prostitutes lingered in doorways, their gazes sweeping over passers-by, searching for clients seeking one last indulgence before returning home.

Ahead, the House of Pansa loomed in the soft light of the nearby taverns; the impressively high doorway was meant to be imposing by design.* The large iron filigree handles lent the door an air of refined elegance, and the intricate circular designs surrounding the lock showed dogs in pursuit of hares amidst flowers and grasses. In the centre of the door, two impressive lion heads held rings in their mouths. Amisusius exhaled and knocked. A voice of an origin other than Latin asked for his identity.

To Amisusius' surprise, the voice didn't emerge from behind the large door. Instead, the porter materialised to Amisusius' right at a smaller entry and beckoned the priest to follow. Amisusius and his entourage passed through the small, secret passageway beyond that wrapped around the main door, leading to the other side of it. Here, a dog as black as night lay curled in a ball. He noted how much like Anubis the dog looked. A good sign, he thought.

As his slaves were whisked off to the appropriate quarters, Amisusius was greeted with the perfumes of wealth and a glistening mosaic floor. The frescoes on the walls seemed to dance as he was led around the tall columns surrounding the *impluvium* pool to the back of the *domus* where he could hear the raucous revelry of a feast in full swing. Natalis had warned him that they would all have

---

* I have pinpointed IX.1.22, sometimes called the House of Marcus Epidius Sabinus, as a possible candidate for Pansa's home. This is due to graffiti around the entrance and the frequency with which graffiti referring to Pansa appears in the vicinity.

THE PRIEST OF ISIS

returned from the games that night. As he stepped into the *triclinium*, the sound of laughter and raised voices dimmed.

'Is this a vision that I see?' Marcus Samellius Modestus bellowed with smiling eyes, flinging his arms wide and sending a spray of wine across the mosaic floor.

Amisusius recognised Pansa's three fellow *aediles* for the incoming year, as well as the *garum* magnate, Aulus Umbricius Scaurus, who lifted his glass cup to the priest as their eyes met. He was seated next to Paquius Proculus, the former *duumvir*, who seemed to be too engrossed in a discussion with a naked female musician to have noticed Amisusius' arrival. Amidst them, Popidius Natalis inclined his head in greeting, his sobriety a contrast to the others. Though Amisusius was aware of the artificial nature of his visit that evening, their feast having already begun and their minds hardly in a state for summoning the spirit of Isis, he nonetheless understood the necessity of fostering ties.

Wasting no time, Pansa gave the signal for Amisusius to begin the rites. At his word, a slave brought the sacred items into the atrium. The guests followed, their laughter and half-slurred prayers rising with every cup of wine, which had grown stronger as the evening wore on. Amisusius rarely performed such rituals outside the temple, especially not within the private homes of Pompeii's elite. The purification of a household was typically reserved for those fully devoted to the cult, or for spaces designated as sacred. But it was hard to refuse the request of one of the city's incoming *aediles*, especially one supported by the temple's worshippers.

Amisusius poured sacred Nile water from the *amphora* into a golden ritual cup, which a slave held aloft. The scent of burning myrrh and frankincense filled the air as he moved through the rooms, the mood shifting as he walked. Where there had been boisterous laughter moments before, now there was a solemn hush.

It felt as if the goddess herself had descended among them. Standing beneath the central opening of the *compluvium*, Amisusius dipped his hands into the cup. The liquid shimmered as he lifted it in offering, murmuring a low invocation to Isis. Then, with outstretched arms, he faced east in the direction of the rising sun, the renewal of life, and raised his hands in the Sign of the Wings of Isis.

'Open, O Heaven! Open, O Earth! Open, O East, West, South and North! The gates of Gaius Cuspius Pansa's home shall be flung wide for you, Goddess Isis!'

At the mention of Pansa's name, Natalis nodded in approval from his spot at the edge of the group. As Amisusius spoke, he turned slowly and marked each direction, inviting the goddess to fill the space. The slaves trailed wisps of myrrh and frankincense from their incense burners as they followed him through each room of the vast home.

On the far side of the large peristyle, two male slaves peered out from a shadowed doorway. Amisusius barely glanced at the first, but the second held his gaze. The young man looked no different from the others, yet there was something in his eyes that caught Amisusius off guard. An instinct told him something was about to change for this one. Something good.

He looked away with a faint smile and continued along the colonnade, sprinkling water at each doorway as the guests looked on in reverent silence. At last, he returned to the atrium and stepped into its centre. Lifting his hands, a slave began to coax the evocative tune on a double piped *aulus*, and Amisusius gave the final invocation to Isis:

'Come, therefore, Winged One, and fill this vessel! O Beloved One, Great of Magic, Beautiful of Wings, Bright of Face: enter into this House and be with your children!'

THE PRIEST OF ISIS

The group solemnly bowed their heads as a breeze caressed their cheeks and hair. Amisusius took it as a sign of her divine and omnipotent presence. He caught Natalis' eye once more, and said, 'The goddess watches over this place.' The music stopped.

The energy of the house felt changed: a warmth had spread through the company, bonding them in a way that only religion could in Pompeii. That, and maybe the games. Pansa beamed at the approval from the goddess that he had just received.

'You must join us for the next course, Amisusius,' Pansa said. 'You would honour me.'

Amisusius shook his head with a faint smile. 'You honour me enough already, Pansa. But I must return. The final rites await, and the temple doesn't rest.'

Heading back into the atrium, Amisusius took a seat as he waited for his slaves to gather his items for the walk back. He could hear the booming voice of Pansa beginning a speech, a self-promotion of his family and their good deeds for the city of Pompeii. Politics never stopped in this city, he thought, as he gazed around at the incredible wealth on display in Pansa's atrium. Once the slaves confirmed all was ready, Amisusius gave a slight nod to the porter and stepped over the threshold of the secret door into the cool night air. At that moment, he heard Pansa's voice cut through the peace:

'Step forward, Petrinus.'

Amisusius smiled knowingly as he walked out into the darkness of the night.

* * *

The sun had not yet crept above the crest of Mount Vesuvius when Amisusius stirred from his restless sleep. The quiet rhythm of a fellow priest's breath, slow and steady in the next bed, was the only sound in their dark chamber. Amisusius pressed his hand to his forehead, trying to grasp the remnants of his dreams. A pit grew in his stomach as the memory returned: Isis herself, radiant and bathed in golden light, had stood before him. But then, she had turned her back. His pulse quickened at the thought. What could it mean? A warning? A test? He would need to meditate on this later.

Gently, he reached over and shook his companion awake. The other priest stirred, groggy but compliant. His stomach panged more sharply than usual, but the morning rituals couldn't wait. The goddess's service came before all else. The bedroom of Amisusius and his fellow priests opened directly onto the southern portico of the temple precinct, its heavy wooden door creaking as he stepped into the crisp, pre-dawn air. The terracotta lantern he carried, imprinted with the cheerful image of the squat Bes, cast a golden glow along his path to the *purgatorium*.

A young slave awaited him there, pale and bleary-eyed, evidence of the toll of his own temple duties. Bowing low, the boy reminded him that today was the third day of Amisusius' ritual cleansing cycle, which required the arduous process of hair removal. A chill hung in the air, making the usual practice of shaving outside unpleasant. Instead, they moved into the dining room where the slaves, accustomed to this task, set about their work with speedy precision, shaving the entirety of his head, eyebrows and eyelashes. The shaving was a practice of deep spiritual significance which ensured that his body, like his spirit, was free from impurity.

Once shaved, Amisusius returned to the *purgatorium*. The horizon above the temple walls was painted with a pale pink light, heralding the arrival of Ra, the Egyptian Sun God. Passing through the doorway, he descended the staircase hidden behind a low wall. The air grew colder as he walked into the crypt, where the wavering lamplight maintained by temple slaves barely cut through the gloom. The room was small but sacred. At its centre lay a large basin

THE PRIEST OF ISIS

filled with water, surrounded by *amphorae* containing the precious Nile water brought from Egypt to Pompeii. On a slightly elevated platform in the corner sat the vessel used to draw the sacred water for ritual use. Amisusius lifted the vessel with reverence as he said prayers to Isis. Pouring the water over his body, he did not flinch at the icy shock of its touch. His whispered words carried his devotion upwards, an offering to the divine. When the final drops splashed into the basin below, two slaves stepped forward, bearing fresh, clean linens folded neatly on their extended arms.

Amisusius stood still as the slaves completed their work, drying his body with the soft cloths and wrapping another long white linen around his torso. They secured the fabric just below his chest, leaving it to cascade in elegant folds. At the bottom were tassels, as was customary for priests of Isis. His white palm-leaf sandals were tied snugly around his ankles; he would need to remove these for the initiation rites later, as part of the ritual purity required. Around his shoulders, the slaves draped a cream-coloured mantel, also made of linen as wool was considered impure for temple service, and tied it in the knot of Isis at his chest. The fabric wrapped tightly around him, offering warmth in the pre-dawn air.

Today was no ordinary day, and his attire reflected that. On his wrists he wore golden bracelets, and from his ears dangled small gold discs. Fully adorned, he ascended the staircase leading back to the portico and made to finish his duties. One by one, the three other priests and the lone priestess descended into the *purgatorium* for their own purification rituals. Amisusius busied himself with the preparations for the morning's dedication. Moving through the temple, he lit oil lamps perched on bronze candelabras shaped like tall lotus flowers, and others resting on simpler clay stands. Each flame symbolised the presence of the goddess within the temple. One by one, the other priests joined the preparation efforts.

Figure 56: Image of a priest of Isis, labelled 'Amisusius', from the House of D. Octavius Quartio (II.2.2.)

Satisfied, Amisusius turned his attention to the sacred objects required for the day's rites. He examined the *sistra*, water vessels and libation cups, checking each surface for clarity and polish. Nothing could be overlooked. Every item had to reflect the goddess's dignity, and anything less would dishonour her. With the preparations complete, the five passed a niche housing a statue of Bacchus at the rear of the temple and began their ascent up the staircase, their voices blending in a low, solemn hymn. Isis, draped for now, was not yet ready to appear. Her daily unveiling would only come once she had been ritually cleansed and clothed.

THE PRIEST OF ISIS

The attendants moved swiftly, their hands lighting the remaining oil lamps that lined the *cella* walls. Attention then turned to the wooden chest near the base of the statue which contained the goddess's most precious items. Amisusius opened the creaking lid with care, and the contents within were revealed. Jewellery that sparkled, even in the dim lantern light; garments to dress the idol of the goddess, alongside small statues of other Egyptian deities, including a tiny bronze amulet of Harpocrates. The goddess's wardrobe was vast, her garments suited to every season and ceremony; today's choice, a dark blue dress, was selected in honour of the initiation that would take place later, symbolising her role as a celestial goddess overseeing the stars, moon and cycles of life.

The morning ritual was as familiar to Amisusius as his own heartbeat. He lit ceremonial incense and watched the first sparks catch, the rich scent of myrrh and frankincense curling upwards in silken plumes. Its heady fragrance filled the *cella* as they lay the goddess's sacred implements before her likeness. With each one, Amisusius said a blessing:

'Thanks to you, Lady Isis, for your compassion, for strength, wisdom and magic, and for your blessing, a reawakening to life. Blessed Be.'

With the rites complete, he opened the wooden shutters of the *cella*, the courtyard beyond coming into view. At his nod, the attendants drew back the heavy curtains that veiled the statues of Isis and Osiris. The effect was immediate. Even after years in her service, Amisusius still felt it: that shiver as her presence seemed to fill the space around him. On an ordinary morning, worshippers would already be seated on the courtyard floor, preparing to greet the sun in silent devotion. But today was different; only Octavius Quartio was watching on. Soon they would gather at the baths of Julia Felix, where his initiation would take place.

Raising his arms, Amisusius began the hymn. His voice, deep and measured, rang out in praise, invoking the blessings of Isis, celebrated as mother, protector and saviour:

> 'Isis, mother of all, mistress of the elements,
> Queen of the dead and the living,
> You who are worshipped in a thousand forms,
> Be present now in your true name,
> Royal Isis, light of women,
> Guardian of the faithful,
> Guide us with your favour,
> Shine on this house, on this man,
> As your will raised him, let your will sustain him.'*

At that moment, as if by the act of the goddess's will, a bright beam of light fell upon the courtyard as the sun peeked over the temple wall. The priestess and other priests joined in with Amisusius, their voices swelling in worshipful unison. The sun rose higher, illuminating the idol and casting shadows across the courtyard, and for a moment, the world seemed to pause, suspended in divine harmony. As the prayer came to an end, the soft jingle of the *sistra* and the pipe played by the priestess trailed off. The temple became silent once more.

* * *

---

* As we hear from the initiate in Apicius' *The Golden Ass*, which describes the initiation into the cult of Isis, but we never find out the specifics of what happens: 'And now, diligent reader, you are no doubt keen to know what was said next, and what was done. I'd tell you, if to tell you were allowed.' The above is therefore a composite of prayers from *The Golden Ass*, spoken by the protagonist.

THE PRIEST OF ISIS

Across town, a gentle breeze slipped through the open doorway of Julia Felix's Venus bath complex, where worshippers waited with anticipation in the entrance courtyard. The air was laced with the aromatic perfume of frankincense, myrrh, lavender and mint rising in slow, fragrant curls from the incense burners flanking the bathing pool of the *frigidarium*. Octavius stood at the edge, his body tense and his hands clasped tightly at his sides, while Amisusius, beside him, prayed as he poured water over the initiate's head from a gold vessel carved with sacred Egyptian motifs. 'May Isis cleanse you,' he intoned.

As the sacred water of the Nile, carried in *amphorae* to Julia's home, ran down Octavius' body, the initiate visibly relaxed, his breath steadying as if the goddess herself had reached out to soothe his spirit. Amisusius exhaled with the solemn certainty of a man who had felt the divine stir the air around him. The goddess was present.

Julia's walled inner garden, or *viridarium* as the elite liked to call so refined a space, was a sanctuary of green, filled with the scents of myrtle, laurel and rose. At its centre stretched the long, glistening *euripus* pool, which had been designed to evoke the sacred Nile. Small bridges arched across its length and, along the marble edges, herms of aged men, spirited women and playful satyrs perched watchfully, gazing down at the fish darting beneath the surface. At the far end of the colonnade, built into the wall that separated the house from the estate's outer grounds, stood a small barrel-vaulted *sacrarium*. It was there that Amisusius led Octavius Quartio for the blessing following his ritual bath.

When the first stages of the rites were finally complete, the procession of the initiate, the worshippers, and the priests and priestess now moved noisily through the streets of Pompeii, gathering a growing crowd as they went. Carts halted out of respect, while hawkers and shopkeepers stilled their calls, watching in solemn awe. The profane knew to withdraw, disappearing into alleyways lest they invoke the goddess's wrath. The hissing shake of the *sistra*, the sharp chime of cymbals and the ethereal notes of the pipes echoed against Pompeii's façades. Temple slaves walked ahead, scattering rose petals in Octavius' path, his bare feet crushing them underfoot as he went. At the temple, the great three-piece wooden doors, usually only partially open, were flung wide and adorned with garlands that lent the scene an air of festivity.

Amisusius stood observing his congregation. At the centre of the gathering knelt the initiate, known today as the *mysta*, whose final rites were about to begin. Tonight, he would symbolically die to his former self. This would be the moment of the dissolution of his former identity, and the terrifying, purifying descent into hallucinogenic darkness before his rebirth. A night of visions awaited him, guided by sacred ritual and potent elixirs, visions that would carry him to the threshold of the realm of Proserpina, goddess of the underworld. There, he would face the gods of below and above and be stripped of all pretence. There, he would be pulled through each element – earth, air, fire and water – before emerging at dawn as a new man, transformed.

Only then would Amisusius and the other priests drape him in the 12 consecration robes representing the zodiacal signs ruled by Isis, embroidered with Indian dragons and hyperborean gryphons of the other worlds. Newly robed, Quartio would ascend the platform at the centre of the sanctuary. The palm leaves prepared for his crown were already laid out, and the flame that would light his torch was burning in earnest. In imitation of the serene idol of Isis, the *mysta* would be revealed to the faithful from behind a curtain, presented as a living statue. The worshippers would then slowly file past his feet, the palm crown around his head radiating like sunbeams, a symbol of his triumph over death.

THE PRIEST OF ISIS

As the congregation stepped inside around the seventh hour, the worshippers moved through to the *ekklesiasterion*, the grand meeting hall at the rear of the temple. The congregation, apart from the *mysta*, who had been fasting for days, sat cross-legged on the floor to share a simple meal of eggs and fish which had been cooked in the temple's kitchen.* The frescoes within were luminous and vivid, but one image drew the eye above all others: Io's arrival in Egypt, where she was received by Isis, after being pursued across the world by Hera's wrath. Her suffering was redeemed in the goddess's embrace. The scene pulsed with symbolic weight, uniting the Egyptian, Greek and Roman worlds. Seated above the muscular form of a river god, his wild hair heavy with reeds, the horned Io extended her hand, half-shrouded in a drape of soft blue and rose. Opposite her, Isis met the gesture with calm authority, a crowned figure of divine composure, one hand grasping the serpent coiled around her arm, the other raised in welcome. Behind them, veiled attendants and sacred emblems, the *sistrum*, a key and a jug hovered in anticipation of the rites to come. The meaning was clear to those who had studied the goddess's mysteries: this was a moment of transformation, of sanctuary and of new beginnings.

Once finished with their meal, the worshippers all gathered again in the temple courtyard for the altar dedication. It was not yet the ninth hour and so, like yesterday, and all the days before that, the image of Isis stood looking down on her congregation from atop her plinth. Though daylight would remain for a few hours yet, the temple's processional lamps had been kindled, a reflection of the stars that burned eternally in the goddess's heaven. At the heart of the courtyard, the main altar had been richly decorated in fresh

---

* As with all objects mentioned in this chapter, the remains of fish and eggs were found in the temple, as were the items on the altar mentioned below, still there from the final dedication.

Figure 57: Io's arrival in Egypt and her reception by the goddess Isis, from a fresco found in the Temple of Isis at Pompeii

greenery, the wreaths and flowers provided by a garden nearby. A knife was handed to Amisusius as he stood over the altar. Beside him, the priestess lifted her hands, her face composed as she recited a prayer. The soft melody of a pan flute carried through the air, its notes weaving into the incantations, while the rhythmic shake of *sistra* echoed through the temple precinct.

The congregation remained still as the first cut was made in the slender neck of a white goose, a faint sigh running through the crowd as the lifeblood of the offering seeped into the sacred fire on

THE PRIEST OF ISIS

the altar. The iron-like scent of blood cut through the perfumed haze, and Amisusius turned to a small pig next, guiding it forward with careful hands. The creature submitted itself without fuss, a good omen. Next, the life of a turtle dove was also taken, its now motionless body being laid to rest beside a bundle of clams, their shells gleaming in the firelight. One by one, their spirits were given over in exchange for divine favour. With each sacrifice, the priests murmured invocations to the goddess.

The *mysta*, adorned in his gleaming white robes, sat apart from the worshippers and watched in silence, his pupils widening as the hallucinogenic effect of Syrian rue, blue lotus and spider-flower fully took hold.* This was the moment of descent.

The libation hissed as it met the altar flame, a brief puff of steam curling into the air. At the top of the steps, near the idol of the goddess, a priest held a vessel of Nile water close to his chest. Below, two others stood on either side of the staircase, their white robes stark against the marble. As the sacred water was lifted towards the heavens, the assembled worshippers instinctively moved forwards.

Beneath their feet, a tremor passed unnoticed, a whisper through the stone foundations. The gods were watching.

A sound, distant yet deep, as if Geb himself, the Egyptian god of the Earth, and father of Isis, had shuddered.

It was slight.

Turning away from the altar to face the temple, Amisusius' gaze fell on one of the lamps on the temple steps. The flame of the lamp

---

* Residues of two hallucinogenic plants were discovered in a jug shaped in the likeness of Bes, dating to the second century BCE. Traces of human bodily fluids were also present, suggesting the mixture had been consumed. Although detailed records of Isis cult initiations are scarce, visionary or hallucinatory experiences are known to have played a recognised role in their rites of passage.

flickered and then, without warning, sputtered and died. For the second time that day, dread gripped him like a vice. A bad omen. He opened his mouth to speak, to assure the people gathered before him, but before he could form the words, the temple exhaled a low, quivering breath.

A deep, guttural roar rumbled up from the earth's core, as if torn from the depths of the underworld. The ground convulsed beneath them, sending a violent tremor through the temple. The great wooden doors groaned on their hinges, and a dish of eggs tumbled to the floor, shattering against the stone.

A scream rang out from the back of the congregation, but it was lost almost instantly, consumed by a sudden, ground-shaking boom that seemed to tear through the bones of the temple. A howling gust of wind ripped through the courtyard, scattering petals and ash into the air.

Amisusius staggered with the faithful, struggling for balance as another shock jolted through the precinct.

Something had awakened.

This could only be an act of the gods.

CHAPTER SEVEN

THE POLITICIAN

THE FIRST HOUR (7.30 A.M.), 25 OCTOBER 79 CE

The heat came first. A wave of searing air, hot enough to blister flesh in an instant. It swept through the streets of Pompeii faster than a man could turn to run. Then came the silence. The eerie, absolute stillness that followed the death of the city, and everyone left in it.

Gaius Cuspius Pansa had heard the final roar of the mountain approaching, the awful thunder of the ash and pumice as they came pummelling down the mountain.

But he did not feel the weight of ash pressing down on him or his last breath leaving his body.

There had been no time for struggle, no moment to brace himself against the inevitable. One instant, he was standing atop metres of pumice and dust, urging a family forward. The next, he was gone.

Would he be remembered? Would his family? What would they say of him? That he had stayed too long? That he had been foolish, believing that the people of Pompeii could be saved from a force much bigger than himself?

For hours, the forum had emptied, the city gates had choked with the crush of fleeing bodies, and yet he had lingered, a man bound to his people and his duty, to the name he had spent his life forging.

A name that, within minutes, would be buried beneath ash.

THE EIGHTH HOUR (1 P.M.), 23 OCTOBER 79 CE

The midday sun cast its rays over the basalt stones of the forum. Merchants bartered beneath the shadow of the market building, arguing over sacks of grain, *amphorae* of wine and baskets of fresh produce. Slaves darted between the colonnades, carrying messages, sacks and jars, their hurried movements ant-like against the unpredictable movement of the crowd.

On the steps of the *Comitium*, the building where magistrates met to conduct official business, issue decrees and oversee the administration of justice, young orators practised speeches with sweeping gestures and fervent rhetoric. Their voices carried across the long, rectangular forum, echoing around the columned walkways, their countenances the perfect embodiment of the Roman masculine ideal of *virtus*: courage, excellence and the pursuit of honour.

Having just concluded a meeting with the current *aediles*, Gaius Cuspius Pansa stepped out of their office at the far end of the forum, his gaze sweeping across the vast space. This was soon to be his political stage. To his back were the offices of the *aediles*, the *duumvirs* and the *curia*, a meeting assembly where policies were debated, alliances forged and the direction of Pompeii steered behind closed doors. The Temple of Apollo to the west was a gran-

THE POLITICIAN

diose reflection of Pompeii's earlier Greek influences, its colonnaded courtyard and altars where citizens left votive offerings, seeking the god's favour in their ventures. Adjacent to the temple, the public weights and measures table, the *mensa ponderaria*, ensured fair trade. Some years before, the city had amended the local Oscan weights to a standard more aligned with that of the Roman state: one of the many changes to bring Pompeii into the first century.* Then there were a couple of Imperial temples, including the Sanctuary of the Public Gods, or *lares*, dedicated to the deities that protected the city and the Imperial family. In the far north-east corner were the warehouses, the city treasury and some public latrines, ironically probably the most frequented area of the whole space.

Pansa's family, arriving after General Sulla stormed the walls in 89 BCE and established Pompeii as a Roman colony, saw the construction of many of these sites. In the late Republic, Rome's dominance over the Hellenistic world transformed the political and cultural landscape of the Mediterranean, and Pompeii, though it had rebelled against colonisation, could not escape Rome's power entirely. Proud and fiercely independent, the city's ancestors had resisted full integration and clung to their own identity even as Roman influence pressed ever closer.

Pansa now stood at the heart of Pompeii's 'Old Town'.† Unlike the neat, gridded streets of the later city, this irregular quarter

---

* The Romans did not refer to their era as the 'first century CE'. Instead, years were usually identified by the names of the two consuls in office, by reference to the reigning emperor (for example, 'in the first year of Tiberius'), or by counting from the traditional founding of Rome in 753 BCE (*ab urbe condita*).

† We now call this the Altstadt, or 'Old Town', and from above you can see how it stands out in terms of its irregular shape. Many archaeologists now accept the theory that this was the original town established by the early settlers of Pompeii.

betrayed its origins as the early nucleus of civic life. In the fourth century BCE, when Pompeii was an Oscan settlement at the crossroads between the towns of Neapolis, Nola and Stabiae, the space had been purely functional: a marketplace and meeting ground used by residents dotted across the surrounding hinterland and within the Samnite walls of the city. Its paving stones were cut from Campania's fertile land, shaped by the restless River Sarno and the looming shadow of Vesuvius. By the second century BCE, Rome's influence had begun to press down upon Pompeii. The forum was enlarged and framed with colonnades and porticoes in the Roman style, and then rebuilt on a scale befitting the city's new status as a Roman colony.

In those earliest years of Roman Pompeii, one of Pansa's ancestors had held the position of a legal magistrate. Since then, his family, the *gens Cuspia,* had made a lasting mark on the city. One had helped to fund one of the city's numerous towers and the wall, while his father and grandfather had completed the refurbishment of the amphitheatre after the great quake.* Standing in the shadow of two statues in the forum, Pansa traced the carved letters on their bases: first his grandfather's name, then his father's, each a record of their political achievements. One day, his own name would join them.

As *paterfamilias,* the head of his household, Pansa took pride in upholding the Roman ideals of authority, duty and public service. In just a couple of months, on the first day of January, he would be sworn in as an *aedile*. He could already picture the purple-bordered *toga praetexta* draped over his shoulders, a symbol of his new office and of the power and expectation that came with it. Four months

---

* A relative of our Pansa is recorded as the first witness in a financial transaction in the wax tablets of the banker, Caecilius Iucundus (CIL IV 3340.12) in 55 CE, showing that he too was a man of substantial standing.

THE POLITICIAN

had passed since the people of Pompeii had elected him to follow in his forefathers' footsteps, securing his place among the city's highest-ranking officials. Alongside the three other *aediles* – his colleague Lucius Popidius Secundus and the second pair, Cnaeus Helvius Sabinus and Marcus Samellius Modestus – Pansa would be responsible for keeping Pompeii running smoothly.* His duties would range from maintaining public buildings and temples to regulating markets and organising games and festivals.

His was a position that required a delicate balancing act: appeasing the plebs without alienating the elite, all while safeguarding his own reputation. His role depended on the support of the people and, being the son of politicians, he had learned at an early age that it was important to appear popular with the masses. The *aedileship* served as a crucial stepping stone to more prestigious positions, possibly even beyond Pompeii. Plebeian support gave him that platform, and public goodwill made him seem indispensable to the daily workings of the city. The city's walls revealed who had fuelled his elevation. The electoral graffiti was overwhelmingly written by the lower classes and freedmen. He was, in every sense, a man of the people.

The citizens, whether they lived within the city walls, now more symbolic than defensive, or out in the *suburbium*, had chosen him to maintain the city and bring prosperity. His role would require a sharp eye and steady judgement. Every decision, from funding public projects to settling disputes, would be under the critical gaze of those who had put him in power. He would oversee street cleanliness, monitor latrines, supervise the water supply and ensure merchants used fair weights and measures. Pansa knew it was a position that demanded constant vigilance. Any failure, no matter

---

* *Aediles* were voted in as pairs.

how small, could spell political disaster. The Pompeians weren't shy about voicing their frustrations and their preferred medium of criticism was graffiti, scrawled in the open for all to see. One complaint, scrawled on the wall in his father's days as *aedile*, still lingered: 'Pansa, we expected more.'

Pansa looked up at the imposing sight of the Temple of Jupiter at the northern end of the forum, its grand staircase leading to the raised podium where marble friezes of the gods had once watched over the city. When Pompeii had been colonised by Rome, the temple had been transformed into a *Capitolium*, dedicated to Jupiter, Juno and Minerva, Rome's divine protectors, as was demanded of every colony. Now, the temple stood hollow, in disrepair from the quakes, its columns fractured and roof exposed to the elements. Its restoration had been delayed for nearly two decades and instead, the people had turned to the smaller Temple of Jupiter Meilichios. But it was not enough. A city like Pompeii deserved a *Capitolium* worthy of its status. As soon as he was sworn in, Pansa would make this happen. Perhaps he could petition for funds at his feast tonight and convince his friends of the benefits of investing in a monument so central to civic life. Surely nothing could cement a man's prestige, or his family's legacy, more than restoring the city's most important temple, the very heart of Roman religion?

Inside the forum, stalls were piled high with meat, fish and fresh produce, their vendors calling out prices over the steady murmur of haggling customers. The stone counters, worn smooth in some places and deeply grooved in others, bore the scars of years of chopping and weighing. The floor was scattered with stray fish scales and vegetable trimmings, the remnants of another busy market day, and the air carried a sharp mix of salted fish and ripe fruit. Pansa was pleased to see Petrinus dart in the direction of the *macellum* market building in the corner of the forum, and the sight of

THE POLITICIAN

him stirred up an idea in his mind. Perhaps today was the day for it.

To Pansa's right stretched the slave market where he had bought Petrinus those many years ago. Once the proud headquarters of the fuller's association, it had been repurposed as the slave market.* Where traders had once set their stalls, now its interior courtyard was thick with bodies; men, women and children herded beneath the marble colonnades. Tablets in the hands of slave dealers listed the names, ages, origins and special skills of the slaves waiting to be auctioned. In the hall beyond, buyers bid beneath the gaze of statues, their voices echoing through the cavernous space. Chains and rope scraped against stone, and the air was warm with the musk of fear and sweat. A fitting use for so fine a building, Pansa thought. Proof of Pompeii's prosperity and place in the growing Empire.

What a steal that had been. The sun had been merciless, baking the marble of the slave market, and the stench of sweat and livestock had turned Pansa's stomach. He hadn't gone looking for an everyday house slave. Instead, he'd intended on buying something useful – a scribe, perhaps, or a strong pair of hands to manage the bakery he had built at the rear of his house. But then his eyes had fallen on Petrinus.

He stood apart from the others, his posture straight despite his circumstance. There was a magnificent stillness to him, something the slave market had not yet managed to strip away. Though young, he neither begged nor pleaded, and his face betrayed not the slightest flicker of fear. Beside him stood a boy of 6 or 7, wide-eyed and trembling, searching Petrinus' face for reassurance. While others

---

* The actual use of the building is still unknown, but it has been inferred that it was used by the fullers, due to Eumachia's association with the college of fullers, as well as for auctioning slaves.

wept or clung to the last threads of their dignity, Petrinus remained silent, composed and unreadable.

Intriguing.

After inspecting his body for injury or disease, Pansa had bid without hesitation, securing both Petrinus and Simplex at a very good price. He had little use for child slaves at the time, but he knew well enough that boys raised under his roof could be moulded into something useful. And he had been right: Simplex became his most trusted advisor and scribe, while Petrinus became a most useful all-rounder. Perhaps he may become even more useful today, he thought.

To the right of the market was the *Comitium*, where the spring election had played out just months earlier. The echoes of the crowd's cheers and jeers still reverberated through his memory. Elections in Pompeii were the pinnacle of civic life, an impressive spectacle that brought together every stratum of society. The city been had transformed in the lead up to the July elections. Walls and columns throughout the city had been covered with such an abundance of electoral slogans that one might have feared the weight of the paint alone could bring the structures crumbling down.* Some slogans had been commissioned, their letters painted with precision, while others were scrawled in haste by zealous supporters. By the election, Pansa had the lion's share of notices by far.

Nevertheless, he had faced a bitter fight from his political rivals. Their barbing words had found fertile ground. Many of them muttered about the erosion of traditional Roman values, blaming politicians like Pansa for encouraging what they saw as the danger-

---

* Graffiti found on a wall in the Basilica (CIL IV 1904) rather wittily said: 'O walls, you have held up so much tedious graffiti that I am amazed that you have not already collapsed in ruin.'

THE POLITICIAN

ous mixing of classes and bloodlines. 'Before long,' Pansa had overheard one of them saying, 'we'll be no better than Carthage, our pure Roman blood diluted by foreign influence. And look where that got them.'

In reality, he thought they couldn't be more right, though he knew expressing this wasn't the way to win the popular vote. Better to get into office and then make the necessary changes.

Pompeii was once little more than a gathering of Oscans, Etruscans, Greeks and Samnites, a tangle of debased roots, unshaped and unruly. Rome brought them civility. Rome gave them law, language and order. Everything this city has become, it owes to her.

Crude though the voting public remained, the campaign wasn't all bad. His friend, Paquius Proculus, a former *duumvir* from 5 years previous and a close neighbour only a few houses down on the Via dell'Abbondanza, had painted a wonderful metrical eulogy in support of Pansa at the entrance to his house. It read:

C. Cuspius for aedile: *if any honour should be given to one living modestly, fitting honour ought to be given to this young man.**

On the hot July day of the election, farmers had journeyed from the surrounding countryside to cast their votes, their bodies and nails cleaned for the occasion so that they might rub shoulders with city-dwelling artisans, merchants and businessmen as they prepared to carry out their democratic right as citizens. Wealthy freedmen with heavy gold rings on their fingers stood beside shepherds and farmers in coarse tunics, their hands roughened by years of toil in

---

* CIL 4.7201. For a wonderful discussion of the poetic electoral graffiti associated with our Pansa, see Kristina Milnor (2015), 288–319.

the fields, and skin leathered by the hot Campanian sun. The sight had reminded Pansa of a cautionary tale he had once heard as a young man studying the art of politics.

Publius Scipio Nasica, an illustrious figure and leader of the Senate almost three centuries ago, had once sought the *aedileship* in Rome. As the story went, during his campaign he shook hands with a peasant and, noticing the man's calloused fingers, had jested, 'Do you walk on your hands?' The rural tribes, offended by what they saw as a slur on their poverty and hard work, had turned their backs on him.*

Pansa took the tale as a reminder of how easily an ill-judged word could unravel a hard-earned reputation. He had seen it himself in Pompeii, how quickly a jest could become graffiti scrawled on the city walls, turning from humour to a smear. Every handshake, every word and smile, had to be measured.

The voting process was, as always, a lengthy one. Each voter placed their ballot of terracotta tiles, or *ostraca*, into the urns under the supervision of the election officials, and each vote was counted in turn. When the results had been announced, the forum had erupted in celebration. It was a moment of triumph, one that Pansa would carry with him long after his *aedileship* ended.

He had won the election by convincing the people he was one of them, a man who respected their labour, understood their struggles and would advocate for their interests. Soon it would be his duty to ensure that every interaction reinforced that trust. As Pansa strolled through the forum's columns surrounded by his entourage of slaves, a passage came to mind from Sallust, a plebeian-born Republican. Trained from a very young age to remember the lengthiest of passages from Greece and Rome's most impor-

---

* Valerius Maximus (7.5.2).

THE POLITICIAN

tant texts, the politician's words had echoed often in Pansa's thoughts:

> The lust for money came first, then for power, this grew upon them; these were, I may say, the root of all evils. For avarice destroyed honour, integrity and all other noble qualities; taught in their place insolence, cruelty, to neglect the gods, to set a price on everything. Ambition drove many men to become false, to have one thought locked in the breast, another ready on the tongue, and to value friendships and enmities not on their merits but by the standard of self-interest, and to show a good front rather than a good heart. At first these vices grew slowly, from time to time they were punished, before finally, when the disease had spread like a deadly plague, the state was changed and a government second to none in equity and excellence became cruel and intolerable.*

Pompeii's wealth had bred ambition in all the wrong quarters. Where the shops had once held the simple wares of local craftsmen, they now glittered with imported luxuries: sparkling jewellery, fine furniture, costly fabrics. Low-born men, swollen with profit, strutted like nobles while the old families watched in silence. Pansa regarded it all with a weary contempt.

* * *

The short walk from the forum to the city gates led Pansa through the ever-moving tide of people making their way to and from the marketplace and shops. As he strode along the pavement, his slaves in tow, the crowd parted around him, an effect he had enjoyed since his election in July. He paused at a small shop with a wooden

---

* Sallust, *Catiline's War* 10.

counter piled high with nuts and dried fruits and the shopkeeper, a wiry man with quick hands, scooped up a handful of roasted almonds.

'For you, Pansa,' he said, waving off any attempt at payment.

Pansa thanked him and tipped the almonds into his mouth, a small snack before his afternoon engagement. One of his slaves scrambled to gather the rest of the gift as he moved on, barely breaking his stride.

He made his way northward, where a group of workmen were busy hauling rubble from a collapsed section of wall. Another casualty of the constant tremors that had plagued the city for years, he imagined. Pansa had certainly earned his place in office at a difficult time. The four *aediles* would soon need to decide how public funds should be spent on rebuilding the city. Various occupational groups had already begun their petitioning, and this was only likely to intensify. He could picture it now: the pressure mounting, the endless stream of self-serving appeals and desperate pleas for funding. It was certain to be an expensive year ahead for himself, too. He knew all too well that power demanded splendour: lavish feasts, grand games, expenses he'd promised in the heat of the campaign. He'd stretched himself to the limit to borrow enough to secure votes and underwrite tonight's spectacles. Hopefully Zosimus will have a solution for me, he thought. And maybe a loan.

Lucius Istacidius Zosimus lived in an elaborate villa just outside the Herculaneum Gate in the north-western corner of the city. Complete with a vineyard, the extensive complex had inspired jealousy in Pansa ever since his friend's renovations. It, too, had been damaged in the great quake, and what an admirable job Zosimus had done at rebuilding. Passing below the gate, Pansa nodded to the watchmen on duty.

THE POLITICIAN

'How goes the day?' he asked as the two men, shocked by his sudden appearance, stood to attention. His eyes flicked behind them to a game of dice they had been playing inside the tower.

'A fair number of carts arriving from other cities for the games later, Pansa,' one said. 'Everyone seems in good spirits.'

'Very good. As you were.' He said this last with a knowing smirk and a nod to the game of dice. He took delight in seeing their faces colour as he turned to leave. It's not like they had anything to protect Pompeii from these days, anyway. There were no more threats to the city under Rome's watch.

Zosimus' villa was located through the *necropolis*, just off and below the main road. Surrounded by verdant gardens, fragrant with the scents of box hedge, flowers and lavender, the building was a vision. As he approached, he caught sight of Zosimus in the porticoed veranda talking animatedly to his farm manager, the *vilicus* Apollonius. In moments like this, Pansa always felt the familiar old bitterness rise. That a man like Zosimus, a freedman of the powerful Istacidii family, once in chains, was smiled upon so greatly by Fortuna, grated on him. But, it was thanks to men like Zosimus that his own campaign had been possible; the freedman's wealth ran deep, and his generosity had been useful. Zosimus, catching sight of his friend, beamed and threw his arms out in greeting. Pansa inhaled deeply and set a magnanimous smile on his face.

'Pansa, what a treat to see you, and on such an important day, too! I thought you'd be busy making arrangements.'

'No, all is well and taken care of for tonight. In truth, I was only a donator. A way to get a platform for a speech, that's all.'

Chuckling, Zosimus dismissed Apollonius with a wave and put his arm around Pansa as he led him inside.

'Are you sure you can't make my feast tonight? The invitation is still open.'

'You know I would have loved to chat with your fellow *aediles*,' Zosimus responded. 'But I have my own feast with fellow villa owners in the area. We're all hoping to discuss the issue of an ambitious local landowner who is trying to start a market on his estate. We can't have him creating a monopoly. Anyway, let's talk of more positive things.'*

The two men walked through the imposing home, passing on their right one of the oldest, and most striking, spaces in the villa: the room of the Dionysiac frescoes.† This was no small distinction in a house where every turn revealed a surprise: a frolicking satyr here, an Egyptian ibis there. No surface was left untouched by the hand of the skilled painters, and no room was without its own dramatic flourish. Its walls were cloaked in vivid red, with life-sized figures moving in an eternal procession in honour of Dionysus, the god of wine, revelry and madness. Some danced while others were mid-gesture in acts of ritual or initiation.

Though he had stood, and dined, in this room many times, Pansa still found himself arrested by the realism of the faces. These were not distant deities or symbolic archetypes, but people, women mostly, who looked disarmingly familiar. Their eyes, their postures, the set of their mouths; they looked like Campanians. Like people he might see in the forum or find gathering olives outside the city walls. That was what unsettled him most: their beauty, yes, but more than that – their ordinariness, rendered

---

* Such an event is recorded by Pliny the Younger in the fifth book of his *Epistulae*, where he relates the dispute between the senator L. Bellicus Sollers and the north-Italian town of Vicetia, who brought a complaint against him for attempting to begin a market (*nundinae*) on his own estate.

† The room was painted sometime between 70 and 60 BCE.

Figure 58: The Dionysiac wedding room, now better known as the Room of the Mysteries in the Villa of the Mysteries, Pompeii

immortal in paint. As they passed the room, his eyes fell, as they always did, on a young woman sitting with heavy-lidded eyes as an attendant combed her hair in solemn preparation for what he assumed was her wedding day. Her piercing gaze, the same seen by others for around 150 years now, seemed to stare right through to his soul.

Reaching one of Zosimus' inner *cubicula*, sometimes used as a sleeping space and therefore one of the more private spots in the villa, the two friends sat down to discuss business.

'So, you want to invest in vineyards. You're fairly late to the game.'

'Better late than never,' Pansa said.

Leaning one hand on his knee, Zosimus reached for the jug and poured Pansa a drink. Pansa's slave Simplex had followed him in and was now waiting at the edge of the room, wax tablet and stylus at the ready.

'First, look to Cato the Elder,' Zosimus began. 'He said to buy land not too far from the city, close enough to reach the markets easily. You'll want fertile soil, though that's a given around here, and a dependable water source: spring, stream, cistern, it doesn't matter, as long as it's reliable. Orientation is important too. If you're planting vines or olives, make sure the slope suits them. South-facing is ideal.'

Pansa glanced at Simplex, who was furiously scribbling on his wax tablet.

'And make sure the land is enclosed, hedged or walled; it keeps out stray goats and greedy neighbours. But most important of all,' Zosimus leaned forward, 'is the man running it. Without a good *vilicus*, like my Apollonius, you may as well throw your *denarii* into the Sarno.'

He took another sip of wine. 'And don't let middlemen bleed you dry.'

Zosimus gestured to Pansa to follow him across the room, where he opened a cupboard to reveal many rolled-up scrolls piled on top of one another. Each time he found one he deemed interesting, he placed it into Pansa's arms, never taking his eyes away from the shelves.

'And profitability?' Pansa shuffled the mound of scrolls in his arms, then, losing patience, dumped them into Simplex's hands. The young slave fumbled to keep hold of them.

'Depends. Here in Campania, we can get up to three or four harvests per year, depending on what you're going to grow. Take wine: Pliny writes about one vineyard of 37 acres bringing in

THE POLITICIAN

400,000 *sestertii*. So, if you do it right, the returns can be extraordinary.'*

After a brief tour of Zosimus' vineyard, where rows of slaves toiled under the watchful eye of Apollonius, Pansa listened with detached interest to instructions on how best to feed and water the slaves; just enough to keep them healthy and working, but always with an eye on cost. He had had his fill of rustic management for one day. With a courteous word of thanks and a wish for a pleasant feast that evening, Pansa made his way back through the streets of Pompeii to his home on the Via dell'Abbondanza, his mind buzzing with ideas. By now, the guards had changed ahead of closing the gates for the night. The sun was sinking low, bathing the sky in soft shades of pink and red as traders pulled down their shutters and the last stragglers made their way towards the amphitheatre.

A spotted brown cat held his small nose to the ground, tracking a rat that had just darted into the cracks of the pavement and out of sight. Pansa watched for a moment. Quick, silent and filthy: it knew its place, surviving by keeping to the shadows. It reminded him of his slaves.

As he neared home, the vendor renting the shop at the front of his house offered a smile and a greeting. The man was lucky, he thought. A prime space on Pompeii's busiest street, even if the rent Pansa charged was deliberately modest. Another small act of generosity that went unnoticed. Pansa acknowledged him with the briefest lift of his hand.

The imposing entrance to his house stood open, giving passers-by a view of the elaborate rooms of his home. Just as he was about to

---

* For context, a common labourer or soldier might earn between 900 and 1,200 *sestertii* per year. Thus, an income of 400,000 *sestertii* from a single vineyard would have represented immense wealth. Saying that, it would also take a lot of wealth to buy this much land.

step inside, he noticed some new graffiti scrawled around the doorway, the voices of the masses pressing in around him, even here: 'Pansa, see that you do it!' A warning to meet his promises.

The transition from the street into the dark, narrow entrance hallway was stark. The passageway's walls, painted in deep reds and blacks, absorbed what little light filtered through the doorway. But as Pansa emerged into the atrium, the space opened up gloriously, bathed in the soft glow of golden light filtering down through the *compluvium*. Its size was both a matter of luxury and a statement of influence; the larger the space, the more clients it could accommodate, a show of his reach and authority. Even the air smelled of wealth and care, faintly perfumed with fresh garlands of laurel and rose that hung from the walls on small nails in draping displays. The *impluvium* gleamed with water, its edges lined in pale stone and the surface reflecting the play of light and shadow from above. Frescoes adorned the walls, depicting mythical scenes and pastoral landscapes in vivid colours. The tiled floor, a mosaic of geometric patterns and swirling designs, had been painstakingly restored after the great quake. His atrium was a powerful symbol of his family's status.

Slaves moved efficiently through the space. One approached with a jug of water and a clean cloth, offering them wordlessly to her master. From the atrium, the rest of the house unfolded in a specially designed sequence of spaces, each one reinforcing his stature in Pompeian society. The further a guest was able to travel, the closer they were to Pansa and his *familia*. To his right, nestled in an ornate niche, was the household *lararium*, their shrine to their household gods. Tiny figurines of *lares* and *penates* stood within, their bronze forms gleaming in the flickering light of the small offering of olives and figs that burned before them.

Passing through his *tablinum*, where Simplex placed the scrolls loaned by Zosimus into the hands of a waiting slave, Pansa climbed two shallow marble steps into the first of two peristyles. Here, the usual, gentle bustle of the house was accompanied by the soft trickle of water from the central fountain, its basin surrounded by flowering plants that filled the space with a subtle, natural aroma. The columns of the small peristyle, painted in bright reds and yellows, rose to support a partially open roof that revealed the deepening twilight sky. Leaving behind the sharp clatter of pots and pans from the nearby kitchen, where the household's cook was orchestrating the preparations for the evening's meal, he walked deeper into his home in search of his wife. Around him, slaves darted back and forth, trays and bowls balanced in their arms, their soft, hurried steps barely audible against the polished floor.

From across the second peristyle, Lucretia emerged, looking elegant as she instructed a slave on some last-minute arrangements for the evening's feast. His wife had a round, noble face; her nose was straight and high, beginning between brows that had been meticulously plucked, and her eyes were lightly lined with kohl. Her lips, small and dainty, bore a faint hint of rouge, matched by the delicate flush on her cheeks, set against her hazelnut-dark ringlets. Though quite a bit younger than Pansa, her demeanour was composed and assured, a mark of her good Campanian breeding and the long-standing heritage of her family.

After greeting Pansa with a gentle kiss on the cheek, they settled in Lucretia's private *cubiculum* off the peristyle, the faint sound of their children and the *nutrix* in the next room reaching their ears through the wall. As befitting of her status as wife and *materfamilias*, Lucretia began reeling off an update for the management of the household. 'Everything is progressing as planned,' she said. 'I have arranged for two of the guests' wives to dine with me in a separate *cubiculum*, and Cuspia will stay with the *nutrix*. The slaves have already arranged for my guests to retire upstairs when the festivities become inevitably louder.' He nodded in approval, reassured by her collected, organised nature. She was everything a man of his standing needed in a wife.

Their marriage had been an arrangement, as was common among the elite, designed to unite his family and hers for social and political advantage. He remembered their wedding day. She had worn the typical orange veil with tiny white flowers in her hair. After only a few weeks, she had shown herself to be a most virtuous wife. He recalled noting this to a close friend: 'She's highly intelligent and a careful housewife, and her devotion to me proves her virtue.'* Looking at her now, he felt affection for Lucretia, not only for her beauty but for the quiet competence with which she managed the household, ensuring its smooth operation even when Pansa's attention was consumed by the demands of public life. Their marriage, though political at its core, had grown into a partnership built on mutual respect.

She had memorised parts of his speeches, in those early days, reciting them back to him in private to help refine his delivery. It was a small but significant act, one that not only proved her intelligence, but also her loyalty to his ambitions. She did not seek life in the public sphere herself, but her support bolstered his position more than she probably realised. Though he would never admit it out loud, he owed a lot to her for helping him to organise his world. And yet, behind her calm exterior, he knew her mind was sharp, a quiet power wielded without disrupting the delicate balance of their lives. Pansa cleared his throat, interrupting his moment of reflection. 'The arrangements are progressing well,' he

---

* The words of Pliny the Younger about his teenage bride, Calpurnia, in one of his letters. At around 15 years old, she was roughly 25 years his junior when they married. Pliny also expressed affectionate admiration for her ability to memorise his writings.

remarked, more to himself than to her. 'You've excelled, as always.' She inclined her head in acknowledgement as their two children entered the room.

They were led by their *nutrix*, the household nurse who had cared for them since birth. The elder, a boy of 14, was on the cusp of manhood, his frame beginning to show the promise of strength, though his movements still retained the awkwardness of youth. He mimicked his father's deliberate stride, his gaze steady and observant. Pansa had not yet made the decision for his son, who also carried the name of Gaius Cuspius, to assume the *toga virilis*, a plain white toga representing adult male citizenship, and enrol him as a citizen at the forum. Even so, his voice had begun to 'crow', and his face held the soft fluff of his first beard.*

Noticing these changes in his son, Pansa had recently discussed with a friend the possibility for young Gaius to leave the period of *ferocitas*, or restlessness, behind, and assume the *toga virilis* on the preferred date of 17 March, at the festival of Liber. As his father, only Pansa could make this decision. But first he wanted to be sure that his son was ready for the public role that a man of Rome had to endure. After formally taking his place in society, his son would step out into public life and assume the familial responsibilities expected of him as Pansa's heir. For now, though, he would stand beside his father and learn the ropes, continue his education in history and rhetoric, and wait for his beard to grow longer, and his voice to grow deeper.

His daughter Cuspia, now 12 years of age, followed closely behind her brother, her dark curls neatly braided in a less elaborate, yet similar, style to her mother's, framing a face that mirrored

---

* 'Crowing' was when a boy's voice dropped at puberty. These were the signs required to begin the step into manhood.

Lucretia's noble features. She had recently experienced her first blood, the *menarche*, and, given her age, Pansa was now free to marry her to whomever he saw fit. They would have to turn their attentions to finding a suitable match soon, ideally a virtuous man in his mid-twenties from an ancient local family with political ambitions. Someone who had already dedicated himself to public life, perhaps with the position of military tribune under his belt, or with plans to later become a *quaestor*, the man in charge of public expenditure.* This would certainly help Pansa's own ambitions.

They had been blessed with two children; the others had not survived childbirth. Lucretia herself had narrowly escaped death, saved only by the skill of her midwives and the strength of her body on the birthing chair. Not all women were so fortunate, or so well bred. She went to the children now, resting a gentle hand on her son's shoulder before bending to kiss her daughter's brow, brushing back a loose strand of her hair. The *nutrix* stepped forward and took the girl's hand, guiding her towards the *cubiculum*. The child glanced back only once, her wide eyes searching her father's face with unspoken longing. He did not return the look. His attention had already turned to his heir. The boy stood tall, his chin raised, waiting. Without a word, Pansa signalled for him to follow. Lucretia gave her daughter one last look, then stepped in line behind her husband and son as they made their way towards the atrium, the night already in full swing.

The boy matched his father's pace as they greeted the first visitors with warm civility. He remained quiet but watchful, absorbing every interaction with the intensity of someone eager to learn.

* To be a military tribune, the minimum age was 20, while to become a *quaestor* at this time, you had to be at least 30. It was common for girls in their early teens to be married to men in their mid- to late twenties, after the girl was considered to have become fertile.

THE POLITICIAN

Pansa glanced at his son, his face betraying the faintest hint of pride. Tonight was the first of many that the boy would shadow him, learning the art of appearances, and witnessing the weight of power and the effort required to uphold it.

The girl, meanwhile, was being settled into her chamber by her *nutrix*, accompanied by the childhood doll that she would soon relinquish on her wedding day. Her absence was not noticed; her time would come when she could serve her purpose as a wife, outside the family home. But not yet.

When Pansa, his son and their guests stepped into the early evening as a group, the torches and lanterns carried by slaves and low-born free people illuminated the darkened streets, their glow catching on the worn stone pavements and casting long shadows on the walls. They soon arrived at the amphitheatre, and Pansa paused briefly in one of the entrance corridors, where the statues of his forefathers looked down on them. Resting a hand on his son's shoulder, he said in a low voice, 'Soon, it will be your turn to carry this legacy forward, to continue the work of your grandfather, his father and of me.'

The boy peered up at the statues and Pansa knew he understood his words' significance. He would ensure the Cuspius name continued to command respect in the city of Pompeii. It would take a lot to stop them.

Pansa entered the amphitheatre with his son at his side and took his place of honour in the stands. When one of the current *aediles* had finished speaking, he rose to address the crowd, his voice cutting through the clamour until their noise fell away. Trained from boyhood in the art of oratory, he spoke with measured confidence, each word deliberate and every pause calculated. The crowd responded on cue, cheering at the right moments, their swell of approval rising and falling like a tide.

Citizens of Pompeii!

You know my name, for it is carved already into the stones of our forum and amphitheatre. My father served this city, as did my grandfather before him, and now it is my turn to bear that duty. From their deeds the city prospered; from mine, it will prosper still more.

As your incoming *aedile*, I will guard our markets, preserve our shrines and ensure the streets of Pompeii reflect the greatness of Rome herself. I will bring games worthy of this amphitheatre, and festivals that honour our gods as they deserve.

The strength of Pompeii does not lie in fortune or chance, but in her people, in men willing to bear her burdens and raise her up again, even when the earth itself has tried to bring her low. My family has always stood firm in that duty. And now, by your will, I will do the same, with honour, with splendour and with results this city will never forget.

Pansa stood tall, letting the moment settle over him as the crowd cheered with approval at his words. When he glanced at his son, he caught the look of awe in his eyes. One day, the boy would stand here too and speak in the name of the *gens Cuspia*.

* * *

The games had been a resounding success, and the feast had begun without a hitch. The celebration was no mere indulgence but a well-designed statement, as these things always were. Every dish, every vintage, had been chosen to impress. Platters piled high with delicacies made their way around the room; the Roman Empire laid out on fine plates. As host, Pansa had played his part smiling, toasting and offering morsels from the hands of his slaves, upholding the sacred duty of *hospitium*, the Roman expectation of a generous welcome. The Greeks called it *xenia*, a bond of mutual respect between host and guest, and tonight he intended to embody it to perfection.

In truth, it was exhausting, for behind the charm he was ever watching, and, in turn, being watched. He noted who laughed too loudly, who remained quiet, who had already drunk more than they should. He listened for snippets of information on the latest from the *curia* and noted grievances for later. He petitioned to the group for future funding for the Temple of Jupiter, and heard words of concern from Scaurus, who had overheard the grumblings of the people in the bath latrines. This was far from a relaxing evening for him.

Beside him, his son reclined and conversed, doing his best to mirror the composed ease of the adults around him. But the effort it required showed in his jaw. He was not yet of age, but he was learning, and that was the point. Alongside their regular lectures, boys of his standing were trained through observation: they learned by shadowing their fathers at banquets, ceremonies, games and debates. Here, he would begin to absorb what was expected of him: how to offer praise that honoured virtue, or *virtus*, and not vanity; how to acknowledge a man's presence without yielding advantage; how to speak with gravitas, to listen with care and to let your expression reveal only what you wanted it to. Most important of all, he would learn never to let the mask slip, for dignity, *dignitas*, once lost was hard won back. Pansa could tell that to his son it all felt strange now, forced and unnatural. But one day, it would come to him with ease. Pansa allowed himself a moment of satisfaction. Soon, he knew, the priest of Isis would arrive.

Natalis had been the one to suggest inviting the priest. Although the rituals of the cult were a mystery to most, including Pansa, the reason why it thrived was not. The goddess's hand was said to calm the seas, shield sailors from tempests and grant favour in times of upheaval. And if there was anything the Pompeians understood, it was upheaval. Who could say when another great quake might strike again? They could do with every bit of protection offered to them, no matter how foreign.

As the final dish was cleared, the priest entered, and a ripple moved through the gathering as heads turned. His scalp was smooth and bare, and his plain linen robes lent him authority. Pansa rose to greet him. They were not friends, but each understood the value of the other. Pansa gestured towards the peristyle, inviting him to step outside.

'Please, begin whenever you are ready.'

The priest raised his hands to the sky, calling upon Isis to bless the household and all within its walls. The company drifted with him through the rooms, murmuring their assent, until at last he withdrew and the guests returned to the *triclinium*. Pansa remained standing. Goblet in hand, he let the silence draw tight as he allowed the weight of his presence to settle over the room. As he lifted his cup, a movement at the edge of the room caught his attention: Petrinus, crouching low and gathering the shattered fragments of a glass goblet someone had just dropped. The sight brought back the thought he'd had earlier in the forum. Yes, he thought. The timing was perfect. He had plenty of slaves, and the evening called for one more display of benevolence, the kind the *gens Cuspia* was known for.

Following his second speech of the day, he let the words leave his lips: 'Petrinus, be free.' They landed just as he'd rehearsed them in his mind, and he paused deliberately, letting the room absorb them. Pansa hadn't expected freeing a slave to feel so energising. The effect was immediate as his guests began to express their surprise and delight at the scene before them.

THE POLITICIAN

This was the kind of gesture that would stick in their minds and, as word spread of his generosity, would bring him far more in return than it had cost him. The magnanimous Pansa. Petrinus bowed low, murmuring his thanks. With a flick of his hand, Pansa dismissed him towards the peristyle. The moment had served its political purpose. He raised his glass and the room broke into toasts. Among the faces he caught sight of his son's proud gaze: another valuable lesson imparted. Later he would explain the finer point to his son, that Gaius Cuspius Petrinus, though freed, was only a Junian Latin and still bound to him as his patron. Pansa savoured the brilliance of his own design.

'To Pompeii,' he said. 'May she stand strong, united and prosperous.'

One by one, his guests made their farewells, their footsteps receding into the night. Pansa lingered in the dimming *triclinium*, watching as the slaves cleared away the remnants of the feast. With feelings of contentment and peace Pansa turned towards the small peristyle on the way to his private chambers, letting the cool air caress his face. The night had been a success. Another step forwards in continuing his family's long legacy in the city.

* * *

Dawn had not long arrived, and a pale blue sky hung over the streets of Pompeii. Inside the House of Pansa, the family gathered for the children's breakfast in a small room adjoining the largest of the two *atria*. Here, a brazier glowed softly, its warmth cutting through the crisp, early morning air. The sound of *sistra* and cymbals echoed over the walls of their home as a procession of Isis devotees passed by on the street outside, their music rhythmic and otherworldly.

Pansa sat on a simple wooden chair, his wife seated across from him, with their children at either side of the low, rectangular table.

Slaves moved about them, tending to their needs. The breakfast was modest yet carefully prepared: bread, baked in their private bakery overnight, served with fruit and a selection of soft and aged cheeses, and a dish of honey for sweetening. Thin slices of smoked fish, sprinkled with herbs, were arranged neatly on a silver platter. Pansa and his wife did not eat breakfast; it wasn't the elite way. It was more important that they show the restraint befitting of their status.

Pansa glanced at his son, who was focused on tearing a piece of bread and dipping it into the honey. The boy's demeanour, steady and composed, belied the dark bags below his eyes, the last remnants of his excitement from the night before. Their daughter, on the other hand, fidgeted slightly, her curious gaze darting towards the open doorway where the procession's faint music continued to drift over the city.

'Eat,' their mother said, her tone gentle but firm. The girl obeyed, picking up a fig and biting into it daintily. Pansa observed the scene with an air of detached satisfaction. Everything was as it was meant to be, under his control.

Once the children had finished their meal, the slaves cleared the table, removing their plates and wiping away crumbs. Pansa rose, adjusting his tunic in preparation for the *salutatio*, the morning ritual where, as patron, he would receive his clients: men of lower rank who offered loyalty, flattery and services in return for favours, protection or a well-placed word. It was less about friendship than obligation, a daily performance of power and dependence that men of his rank practised. His wife and children withdrew, as was customary: she to her weaving, they to their lessons with the visiting tutor. Simplex appeared silently at his elbow, as ever carrying his wax tablet and stylus, ready to note pledges, promises or names worth remembering.

THE POLITICIAN

In his *tablinum*, the faces of Hermaphrodite and Silenus gazed down at him from the painted plaster. Opposite them, a group of cupids tumbled and jostled with the goat-legged Pan. Silenus, the old companion and tutor of Dionysus, was a symbol of revelry and wine-soaked wisdom, while Pan, the rustic god of fields and flocks, evoked a wilder, earthier harmony. Both were chosen carefully. Pansa had designed it all with intention. The images of gods, groves, hillsides and myths reflected not only his sophisticated taste, and awareness of Greek style, but also his Roman lineage. He wanted visitors to see his roots in the land and his kinship with the traditions of old Italy, without ever needing to muddy his hands.

The Roman obsession with Greek culture was everywhere: in the frescoes that covered the walls of their grandest rooms, in the marble statues nestled between garden columns, in the delicate silverware passed around at banquets. Since the Samnites began their emulation of Hellenistic culture some three centuries ago, men like Pansa had filled their homes with tales of gods and heroes in the statues, libraries and paintings they displayed, wrapping themselves in the legacy of a culture they had once conquered and yet never stopped admiring. A Greek myth, artfully interpreted, could lift a man's name. What better way to command respect than to cast yourself in the image of a hero, or claim Jupiter's favour outright? Pansa relished the thought that Rome had taken Greece's vaunted legends and bent them to its own ends. What the Greeks had dreamed, the Romans had mastered.

From behind the curtains dividing his *tablinum* from the atrium, Pansa could hear that it was already filled with his clients, men of varying stations who waited patiently to be seen. Many wished to visit him that morning to thank him for the games. Others hoped to lace their courteous visits with pleas for his assistance. Pansa took a seat beside his large chest of money and valuables, its size a show of his wealth and status, and prepared for the steady procession of petitioners. But before he could call for his first client, a familiar face appeared through the curtain: red cap, red eyes and the unmistakable flush of tears. Pansa noted it with mild satisfaction. No doubt he had been crying in gratitude of Pansa's clemency.

'Gaius Cuspius Petrinus, come in!' he said, gesturing with the warmth of a man performing generosity. He indicated the stool opposite him. 'Please –' Hesitating briefly, he considered the best place for a man who was only yesterday a slave, to sit. He swiftly moved his hand over to the marble step leading out to the peristyle. 'Sit.'

Petrinus hesitated, then obeyed, perching like someone unaccustomed to sitting. Pansa thought about what a former slave like Petrinus might need to know, being so unprepared for civilised life. He would need lodgings, of course. Dropping Pansa's name would certainly help there. He might even have Simplex write a short letter of introduction for him to seal with his carved *intaglio* ring, unique to his hands only. Not an extravagant letter, just enough to show that Petrinus hadn't crawled out of the gutter.

He paused in giving his advice and looked at the wretched, scrawny figure crouched on the step. Next to him, Simplex, who often ventured out into public life with Pansa, looked far more respectable in clean, nice clothes, his face and hands free of dirt. Pansa spied the dirt under Petrinus' nails and the corner of his lip curled in response. It figured. Slaves were little better than animals. Why would he know how to care for himself? As he reeled off some advice about basic cleanliness, he thought to himself: is no one capable of doing anything without needing my advice first? It was exhausting.

Then again, he reminded himself, this wasn't only done out of the kindness of his own heart. Petrinus was now attached to his

THE POLITICIAN

family's legacy. A gesture like this would be remembered, especially by those watching. A man who could afford to free a slave and then set him up for success was a man worth aligning with. And, relatively speaking, Petrinus had cost him little. He watched his former slave nod solemnly as he absorbed Pansa's wise guidance and received, with shaking hands, the *peculium* savings that would take him into his new life. He was the picture of devotion. Just as it should be.

A thought crossed Pansa's mind, not for the first time that week: what a fine example of a man I am. A true Roman, generous and benevolent. The very model of *Romanitas*.

Attuned, as ever, to appearances, Pansa made the calculated decision to walk with Petrinus into the atrium, his hand held at the man's back, close enough to imply paternal guidance but careful not to touch.

'*Bona fortuna*, Gaius Cuspius Petrinus,' he declared, his booming voice filling the space. 'I wish you all the best in your new life as a freedman bearing my family's name.'

The waiting group burst into applause and Pansa soaked in the approval. Yes, it was going to be a good day.

One by one, Pansa's other clients were ushered into the *tablinum*, each presenting their case with a mixture of humility and hope.

The first client, Clodius, came with a petition. '*Salve*, Pansa. I come as ever with respect, and only because I find myself without remedy.'

'You've never come with idle complaints, Clodius. Speak freely.' Pansa settled himself on the cushioned stool next to his strong box as his listened to his low-born client.

'My wealthy neighbour, Gallus, burned down my tree in the night. He'd been complaining for months that it blocked his sun, but it did him no harm and brought me so much joy. Thank the gods for the men of my neighbourhood who stilled the flames. I'd have no house left if it weren't for them.' He paused, his expression clouded with thought. 'Beneath that little tree I used to imagine myself in the forests of the rich. Now it is gone.'*

'This will need to go to court, and when it does, I'll help where I can. I can't see the outcome going in his favour; it was a hostile act, both against your property and the *Laws of the Twelve Tables*. A man is only allowed to demand a tree be removed if it's fallen onto his land, not if it's still standing. And boundary disputes, as you know, must be settled by a third party. He did neither.'

Pansa paused, then said more gently, 'Speak to Simplex before you go. He'll make a note of your case, and the names involved. Justice may move slowly, but it will move nonetheless.'

Simplex, standing close by, whispered in Pansa's ear: 'He is a scaffolder, just finished reparations at the Temple of Venus. Perhaps he can help in the upcoming renovations around the city?'

Pansa's expression didn't change, but he looked back at the man, assessing him anew.

'I seem to remember you've done work near the Temple of Venus, haven't you?' he enquired. 'Scaffolding. Your business seems to be doing well.'

'Yes, Pansa, I suppose it is, but I –'

'Wonderful. When the call comes, I am sure you will be delighted to assist your patron and your city.'

With a deliberate glance past the astounded face of Clodius to the next petitioner waiting behind the curtains, Pansa brought the meeting to an end.

---

* This wording is taken from a real court case between a rich man and a poor man in Seneca's *Controversiae* (5.5.24). The poor man won the case.

THE POLITICIAN

By the time his final client had departed, the large atrium was quiet again, save for the soft trickle of the fountain in the *impluvium*. Pansa leaned back in his chair, his eyes closing as he rubbed his temples. The dull throb behind his eyes was an unwelcome reminder of the Falernian wine he had indulged in the night before. It wasn't often that such fine wine left him feeling this way; it must be an imbalance in his body, he thought, coupled with the late night and an early start. Rising from his chair, Pansa made his way to the peristyle, where a small, practical *prandium* lunch awaited him. The meal was simple but sufficient: slices of cold salted fish, bread, olives and a wedge of hard goat's cheese. A small bottle of Scaurus' flower of *garum* sat to the side, the sharp, salty aroma rising faintly from its mouth. As he sipped watered-down wine from a cup, his thoughts turned to the tasks ahead.

* * *

After his meal, Pansa set out for the Stabian Baths, the sound of his sandals echoing as he walked along the Via Stabiana. He nodded occasionally to passers-by, maintaining his air of authority without pausing for pleasantries. The baths loomed ahead, a hive of noise and motion, though today he had not come to enjoy their comforts. He was expected in the *palaestra* of the baths where Marcus Casellius Marcellus and Lucius Albucius Celsus, the *aediles* currently in office, were overseeing the new scaffolding. By the time the work was complete, its upkeep would be his responsibility, which was reason enough to take an interest now.

The city's relentless tremors had taken their toll on the structure, making repairs unavoidable. Now a lattice of wooden scaffolding lined one wall, and slaves and labourers clambered up and down the beams, wary of the weakened masonry beneath their hands.

'Marcellus, Celsus,' he said. 'It's good to see progress, though I see the walls are still arguing with the earth.'

Marcellus gave a half-smile. 'They've stopped groaning, for now. Let's not tempt the goddess Fortuna.'

Pansa's gaze rose to the framework overhead.

'I may have someone for you,' he said. 'A client of mine, a scaffolder by trade. Capable, dependable and, more importantly, enthusiastic. He'd be grateful for the opportunity, and I can vouch for his steadiness.'

Celsus exchanged a glance with Marcellus, who nodded. 'We're not short on work. If he's as keen as you say, have him report to the foreman tomorrow. The sooner we have trusted men on these beams, the better.'

After spending some time appraising the work – or, at least, enough time to be seen as useful – the *aediles* had asked if Pansa would sort a quick trading issue for them at the Marine Port across town. Already offloading their duties, Pansa thought. No matter. If Pansa was going to make a good impression as an *aedile*, he needed to start managing these relationships now. The air grew saltier as he approached, and the cries of gulls cut through the rising din of dockworkers shouting orders over the clanks of *amphorae* and the creak of rope and timber. The problem was simple enough: a storage bottleneck at the port was delaying the unloading of grain, and the merchants were growing restless.

The *aediles* had insisted he meet with one of the key figures overseeing the docks, Gripus, a man whose influence would be invaluable come January. As he strode down to the waterfront, he took in the chaotic rhythm of the docks, the smell of fish and the sea's salty brine threatening to overwhelm him. Workers were hauling crates and *amphorae* onto carts, but the operation seemed slow and disorganised. The city's reliance on the water was undeniable,

THE POLITICIAN

but its infrastructure was beginning to show its limitations. Standing at the edge of the dock, he regarded the ships bobbing in the harbour. Perhaps they could expand it.

Pansa pivoted and came face-to-face with Gripus. Broad-shouldered and weathered by years of salt and sun, he had the look of someone who kept the docks running through sheer force of will. If there was a problem with shipments, this was the man who could fix it or, indeed, make it worse. Pansa immediately recognised him as the sort of man who did not give a fig about bloodlines, speaking to everyone as though they were equal. As they spoke, a low rumble stirred beneath their feet, so slight that Pansa almost dismissed it as his imagination.

Then the sea itself seemed to draw breath. The gentle lap of waves grew restless and pulled away from the shoreline in a sudden retreat, leaving the wooden pylons of the docks exposed in the dry air. Small boats tilted awkwardly in the mud, their crews shouting and scrambling to secure them. Overhead, the seabirds that had been circling lazily now erupted into a cacophony of panicked cries, wheeling wildly before flying out to sea.

Gripus sprang into action, but Pansa froze, pulse quickening. He had heard sailors' tales of such things, the sea's retreat from the shore a terrible omen and harbinger of something unnatural.

The faint rumble returned, louder this time, followed by an ungodly crack from the direction of the mountain. The air caught in Pansa's throat as he turned to face it, its imposing silhouette now marked by a curling plume of dark smoke that was twisting upwards and thickening at an astonishing speed.

It was then that the realisation struck him.

The ancient writings of those who had speculated about their mountain rushed into his memory: Strabo, Vitruvius, even Diodorus Siculus, each speaking of the mountain's scorched summit, which bore traces of the ancient fires that had once raged within.

Like many, Pansa had dismissed their thoughts as mere speculation, but their words now rang in his mind with terrifying clarity.

The tremor grew stronger, and Pansa could see workers along the docks beginning to panic. Some pointed towards the mountain, while others scrambled to secure their goods, uncertain of the cause yet gripped by the sense that this was no ordinary quake.

A dusty blast of wind blew through the harbour, carrying with it an odour of sulphur that stung his nose and throat.

Pansa's instincts took over. He barked orders to the dockworkers, his voice cutting through the rising din. Nearby, the dock overseer was a step ahead of him, shouting commands of his own.

'Secure the *amphorae*, don't let them smash! If your cart is loaded, get it moving now!'

The harbour, under the dock overseer's care, didn't need his leadership now. Pompeii did.

Another tremor, stronger this time, sent ripples through the water. The wooden pylons groaned louder. A ceramic jar toppled from a cart and shattered, spilling its cargo of salted fish onto the planks. Pansa cast one last glance at the chaos unfolding along the waterfront but his feet were already moving unsteadily towards the city as the ground rippled beneath him.

The mountain was awake.

Running up the incline from the port, Pansa was at the forum in a matter of minutes. People were emerging from buildings, their faces pale with fear, while others ran aimlessly about clutching bundles of belongings.

Pansa's mind raced. The city had no precedent for this, no plan. Yet it fell to him, as an incoming *aedile*, to impose order. Without men like him they'd crumble into an hysterical mob. He began

THE POLITICIAN

yelling instructions to the gathering crowds, his voice hoarse but unwavering.

'Get to shelter! Stay away from buildings that might collapse! Gather water and provisions!'

Pansa strode through the panicking crowd with purpose. He had to protect the people of Pompeii.

CHAPTER EIGHT

THE FINAL HOURS

AROUND THE EIGHTH HOUR (1 P.M.), 24 OCTOBER 79 CE

Petrinus' breath was shallow. He had remained for a short time in Julia Felix's garden, away from falling buildings. But now the air was thickening with dust, turning the midday light into an eerie twilight, and the garden was under siege. Pumice rained down in a relentless cascade, striking the rooftops with sharp, hollow clatters. He had to find Pansa. He would know what to do, and Simplex might be with him. Perhaps Pansa would even know what was happening. Petrinus had spent so long in Pansa's shadow that moving without his direction felt how sailors must feel when the clouds swallow the stars at sea.

Behind him, Julia's female slaves had rushed to her side, their faces pale as they reached for their mistress. All at once, their eyes turned skywards. The column of ash was writhing into the sky, swallowing the light. 'It's reaching the heights of the gods,' one of them mumbled, her voice thin with terror. Another shock rolled through the earth, deeper this time. The women shrieked. They clutched at Julia and broke into a run, forcing her along with them.

Reaching the gate, they spilled onto the street, joining the flood of bodies surging through the streets. From every side came shouts, voices of those who had survived the great quake, their warnings cutting through the chaos.

'Away from the columns! Into open spaces! The roofs will fall!'

Petrinus ran in the opposite direction, pushing against the tide. Every muscle in his body burned but he didn't slow. He wove through the panicked masses, past the crumbling *palaestra*, through the arched gateway, and onto the road where, not long ago, he had sat with a cup of wine in Euxinus' inn. A solid collision. Petrinus stumbled back, eyes locking onto a familiar face. The innkeeper.

'Where are you going?' Euxinus asked him.

Petrinus wiped a streak of ash from his face. 'The forum. My master, I mean, patron, might still be there.'

Euxinus and Petrinus stood, two pillars in a sea of turmoil as people ran about in panic. Euxinus glanced up at the ever-thickening cloud, then in the direction of the city gates. 'If it keeps going like this, I'm leaving through the gate. But it'll stop soon. It has to.'

They exchanged one last word of good fortune before turning, one towards the forum, the other darting into his inn to gather his belongings and his people.

The ground rumbled again, longer this time. Euxinus found his slaves and barmaid cowering below the vines at the back of his inn. The customers had already fled. Seeing them, he shouted at them to get moving and gather anything useful or valuable. Looters were bound to take advantage.

'We're going to leave the city on foot and wait for it all to blow over,' Euxinus ordered.

THE FINAL HOURS

Biria tried to contain the panic in her voice. 'What's that cloud? What's happening?'

'I have no idea. But we haven't seen the likes of it before.'

*   *   *

On the other side of the city, Scaurus steadied himself as a quake shuddered through his friends' house. The painted cupids around him tumbled as cracks shot up the frescoed walls. That was enough for him; he didn't wait for his friends, didn't linger to see if the walls would hold. He turned sharply on his heel, striding through the peristyle and out through the entrance, telling a slave on the way out that he would be in touch once whatever this was had subsided.

Merchants and traders stood frozen on the Via di Mercurio, as if debating whether to guard their wares or abandon them entirely. Carts rattled, their goods shifting dangerously, some spilling onto the street as the mules reared in panic. A man cursed as *amphorae* crashed to the ground, oil seeping into the dust. Scaurus moved more quickly. Further along, traders closed the shutters over their shop fronts. He saw it in their faces: the indecision, not knowing whether this was another earthquake, or something bigger.

It had been like this for months, years even. They had learned to live with the shaking earth. But as Scaurus pressed forwards, a voice at the back of his mind whispered: Had they all been this strong? As a fisherman, he was trained to sense danger, a slight change of wind or foreboding signs on the horizon. The thought nagged at him as he reached the corner of the Via di Mercurio and stepped into the forum. It was there that he came to a halt.

Clusters of people huddled in tight groups, their heads tilted back and faces drained of colour. The usual cries of haggling and gossip had vanished. Save for the rumbling, a strange and unnatural silence clung to the forum. Scaurus turned to follow their gaze.

Above the city, a vast column of smoke and ash was rising fast, twisting and swelling as it climbed. It wasn't like that from a normal fire, but rather an uncoiling monster blotting out the sky. Darker than anything he had ever seen, it pulsed upwards, vast and terrifying.

This was different, he thought. Wrong.

Scaurus tried to steady his breathing. The forum was far from the mountain. They were safe here. Weren't they?

By now, small pieces of sponge-like stone were falling in earnest. They struck the ground with sharp, percussive clatters. It reminded him of hailstorms on the open sea, the way the drops would lash at the deck and roll in drifts, relentlessly. Yet these drops were not the icy cold of Jupiter's rain clouds. They were warm.

To his left, his friend Gaius Cuspius Pansa, *aedile* elect, stood with arms outstretched, shouting to the people as the pumice grew thicker around him. Slaves darted about obeying his orders as they rushed to get supplies for the people now taking refuge in the most secure places in the city, away from falling walls. Seeing the anxious look in Pansa's eye, Scaurus hurried onto a side street towards his own villa. By the time he reached it, his wife and family were in the garden avoiding the perils of indoors, hiding below a sheet held by a few slaves, their faces tight with unease as the pumice gathered atop their cover.

Inside, as plaster rained down from the walls and objects shattered around them, the rest of the Umbricii family's slaves rushed to gather the most valuable items. They hid prized statues and possessions inside rooms and stuffed valuable objects into chests or covered them with cloth. Scaurus exhaled, steadying his mind. He would need to stay calm for his family. The tremors had not ceased, but neither had they worsened, and the sky, though filling with smoke, had not yet turned entirely to night. For now, they would wait, overlooking the sea. Surely it must end soon?

*   *   *

Petrinus pushed through the disorder, the crowd pressing around him in frantic desperation as a fresh cascade of roof tiles shattered onto the paving stones. Pumice drummed against the earth as it bounced off stone, striking flesh and rolling in uneven piles beneath their feet. He caught sight of a familiar figure standing firm amidst the shifting throng in the forum.

Pansa.

The man's voice cut through the noise, sharp and unwavering. While others ran in panic, he directed anyone who would listen towards the granaries and the Stabian Baths, any structure with thick walls which might withstand the ongoing tremors. But why was there so much dark cloud in the air? Petrinus stumbled towards him, coughing against the thickening mist. His tunic and skin were dusted grey, the grit settling in his teeth and lungs.

'What can I do?' he managed.

Pansa didn't hesitate. 'Get a message beyond the city. We need help: carts, food, supplies. When this all dies down, it'll be far worse than the fallout from the great quake. Simplex has gone to send word to Lucretia and the children to get out of the city. This is not like last time. Vesuvius is no ordinary mountain.'

Petrinus nodded, already turning to go. His feet felt leaden, his body worn thin from running, but he did not stop. As he struggled forward into the crowd again, he spared a final glance at Pansa. His former master was still shouting orders, trying to hold Pompeii together with as much authority as he could muster.

Petrinus found Lucretia, their children and the *nutrix* readying a cart outside their home, the floor beneath them becoming difficult to traverse in the rising pumice. Every step was a struggle as the mule's feet sank into the uneven, shifting ground. He gripped the mule's reins with one hand and steadied Lucretia with the other as she climbed onto the cart, shielding the children with his body as a large stone clattered to the ground nearby. He grabbed the edge of the cart and helped the *nutrix* up next. As the mother and nanny clutched the two children to their sides, Simplex stepped out from behind the cart and Petrinus' heart jumped in relief as the two lovers' eyes met.

'Thank the gods. I thought I wouldn't find you.' Petrinus looked at Simplex and recognised the same expression he had worn at the slave auction all those years ago. 'I've sent Pansa's word to the messengers at the gates. They should be sending help now.' Petrinus took Simplex's hand and squeezed.

'We will get out of here. We have to.'

Petrinus and Simplex began leading the mule through the ash and falling pumice. They passed a small family with two young children standing hopelessly in the sea of people moving out of the city, and Lucretia cried out:

'Stop the cart!' She gestured down to the family. 'We have room. Please, join us, while you can.'

Hearing the noblewoman, Lucius turned to Fortunata, an urgency in his voice. 'Take the children,' he said, hands firm on her shoulders, the heat of his palms pressing through her tunic. 'Go ahead. I'll find you. I promise.'

He nodded towards their own mule, shifting restlessly nearby. 'I'll go and find my family,' he said. 'I can't leave them.' He managed a small smile, though it didn't reach his eyes. 'I'll be right behind you. Whatever this is, it'll pass. Just keep going, and don't look back.'

THE FINAL HOURS

There was no time to argue. The sky was falling in, and the air was growing thick and bitter. Taking Lucretia's hand, Fortunata climbed onto the cart as Lucius lifted the children up, kissing each one on the cheek.

'Can we join you?' came a voice.

Julia Felix, surrounded by her female slaves, peered up at the people in the cart with remarkable composure. Imploring them to hurry, the two families shifted aside as Julia and her slaves climbed onto the cart. As it jolted into motion, Lucius' hand brushed Fortunata's. And then she was gone.

END OF THE DAY (4 P.M.)*

The boats were already being loaded when Scaurus and his family arrived at the docks. When the walls of their home had started to crack and fall, Scaurus had made his decision: it was time to leave. They would sail to a friend's villa across the Bay and wait. Their slaves staggered under the weight of silverware, scrolls and decorative items, anything worth saving, as the family of three generations shoved their way through the crushing crowd to the edge of the dock. Scaurus' wife held a small box of jewellery tight in her hands. The children huddled close to their mother and grandmothers, silent and wide-eyed.

Panic rose in the group as large swathes of terrified people pleaded with sailors for passage. Many boats had already left, and desperation was setting in for those still ashore. Scaurus hurried his family on board his fishing boat. There was no room left for anyone

---

* There are only 12 hours in a Roman day, so the end of the day was just after 4 p.m. in modern time.

else. The small vessel was covered in the ash which had settled on Pompeii like a blanket.

'Take us across the Bay,' he ordered his boatsmen. 'To Misenum. My friends will take us in.'

As the boat pulled out into the sea, it rocked hazardously beneath them. Scaurus looked back towards the city. Smoke and fire clawed at the sky above the mountain, and hot pumice crashed down in fist-sized lumps. One struck the edge of the boat, splintering wood. Another smashed into the arm of the captain, burning his skin. The family pulled their cloaks tighter, the wool providing little protection against the hot stones falling from the sky, as the children screamed, their throats raw with terror.

Scaurus shouted for the slaves to begin rowing, urgency pressing into his voice. A young woman stranded on shore, her tears carving wet streaks through the ash on her cheeks, pushed forward at the last minute, desperation etched across her face. She held out a bundle wrapped in cloth to the family, her hands shaking. 'Save her, please. Take my baby. Her name is Aelia.'

His wife didn't hesitate. Reaching out, she dragged the baby from the mother's grasp as the boat lurched forwards into the crowded harbour, waves churning with the force of the quakes and the fleeing vessels.

ONE HOUR AFTER THE END OF THE DAY (5 P.M.)

The sun was little more than a memory, its feeble glow swallowed by the monstrous cloud that now reigned over the sky. What light remained was a strange colour, casting an eerie, ochre hue over the falling ash. Many whispered in fear that the gods had abandoned

THE FINAL HOURS

them. Some called it a punishment. In the forum, a man with hollow, wild eyes pointed to the darkest point of the cloud above the mountain: 'The Giants! Can't you see them? They're rising up! This is the end!' He pointed now at the crowd around him. 'I warned you all, our time was near. The Giants long trapped beneath the mountain revolt at last!'*

The Temple of Isis trembled. Below it, the earth itself seemed to shudder under the weight of the sky. The once-bright frescoes of Isis and her divine retinue were fractured by deep, creeping cracks, the painted figures splitting apart. Flakes of plaster drifted down with the falling ash, collecting in ghostly piles at the base of the columns.

The floor of the sanctuary was thick with pumice, knee-deep in some places, forcing those gathered within to wade through the shifting mass of stone. Amisusius could feel it pressing against him, dragging at the folds of his robes as he knelt before the goddess, his hands lifted in prayer, steady despite the weeping of the faithful around him. The goddess had carried her people through chaos before. She would not abandon them now.

Another tremor. Stronger this time. The great wooden doors groaned, their hinges straining. A fresh crack splintered through the mosaic floor beneath him, racing towards the altar.

Still Amisusius did not move.

He had seen this darkness before.

During his initiation into the cult of Isis, he had been led through the rites of death and rebirth, blindfolded and stripped of all worldly ties. He had descended into the depths where only the

---

* Writing of the eruption some years later, the Roman writer Dio Cassius talks of the people who reported seeing figures resembling Giants in the ash clouds of the eruption, with some believing these long-subdued dwellers of the caverns below the mountain were rising up in revolt (66.23).

gods dwelled, where all light was gone. He had trembled at the threshold of Proserpina's realm and passed through the gates of death. He had advanced through all the elements and had still returned. He had entered the presence of the gods below and the presence of the gods above, and paid due reverence before them, afterwards being reborn beneath the light of the sacred torches. Now, as he knelt once more in the temple of his goddess, it was as though he had returned to that same darkness, the same choking void where all things ended and began.

A deep, violent crack split the air. The ceiling above the sanctuary shifted, groaning under its own weight. The great column to the right of the temple trembled. Amisusius turned his head just in time to see the fractures racing up its length, jagged like lightning.

With a final, tortured moan, the column gave way.

A roar of collapsing stone filled the air as dust and debris rained down in a choking cloud. The faithful screamed.

Amisusius saw no more.

THREE HOURS AFTER THE END OF THE DAY (7 P.M.)

Lucius had no choice but to abandon his cart. He had left it near the *palaestra* latrines when the pumice grew too deep, the wheels locked fast, half-buried beneath the relentless rain of stones. After Fortunata and the children had escaped the city, he had tried to reach the far side of town, desperate to find his parents, but the streets were no longer the streets he knew, just shifting grey mounds of ash and ruin. Defeated, he had turned back towards the *palaestra*, where he had since stayed, hoping to at least be there when his family returned, to guard what little they had left. Without his mule, and their garden, they had nothing, and now, with no cart and no path, and the debris rising fast, he saw his situation for what it was: it was too late.

The city was lost beneath a darkness that defied night, a thick, choking blackness cast by the towering cloud above, stretching far beyond the walls, over the mountains and out across the sea. Somewhere within its churning mass, flashes of lightning tore at the sky, illuminating ash and fire in brief, terrifying bursts. Was Jupiter at war with the other gods? Was this the reckoning they had all feared?

People moved like ghosts through the shifting haze, lanterns lifted in front of them, casting dim, feeble pools of light as the stench of sulphur burned the backs of their throats. Some walked blindly, hands outstretched, calling for lost loved ones. Others did not move at all, having fallen to their knees in the street, faces contorted as they fought for air. From every corner of the city, cries rang out: shouts of names, appeals to the gods who had abandoned them, screams swallowed by the darkness. The world had lost any sense of shape or order. It felt like the city had been transported to the endless labyrinth of Pluto's halls in the underworld.

Lucius had heard of such places before. He'd been told about gates to the underworld, passages to hell itself across the Mediterranean. He had listened to travellers' tales of cavernous mouths in rock that belched vapours, of hot springs that churned like a cauldron stirred by the hands of unseen Giants, long since subdued by Heracles, and of sacred grottos where the breath of the earth was said to steal the lives of those who ventured too close. Was another opening up before them?

THE LOST VOICES OF POMPEII

FOUR HOURS AFTER THE END OF THE DAY (8 P.M.)

Across the Bay in Misenum, Scaurus' family had bathed and eaten, and were trying to settle themselves. Yet as Scaurus stepped back outside, a cold weight pressed against his chest.

He could no longer see Pompeii.

There was no moon that night, and the only light came from the fires of the mountain, as bursts of molten rock lit the sky in brief, violent flashes. The mountain burned with an unnatural glow, and the monstrous cloud had now completely swallowed the land beneath it. Lightning ran in shocks through the mass, illuminating the anarchy only for short, terrible moments. The sea, once an, albeit treacherous, lifeline for those fleeing, was now filled with the debris of shipwrecks. Scaurus stood motionless, knowing there was nothing he could do. The city he loved was vanishing.

As he turned to pull his eyes away, no longer able to take in the destruction before him, something happened.

Part of the column above the mountain collapsed. Scaurus watched helplessly, stuttering words of horror as a monstrous wave of ash and fire raced down the flanks of the mountain, devouring everything in its path. Beside him, the women let out raw, involuntary sounds, shrill and guttural, the kind of cries that come when the body understands devastation before the mind can form a thought. It fell in the direction of Herculaneum.

He could picture the villas with their painted *loggias* facing the sea, the neat colonnades where merchants gathered, the bustling workshops and wineshops along the marble-lined streets. Only hours before, those people would have been haggling over fish, pouring measures of wine, arranging *amphorae* for transport. Now all of it was gone, smothered beneath the black tide. He thought of the men he had bargained with, the women he had nodded to in the market, the children who played in the streets. Their voices, their lives, snuffed out in an instant. The thought twisted in his gut. Perhaps there was hope still for Pompeii; the same hadn't yet happened to their beloved town.

It dawned on Scaurus then. The wind was blowing in the direction of Pompeii, and the column had to come down at some point.

FIVE HOURS AFTER THE END OF THE DAY (9 P.M.)

For hours, Pansa had been moving through the city, helping wherever he could, digging survivors from collapsed buildings and guiding families towards shelter, all the while wondering if his family were safe. There was no guarantee that their escape from Pompeii meant safety; there was every chance that this was the end of the world.

Again and again he came across groups of men pounding on doors, clawing at fallen thresholds, digging bare-handed through the pumice that had swallowed the ground floors of homes all over the city. By this point, huge pumice stones were falling at terrifying speeds, cracking rooftops and decimating beams. The city was being pummelled from above.

The onslaught was relentless and unending. Roofs sagged. Houses collapsed with muffled crashes. Chained dogs howled in a chorus of terror, their cries intertwined with the shrieks of mothers who had lost their children, and with the strangled screams of the dying. The streets were an obstacle course of broken beams, fallen tiles and shattered statues. Those who moved forwards were forced to weave through the bodies of the dead, stepping over the fallen as they tried to reach safety.

EIGHT HOURS AFTER THE END OF THE DAY (MIDNIGHT)

Buildings continued to collapse one after another, crushing the people trapped inside. The crash of stone, the splinter of wood and the muffled cries of those trapped echoed through the streets in a dreadful, inescapable cacophony.

Pansa was still trying to help anyone he could, dragging the wounded to safety, lifting fallen structures and digging through pumice-choked doorways in search of those trapped behind them. He called out to anyone who might still be alive. But with every passing moment, as the streets grew heavy with the litter of bodies suffocating from the dense air and falling debris, he felt in his heart that this was the end.

TWO AND A HALF HOURS BEFORE SUNRISE (5 A.M.), 25 OCTOBER 79 CE

Following several more strong tremors, the pumice had stopped falling, and with it the city grew quiet. After hours of chaos, the sudden stillness felt heavier than the noise. Only the distant groan of collapsing buildings and the stifled cries of those entombed below debris broke the silence. The mountain still rumbled in the near-dark, a low, constant roar.

Euxinus had followed his plan and had left the city by mid-afternoon. Taking the road towards the neighbouring town of Nuceria,

THE FINAL HOURS

he and a number of other refugees had sheltered in a villa along the way, forced to stop as the road became congested with ash and pumice and larger stones began to fall. Though the fallout lessened the further they travelled, the horror of the eruption did not.

'Has it ended?' A woman in the group asked with hope.

Euxinus stood to peer out of a window. 'We have to go straight away. They'll need our help. Only the gods know how many people are stuck under buildings.'

One of the men looked at Euxinus. 'You sure about this?'

Euxinus nodded. 'If there's a chance to help, it's now. We wait any longer, we're just digging up bodies.'

The men didn't argue but left their wives and children cowering in the dark of the villa. It would take at least an hour to get back to the city, longer even in these conditions.

The road back to Pompeii was strewn with bodies. Arriving at the gate to the city, they found a place they no longer recognised. Landmarks had vanished, doorways were half-buried, and the skeletal remains of buildings loomed out of the blackness.

Still, they pressed on.

ONE HOUR BEFORE SUNRISE (6.30 A.M.)

To the south of the city, Pansa was straining beside a group of men, their shoulders pressed to a beam that had come down across a doorway, sealing a family inside. A child cried out from beyond the doorway, its cries muffled by dust. Around them people began emerging where they could from gaps or through high windows. Though there was a lull in the pumice fall, ash clogged their throats and sweat streaked the grime on their faces. It was becoming harder to draw breath with each passing moment.

A man stumbled towards them, coughing from the dust, his tunic torn and scorched. He grabbed Pansa's arm.

'It came down like a wave,' he gasped. 'From the mountain, like the gods had cast it. The whole north wall shook, and we thought it would break, but it held.'

Pansa stared at him, panic rising. 'What was it?'

'It was like an avalanche, but hot. And so fast. I was standing all the way back down the street leading to the Vesuvian Gate when it came. We all ran but it didn't make it over the wall.'

Pansa didn't speak. That deep roar he had heard earlier; now he knew what it had been. He looked north, though there was nothing to see but smoke and falling stone. The mountain was not finished.

Across the Bay, Scaurus had slept, though only lightly, and only after he and his wife had settled the children on borrowed cushions in the corner of the garden courtyard. A brief calm had fallen over Misenum in the early hours, and it had seemed, for a moment, as though fortune might have turned again. But sometime after dawn, the ground had begun to heave once more.

Scaurus was already awake when a servant ran into the peristyle, breathless and white-faced. 'The sea's pulled back again,' he choked. 'There are sea creatures flapping on the sand and the shore has grown.'

Scaurus didn't reply. They couldn't stay here.

Around the villa, panic was taking hold. Some of their hosts' neighbours were shouting, trying to gather their belongings and urging everyone to head for the harbour. Down by the quay, people shoved their things onto overflowing carts.

But Scaurus stood at the threshold, eyes fixed on the choppy sea, too violent to traverse.

'We're not going to the boats,' he said. 'We will make for Puteoli. By road.'

THE FINAL HOURS

His wife stared at him. 'You're sure?'

'Yes,' he said. 'The sea's no safe passage now.'

Ash was falling again, dry and soft at first but building rapidly. He took the baby they had rescued and wrapped a spare tunic across its face, gesturing for the others to cover their mouths. A wave of sulphur washed over them. His grandson clutched his mother's hand as Scaurus reached back for his daughter, linking their hands together, one after the other, in a human chain. The gloom was deepening. Behind them, the sky cracked again with violet lightning and a black cloud began its quick descent, obscuring the peninsula and drawing a mantle over the island of Capri lying off the headland of the Bay.

A darkness fell over them, suffocating and heavy. It wasn't like a cloudy evening, or even a night without the moon; it was the kind of darkness that comes when a door is shut tight and every lamp has been blown out. People stumbled and cried out, calling for parents, children and the gods who had abandoned them. Voices rose in confusion and fear. Somewhere, someone was screaming that Misenum was falling, that the harbour was aflame. The Umbricii walked on, fingers laced together in the dark, refusing to let go.*

* * *

Far from the ruined city, Julia Felix sat in a cart jostling over the uneven road, surrounded by a group of weary travellers. Among them was Lucretia Pansa, her two children and their *nutrix*. Curiously, the freedman in the red *pileus* Julia had glimpsed in her peristyle sat opposite her. He held the hand of a male slave whose

---

* These are the descriptions we get directly from Pliny the Younger (written to the historian Tacitus, years later), who describes his first-hand experience of that evening from his position in a villa in Misenum, overlooking the Bay of Naples.

face was drawn tight with shock. They had not spoken for the entire journey. Lucretia's little girl, cradling her doll to her chest, had fallen asleep against her mother. The boy, however, remained wide awake, eyes fixed ahead, a stand-in *paterfamilias*.

The people around her were coated in ash, their faces drawn with exhaustion, each clutching whatever they had managed to save; their most precious belongings, and the last remnants of the life they had left behind. The events of the day before had been a leveller, reducing them all to the same status by circumstance. All around them, carts carried their passengers forward, some stopping at towns along the way, others continuing on to Rome, their wheels creaking under the weight of people and their possessions.

As the cart carried them northwards, the land stretched wide before them, Rome's fields rolling in golden waves, dotted with figures labouring in the early morning light. The cloud which had risen so high into the sky was long behind them, now out of sight. To their right, the sun rose over the horizon and bathed the earth in a light made hazy by the travelling ash. Julia watched as slaves toiled hard in the fields, their movements steady and methodical, oblivious to the destruction that had unfolded miles away. She wondered if the pumice had stopped falling, if the quakes had ceased, or if anything remained of Pompeii at all.

A messenger on a horse shot past the cart, bound for Rome at breakneck speed. Soon, she too would send word; a messenger would be dispatched from her relatives' home in Rome to learn the fate of the city. But for now, there was nothing she could do but sit and watch as the countryside gave way to the outskirts of the great capital. Life, it seemed, carried on.

THE FINAL HOURS

FIRST HOUR (SUNRISE, 7.30 A.M.)

Euxinus had been pulling people from the debris when he had heard it: a petrifying roar in the distance, followed by a wave of terrified screams. In the hour that had passed since then, the sound had lodged in his chest like a stone. Struggling to breathe even more than before, the air now choking his lungs with a thicker dust, Euxinus laboured through pumice and debris to the outskirts of the city near his inn. The sun barely pierced the thick veil of dust that cloaked the Bay, casting the landscape in a ghostly half-light. Morning arrived not with brightness but as a dull, greyed-out dawn, creating a strange, haunting twilight.

Hearing voices, Euxinus finally stopped at a vineyard and orchard near the city wall. At the rear of the plot, he discovered a group of 12 people huddled together, men, women and children from his neighbourhood. They were perched atop mounds of pumice, having climbed out from their hiding places during the lull. He hauled himself over the orchard wall, something that would have been impossible only yesterday, but was now easy with the metres of pumice and ash in the streets. His sandals crunched on the shifting stones as he landed. Even in the dim light, he could see that the orchard looked barely recognisable.

The trees, once vibrant, stood lifeless, their branches sagging under the weight of ash. The vines lay smothered, jutting through the metres of pumice like broken fingers clawing their way out of a grave. He took a breath, though it burned to do so, and sat for a moment among the others. His limbs ached from the day's ordeal, from the endless walking and running, from the fear. Around him, his neighbours huddled close as the ground convulsed beneath their feet, more violently, it seemed, than before. Their bodies tensed once more, drawn tight with terror at the rumbling sounds and the scenes of death around them. The smell of panic and sulphur clung to the air. The group's silence was broken only by quiet whimpers.

* * *

The air was worsening rapidly as Pansa arrived at his street, the Via dell'Abbondanza, to find his home half buried. He didn't go inside, knowing that he had ordered the evacuation of his family. He presumed his slaves had left with them. He offered a silent thanks to the gods for sparing him the fate of so many others up to this point, those crushed beneath falling buildings, or with lungs too weak to withstand the choking ash. He thought of his wife and children and hoped beyond hope that they were safe.

The pumice had reached high up the doorways of houses and shops, transforming the once-bustling street into a ghostly wasteland of half-buried buildings and skeletal façades. As he stumbled forwards, trying to steady himself against a forceful tremor below, a sound cut through the shaking buildings further down the street: the whimper of a dog.

He turned towards the noise and found that it was coming from the home of his friend, Paquius Proculus. Clambering over the drift of pumice piled in the doorway, he edged towards the first side room, peering through its narrow window. Beneath a bed with iron legs, the hunched form of a dog was just visible, trembling in the dust. Its body was pressed low to the ground and its eyes were wide with alarm. The room was strewn with debris, with shards of pottery scattered across the bed. He stepped forward, ready to free the poor creature from its misery – and then he heard it.

Voices.

Abandoning the dog, he ran down the street, lungs burning. A few doors down, tucked between two shops, he found them: a

THE FINAL HOURS

family he recognised still sheltering inside their home. How had they waited this long? The pumice in their hallway was already knee-high. They huddled together in the atrium, faces streaked with dust, hoping the walls might yet protect them.

'There's no time. You can't stop here. The buildings aren't safe,' Pansa urged as he stepped inside, motioning for them to follow.

He helped them over the wreckage, one by one. In the half-light their ornaments caught the eye, glinting against the dust and ruin. First came a young girl, her gold earrings, fine wire knotted at the ends, flashing as she moved. Then a man, the bronze of his ring dulled, but the carnelian *intaglio* of Fortuna still burning red. Behind him, a woman whose arms shimmered with gold armlets, her fingers heavy with more rings than any ordinary day would allow. They had dressed themselves in panic, it was clear, gathering what treasures they could before fleeing their home. But the group of eight had been forced to take shelter inside the house of a stranger during the final quakes. Now only seven remained. As they stepped over the fallen body of a woman crushed beneath rubble in the entranceway, one of the women cried out in vain.*

Behind Pansa, their *paterfamilias* lingered, refusing to leave until everyone else was out.

* * *

In the orchard across town, Euxinus and the others lay on the ground as the trembling grew, shielding the children beside them. A boy of no more than 10 curled up beside his mother in the

---

* This is the House of the Priest Amandus (I.7.7), where nine skeletons were discovered.

foetal position, his small body shaking as she whispered softly, singing a song meant to soothe, though her voice quivered with fear.

* * *

Lucius was still sheltering in the *palaestra*, huddled in a corner that had managed to hold up against the destruction. The great open courtyard had so recently been so full of life: men exercising in the sun or scraping sweat from their bodies with *strigils*, the air filled with laughter and the scent of oil and wine. His wife hawking food. She had looked so beautiful.

Around him sat the remnants of that time, already so distant somehow: a bronze cooking pot, a long-handled pan, a strainer. All left over from a meal cooked under the columns. *Strigils* and bronze vessels lay discarded. Nearby, the iron trident of a gladiator had been abandoned, its prongs buried in the pumice.

Lucius stared at the cooking pot. He and his wife owned one just like it.

Would he ever see her again?

A wave of sadness and panic overtook him then, gripping his chest in an unrelenting vice as he struggled to breathe the suffocating air. He should have left with them. How could he have known? Crouching down, Lucius drew his knees up against his chest and pressed his back against the wall of the east end of the south portico. He closed his eyes against the darkness.

* * *

They all heard it at once: Pansa, Euxinus and Lucius.

A new sound, unlike any of the others.

Pansa shouted urgently at his group to move forward as a new tremor shook the ground.

THE FINAL HOURS

A deep, rolling thunder that was neither from the sky nor the earth.

Euxinus propped himself up on his elbow and leaned over to comfort the shaking boy.

It was coming for them.

Lucius covered his mouth in panic, thinking of the faces of Fortunata and his children, his eyes shut tightly against the world outside.

The great wave of heat and ash rushed forwards at an impossible speed, roaring through the city like a tide of fire.

Then, nothing.

THE AFTERMATH

The eruption began between midday and 1 p.m. on the afternoon of 24 October 79 CE. From Vesuvius, a vast column of ash and gas surged skywards, reaching heights of up to 26 kilometres. The sheer weight of this column would cause it to buckle and collapse again and again over the hours that followed. Each collapse would send pyroclastic currents in a different direction, striking towns and villas at staggered times. The direction of the wind blew the volcanic fallout in a south-easterly direction over Pompeii, burying the town in over 6 metres of pumice, with many buildings and roofs buckling beneath its weight. One third of the casualties at Pompeii were in this level of the eruption layer.

Herculaneum, closer to the mountain, escaped that rain (a layer of only 1–2 cm of pumice and ash has been uncovered at Herculaneum), but the town arguably met an even crueller fate than Pompeii. There, the first pyroclastic flows, torrents of burning gas, ash and debris that tore down the slopes with impossible speed, seared and suffocated everything in their path between 7 and 8 p.m. on the first day.*

---

* This was originally set at between midnight and 1 a.m., but recent research has determined a much earlier time.

It was not until 6.30 a.m. on the second day (25 October) that the first pyroclastic surge thundered down the volcano and reached Pompeii's northern walls, forcing its way some 200 metres into the city before losing momentum.* This would have made breathing even harder than it already was to anyone remaining in the city. Then, between 7.30 and 8 a.m., the entire eruption column above Vesuvius collapsed under its own weight. This time there was no reprieve. Another pyroclastic flow thundered down the volcano at hundreds of kilometres per hour and engulfed Pompeii, its temperature reaching between 180–380°C (356–716°F). Those who had remained, or who had returned in the pumice lull in the early hours, were killed instantly, their bodies contorted into the rigid 'boxer pose' as the heat contracted their muscles. Two more flows struck Pompeii after this, bringing the total number unleashed during the eruption to six. The flow of volcanic material was so considerable that it created a blanket of 6–7 metres of pyroclastic deposits over Pompeii and extended the shoreline by over a kilometre westwards into the Tyrrhenian Sea.

ANCIENT RELIEF EFFORTS

The eruption of 79 CE struck just a month into the reign of Emperor Titus. His response was immediate. He travelled south to Campania to oversee the relief efforts in person, while his adminis-

---

* Volcanologists use pyroclastic density current (PDC) as the umbrella term for the fast-moving avalanches of hot gas, ash and debris that sweep down a volcano. Within this, they distinguish between heavier pyroclastic flows, which hug the ground like a torrent of molten rubble, and lighter pyroclastic surges, which are more turbulent and can leap over walls or spill across water. Both move at terrifying speeds and reach lethal temperatures.

THE AFTERMATH

tration organised emergency aid for the affected population. Survivors were resettled in nearby towns such as Nola, Naples, Sorrento and Capua, which in turn were granted special privileges and financial support for taking them in.

Property belonging to those who had died without heirs was redirected to a relief fund, and a senatorial commission was appointed to consider whether the buried towns could be rebuilt. Their ruling was decisive: the scale of the devastation, and the depth of volcanic deposits, made reconstruction impossible. Pompeii, Herculaneum and their neighbours were to remain entombed.

Despite this, survivors and opportunists soon returned to Pompeii and made use of what remained, living in upper storeys above the ash and adapting former ground floors into cellars, ovens and workshops. Pompeii became less a city reborn than a fragile settlement clinging to its ruins, a place where memory, necessity and survival briefly overlapped before history swallowed it up. Within a few years, Pompeii disappeared from official records. Apart from a brief appearance centuries later in the fourth-century *Tabula Peutingeriana*, an illustrated Roman road map, the city was remembered only by the word *civita*, a loose term meaning 'the settlement' or simply 'a community of citizens'. The vague term reflected how little was left to distinguish the site but nonetheless acknowledged a city had once existed there.

Life resumed in the surrounding region in the succeeding months and years; the fertile volcanic soil continued to be beneficial for agriculture and, eventually, people returned to farm and populate the land. Vineyards, fields and new buildings gradually crept across the desolate landscape, covering not only the ruins of Pompeii and Herculaneum, but all that surrounded them. In time, Pompeii and Herculaneum became mere footnotes in the letters and histories of Rome's greatest writers, and a local legend.

WHAT REMAINED?

When survivors returned to what had once been Pompeii, hoping to salvage belongings, recover valuables, or simply to make sense of what had happened, they found that the thick blanket of ash and pumice had buried everything. Over time, this solidified and was made even harder by rainfall. In the immediate aftermath, it was still possible to dig through the softer layers, and some attempted to tunnel down, guided by the tops of buildings that still protruded above the surface. The upper levels of the amphitheatre, and a few walls and fragments of rooftops remained visible, serving as markers for those trying to recover their possessions. However, as the months passed, the volcanic material became cement-like, locking Pompeii beneath and making further digging almost impossible.

For more than 16 centuries the cities lay hidden, preserved in silence beneath the volcanic crust, until the Bourbons, under the direction of the King of Naples, began to dig. Excavations started at Herculaneum in 1738 and at Pompeii in 1748. In Herculaneum, the first excavators were struck by the lack of human remains and assumed that most of the population had escaped. That belief held until 1982, when archaeologists uncovered a grim truth along the ancient shoreline: over 300 skeletons huddled in the boat sheds and found sprawled on the beach. Mostly women, the elderly and children had taken shelter in the vaulted chambers. The remains of men and soldiers were found along the beach, as if trying to help others flee by boat. It is only a small comfort to know they would have died instantly, the heat killing too fast to bring pain.

That heat also shaped what was left behind. At Pompeii, the pyroclastic flows did not reach the extreme temperatures required to carbonise organic material. As a result, wood was often inciner-

THE AFTERMATH

ated, rather than preserved. In contrast, Herculaneum was struck earlier by hotter and denser pyroclastic flows. These conditions carbonised wooden objects, furniture, shelves, beams and even a baby's cot, preserving them in extraordinary detail. This difference in thermal exposure explains why Pompeii has far fewer surviving wooden structures than Herculaneum.

THE DEATH TOLL

As of 2002, 1,049 bodies had been discovered in the two-thirds of the city that had been excavated. This number has since risen with ongoing excavations, though many recent discoveries remain unpublished. When extrapolated across the full extent of the city, estimates place the likely death toll at around 1,600 to 1,700 individuals. Population estimates for Pompeii range widely, but a figure between 15,000 and 20,000 is generally accepted, towards the higher end if enslaved people are included. Based on this, the city's mortality rate was probably in the range of 8–11 per cent: a lower proportion than might be expected for a disaster of such scale, but still a devastating loss of life.

While many seem to have escaped the city, many more would have perished in the immediate suburbs and countryside, either from pumice fall, the effects of tremors (for example, falling buildings), suffocation from ash, or the pyroclastic currents. Many bodies have been found outside the city gates, with the remains of one man even found in a tree outside the Nola Gate. A further 48 were found by the River Sarno, likely awaiting rescue, while others were found in the many villas surrounding the city. Because of the developed nature of the areas around Pompeii, undoubtedly many will never be found.

THE LOST VOICES OF POMPEII

During the initial pumice fall, many who had not escaped were trapped and buried in their homes or shelters, but not all. Around two-thirds of the final body count survived the first phase and were able to move through the city for many hours, rescuing others and retrieving items. The skeletal remains found in these layers suggest that they died when roofs and walls collapsed under the weight of accumulating debris, compounded by tremors. Later, as the first pyroclastic flow to breach the city walls smothered the city, anyone still present would have died instantly from thermal shock, their bodies frozen in the positions they had occupied at the moment of death, whether on top of pumice, in buildings, on rooftops or along the roads leading out of Pompeii. Asphyxiation most probably took the lives of many before the heat reached them.

Unlike the earlier victims, those caught in the pyroclastic flows were encased in a fine volcanic ash that hardened over time. When their soft tissue decayed, it left behind voids in the layers of ash. Thanks to a technique pioneered by Giuseppe Fiorelli in 1863, archaeologists have been able to fill these voids with plaster, creating casts that have preserved the forms, clothing and even facial expressions of the victims with haunting clarity. To date, just over a hundred casts have been made.

Almost as many bodies were found in the streets as inside houses, and most victims were discovered in groups, often assumed to be families. Advances in DNA testing are starting to tell us more about these groups. For example, one study has found that a group found under a staircase, originally thought to be a mother and father with two children, were in fact all male and unrelated.*

---

* Pilli et al. (2024), Ancient DNA challenges prevailing interpretations of the Pompeii plaster casts. *Current Biology* 34 (22).

THE AFTERMATH

THE FATES OF THE CHARACTERS IN THIS BOOK

Some made the fatal choice of returning during the brief lull between phases of the eruption, only to be caught in the deadly pyroclastic surges that followed. I have written Euxinus' fate this way, placing him among the other victims in the Garden of the Fugitives (I.21.6). Their bodies, preserved in plaster casts, remain on display in the garden today, a moving monument to their final moments.

Others, like Scaurus and his family, did escape by sea, though few would have managed it. Even at the outset it was perilous: tremors shook the shore, pumice rained down and tsunamis likely churned the waters. For many, the roads provided the only real chance of escape, though even that was fraught with uncertainty. Fortunata and her children, Julia Felix and her household, and Petrinus and Simplex take this route, desperate to outrun the disaster on the back of a cart. You may have also noticed in the narrative a horse passing their cart at speed on the way to Rome; messengers would have been sent to the emperor in haste to inform him of the disaster happening in Campania.

Amisusius meets the same end as a priest who was found in the Temple of Isis by excavators under a column which had fallen during the eruption. Pansa's death I have placed in the so-called House of the Priest Amandus (I.7.7), just a few doors down from what I believe is the most likely candidate for Pansa's own home. In this small house, archaeologists uncovered the remains of nine victims, found in pumice layers above the ancient walking surface depths of 10 to 60 centimetres. It appears they initially sought shelter inside before making a final, doomed, attempt to escape. They never made it beyond the threshold. Among them was a man whose head and shoulders were preserved in a plaster cast by excavators. His features remain eerily distinct: a high forehead, a prominent nose, and, unlike so many others, a face not twisted in agony but almost nearing peace. The fabric of his clothing, still draped over his shoulders, lingers as a ghostly reminder of the life that had been so abruptly stolen.

I chose to give Lucius the story of the muleteer whose body was found pressed against a wall in a squatting position, his cloak wrapped around him and hands covering his mouth in a final, futile defence. He was discovered near to a two-wheeled carriage in the *palaestra* near the amphitheatre, part of a group of nearly a hundred individuals unearthed between 1935 and 1939. To this day, it remains the largest single concentration of victims found in Pompeii. Sixty-five of them were found in the pumice layer, suffocated or crushed beneath the weight of falling debris, while the rest perished in the pyroclastic flows.

Among the victims was a horse, its head resting on a mound of ash and its legs folded beneath its body as if kneeling. Around its neck were decorative glass beads, in the same style still used on horses in Campania today. Just a metre away lay its owner. Also found in the *palaestra* was the body of an athlete, a striking figure whom Amadeo Maiuri described in his excavation diary on 2 November 1937: 'One of those strong, agile young men from Campania, with athletic legs made for running, for the last gasp of the race.'

We will never fully know the true fates of the men, women and children whose stories I have reimagined here. All we can be certain of is that on that day, they lost a home, if not their lives. Some left behind their names, inscribed in stone. Others remain only in the places they lived, the objects they touched and the imprints of their final steps. And for those who left only the slightest tangible mark

THE AFTERMATH

on the city, like Petrinus, I have attempted to give them a voice of their own.

Buried for centuries, their stories might have faded into silence. But human memory endures and resurfaces in ways they themselves could scarcely have imagined. In this way, I feel, their voices were never truly lost.

AUTHOR'S NOTE

THE PEOPLE IN THIS BOOK

I selected each of the characters featured in this book with care, using a variety of methods to reconstruct a plausible, everyday narrative for them. Some of these figures can be tied to real people we know from inscriptions and archaeology, while others are composites, pieced together from the patterns left by objects, spaces and evidence both inside Pompeii and beyond it.

I wanted to begin with the most elusive of all individuals in Roman society: the slave. Due to the nature of their existence, enslaved people are among the hardest to recover in the historical and archaeological record. They rarely appear unless tied to transactions, punishments or ownership, and even then, their presence is often reduced to a name or role. Petrinus, the slave introduced in chapter one, is one such figure. He appears only briefly in a loan contract and is listed as collateral between two women.* The

---

* The wax tablet was found with two other *libelii* and a silver set in the furnace area of a house later converted into an exercise complex, likely brought there by people seeking shelter from the eruption. We can infer from this that either of the two women (Dicidia Margaris and a Poppaea Note), or else their family or dependents, were responsible for leaving these records here.

Petrinus in this book is a composite of multiple slaves, grounded in that fleeting reference but shaped by wider patterns drawn from the lives of enslaved individuals in Pompeii. A striking example is the unique slave room excavated at Civita Giuliana, a suburban villa just outside Pompeii, along with the bakery that doubled as a prison for enslaved individuals inside the city. Petrinus' story reflects not a single biography, but a composite, constructed to give voice to the many people who would otherwise remain almost entirely invisible.

Though women were also commonly underrepresented in the written record, one woman in Pompeii left an especially clear mark. A wealthy businesswoman and property owner, Julia Felix adapted part of her estate after the 62 CE earthquake to include rental apartments, shops, private baths and garden spaces. Her response to this crisis was both entrepreneurial and spiritual, reflected not only in the transformation of her property, but also in its decoration and garden *lararium*, which tells us she was a dedicated worshipper of Isis. The material remains uncovered on her estate provided a rich foundation from which to reconstruct a plausible day in her life. Yet while we know a great deal about how she lived, we know far less about Julia herself. From the advertisement on the outside of her property, we can infer that she lived and operated businesses independently, but we do not know why. Nor do we know whether she was widowed or unmarried. Whether through choice, circumstance or loss, her situation invites questions that the evidence cannot fully answer.

Julia became the starting point of my attempt to trace the lives of other women in the same neighbourhood and beyond, to give them their dignity back (women still all too often being spoken of within the frame of prostitution, and little else). Jumping down the female-Pompeian rabbit hole, I was surprised by how many were

AUTHOR'S NOTE

engaged in commerce, moneylending and even political messaging. Though barred from formal power, women throughout Pompeii found ways to assert their independence. While their names often come up only in passing – scratched or painted on walls, mentioned in contracts or carved onto dedicatory statues – together they reveal patterns of agency and ambition in a world that rarely paused to record them.

Chapter three is dedicated to the fish-sauce merchant Aulus Umbricius Scaurus, who by 79 CE had become a household name in Pompeii. Scaurus is perhaps the best-documented individual from the city. We know which Roman tribe he belonged to, where he lived, what he sold, how he marketed it, and even when he became active in business (25–35 CE). We know that his son had predeceased him, commemorated on a marble tomb outside the city walls, and we also now have evidence that at least some members of the *gens Umbricia* seem to have escaped the eruption and later re-established themselves in Puteoli.

His branded *amphorae* and *urcei* (small *garum* bottles) have been found not only across the city but as far as southern Gaul (modern-day France), demonstrating the sheer reach of his commercial network, or 'empire'. In the atrium of his house, mosaics depicting these very containers, labelled with his name and the type of fish sauce they once held, were installed between 35 and 25 BCE, likely by his grandfather (given the usual generational gaps). This is thought to be one of the earliest instances of branding from the ancient world. In this book, I refer to him as 'The Everyman' because there is something disarmingly modern, even theatrical, about the way that he and his forefathers broadcast their identity and success: something of an ancient Richard Branson.

Perhaps most compelling is what we can learn about the people who worked for him. Scaurus is thought to have owned at least seven workshops in Pompeii and employed a network of freedmen and freedwomen, including his *liberta* Umbricia Fortunata, whose name appears alongside his on *garum* bottles. This is a clear sign that she continued working for him after her manumission. Such details bring us unusually close to the workings of real economic life in Pompeii and the relationships that structured it. In Scaurus, we glimpse not just one man's ambition, but a whole world of production, branding, family and labour.

This brings me on to the 'working poor family'. The application of modern class systems to the ancient world is generally argued against, and for good reason: they are rooted in capitalist structures that come out of specific economic transformation during the Industrial Revolution. I chose to swap the modern term 'working class' for 'working poor'. This is because 'class' structures have no direct equivalent in antiquity. However, the term 'working poor', I felt, communicates 'working-class' conditions without imposing the baggage and associations of the modern term: they made their living by selling their labour; they did not own their business; they were not skilled in the sense that they had a trade (for example, a blacksmith); they lived without financial security; and they had little or no access to education, networks and opportunities.

I chose Umbricia Fortunata as the mother of the working poor family in chapter four to explore the possible circumstances and life histories within which such a family, and a working freedwoman at that, might have lived. I borrowed her husband's name, Lucius Aelius, from a simple funerary urn discovered just outside Rome, to give shape to a figure who, while unattested, represents many like him. More specifically, I wanted to give life to at least one of the hundred or so plaster casts recovered from Pompeii.

Their family is imagined as existing on the site now known as the Shop-House Garden (1.20.5), a modest property with a

AUTHOR'S NOTE

productive garden which I had studied extensively during my doctoral research. Serendipitously, while reviewing excavation notes after writing their story, I found that a bottle bearing Scaurus' brand had been discovered by the cistern in this very garden. While this does not confirm the family's involvement in the *garum* trade, because many people in Pompeii enjoyed Scaurus' *garum*, it does suggest a closeness to the networks and products that shaped daily life in this neighbourhood, including Scaurus' *garum* workshop located just around the corner. It felt like a moment in which the archaeology echoed the narrative I had already begun to build.

Also close to the working poor 'Shop-House' was another property I came to know very well during my doctoral research: the *Caupona* of Euxinus. The name of Euxinus appears in at least two places within the property: in electoral graffiti on the exterior wall beside a painted phoenix, and in an inscribed label on an *amphora* found inside, detailing his name and delivery address.

This is one of the few instances in Pompeii where we can be almost entirely certain about the owner and/or manager of a property. While often dismissed as marginal figures, innkeepers were essential to the rhythms of urban life, and Euxinus, like many in Pompeii, was altogether a businessman and neighbour, employer and host. I felt his world offered an important glimpse into the social economy of the city's lower classes.

Then there is the spiritual world of Pompeii, a vital and deeply rooted part of daily life in the city. The Egyptian cult of Isis, fully blended into Pompeii's religious fabric by the first century CE, played a prominent role in the years following the earthquake of 62. Its temple was among the first to be restored, and unlike many forms of Roman devotion, Isis attracted worshippers from across the social spectrum. Despite its popularity, however, the cult remained a mystery religion: many of its rituals were intentionally concealed, creating a compelling tension between public visibility and private experience.

It was this tension that made the figure of the priest especially intriguing. I chose to include the priest of Isis as one of the protagonists in this book because he offered an opportunity to explore how religion, identity and politics overlapped in Roman antiquity. Remarkably, he is also one of the few individuals in this book whose fate may be known, a detail I have worked into his narrative. Amisusius Loreius Tiburtinus, a priest of Isis, appears in a fresco from the so-called House of Octavius Quartio, a name assigned to the property after a seal ring bearing that name was found during excavations. The fresco was located in a room now thought to have functioned as a *sacrarium*, based on its position at the end of a *euripus* water feature, much like the one found in the garden of Julia Felix, where a similar Nile-like canal led to her own *sacrarium* dedicated to Isis.

This was also why I chose to have Octavius Quartio undergo his initiation into the cult of Isis. As there is no direct evidence for such a ritual in his case, I used Apuleius' *Golden Ass*, one of the only surviving ancient accounts of Isis initiation, to animate what this deeply personal and undocumented experience might have entailed. In this sense, the reconstruction once again becomes a form of critical fabulation: an effort to bridge the silences of the historical record through informed imagination, grounded in the spaces, objects and practices the cult left behind.

Finally, Gaius Cuspius Pansa, who ran for the office of *aedile* in the final year of Pompeii's existence, is another one of the best-documented figures in this book. His name shows up in at least 50 electoral *dipinti* across the city. In the 1980s, scholars developed a method to date Pompeian election graffiti by looking at how the inscriptions were layered on top of each other. If one was painted

AUTHOR'S NOTE

over another, it meant the upper one came later. When several names appeared together, it helped link them to a specific election. Some graffiti could even be tied to particular years, for example, if they referred to the major elections held every 5 years (as in 75 CE), or if they were consistently found as the top layer, such as those linked to the candidates of 79 CE.

For this reason, Pansa is often identified as the *aedile* of 79. I chose to more specifically portray him as an *aedile*-in-waiting; Roman elections typically took place in July, with the successful candidates taking office on 1 January of the following year. Given the positioning and phrasing of the graffiti, it seems likely that he had not been formally installed at the time of the eruption.

I also wanted to choose a suitable address for Pansa, because we are still not certain about where he lived. Graffiti bearing his name outside one property led early excavators to name it the 'House of Pansa' (VI.6.1). Yet I would argue that a more probable candidate for his residence is the House of Marcus Epidius Sabinus (IX.1.20), based on the number of Pansa's endorsements on and around that house. That said, graffiti alone is a precarious basis for determining ancient property ownership. Still, the house remains a valuable example of elite domestic architecture in Pompeii, and a fitting backdrop for exploring the political ambitions and social expectations of men like Pansa.

While writing, I imagined a scene in which the priest of Isis visits Pansa to offer his political support. Only later did I come across a piece of graffiti outside the Temple of Isis, in which Popidius Natalis, Pansa's client and a member of the family who rebuilt the temple after the earthquake, declares that the worshippers of Isis 'call for the election of Cuspius Pansa [as] *aedile*'. It was one of those rare moments where the evidence seemed to affirm an imagined choice I had already made.

Or perhaps it was simply that history itself was already telling the story, of patronage, faith and ambition, waiting for us to listen.

SOURCES

MODERN SOURCES

Allison, P.M. (2004) *Pompeian Households: An Analysis of Material Culture.* Routledge.

Apuleius (trans. P.G. Walsh) (2008) *The Golden Ass.* Oxford University Press.

Beard, M. (2010) *Pompeii: The Life of a Roman Town.* Profile Books.

Berry, J. (2013) *The Complete Pompeii.* Thames & Hudson.

Betts, E. (ed.) (2017) *Senses of the Empire: Multisensory Approaches to Roman Culture.* Routledge.

Butterworth, A. and Laurence, R. (2006) *Pompeii: The Living City.* Weidenfeld & Nicolson.

Cooley, A.E. (2023) *Pompeii.* Bloomsbury.

Cooley, A.E. and Cooley, M.G.L. (2014) *Pompeii and Herculaneum: A Sourcebook.* Routledge.

Ellis, S.J.R., Emmerson, A.L.C. and Dicus, K.D. (2023) *The Porta Stabia Neighborhood at Pompeii. Volume I: Structure, Stratigraphy, and Space.* Oxford University Press.

Flohr, M. (2020) *Urban Space and Urban History in the Roman World.* Studies in Space and Urbanism. Routledge.

Flohr, M. and Wilson, A. (2016) *The Economy of Pompeii*. Oxford University Press.
Foss, P. and Dobbins, J.J. (2008) *The World of Pompeii*. Routledge.
Hales, S. (2003) *The Roman House and Social Identity*. Cambridge University Press.
Jashemski, W.F. (1979–93) *The Gardens of Pompeii*. Caratzas Brothers.
Jashemski, W.F. and Gleason, K. (eds.), *et al.* (2018) *Gardens of the Roman Empire*. Cambridge University Press.
Jashemski, W.F., Jashemski, E. and Meyer, F.G. (2002) *The Natural History of Pompeii*. Cambridge University Press.
Laurence, R. (2007) *Roman Pompeii: Space and Society*. Routledge.
Ling, R. (2005) *Pompeii: History, Life and Afterlife*. Tempus.
Milnor, K. (2014) *Graffiti and the Literary Landscape in Roman Pompeii*. Oxford University Press.
Moormann, E. (2015) *Pompeii's Ashes: The Reception of the Cities Buried by Vesuvius in Literature, Music, and Drama*. De Gruyter.
Platts, H. (2019) *Multisensory Living in Ancient Rome*. Cambridge University Press.
Pliny the Younger (trans. P.G. Walsh) (2009) *Complete Letters*. Oxford World's Classics.
Poehler, E. (2017) *The Traffic Systems of Pompeii*. Oxford University Press.
Roberts, P. (2013) *Life and Death in Pompeii and Herculaneum*. British Museum Press.
Roberts, P. (2019) *Last Supper in Pompeii*. Ashmolean Museum.
Wallace-Hadrill, A. (1994) *Houses and Society in Pompeii and Herculaneum*. Princeton University Press.
Wilkinson, P. (2019) *Pompeii: An Archaeological Guide*. Bloomsbury Academic.
Zuchtriegel, G. (2025) *The Buried City: Unearthing the Real Pompeii*. Hodder Press.

SOURCES

ANCIENT SOURCES

Apuleius, *Metamorphoses* (commonly known as *The Golden Ass* XI.1–30) – the only complete Latin novel to survive from antiquity; its closing books describe the protagonist's initiation into the cult of Isis, offering valuable parallels with Isis worship in Pompeii and wider Roman religious life.

Cassius Dio, *Historiae Romanae* (Roman History LXVI.21–24) – gives a detailed narrative of the eruption of 79 CE and its aftermath.

Cato the Elder, *De Agri Cultura* (On Agriculture) – on agricultural management; reflects attitudes similar to those seen in Campanian villa culture.

Columella, *De Re Rustica* (On Country Matters) – Campanian landowner writing about farming, gardens and villa life; invaluable for reconstructing Pompeian agriculture.

Diodorus Siculus, *Bibliotheca Historica* (Library of History IV.21–22) – early description of Campania's geography and fertility.

Juvenal, *Saturae* (Satires III.5–10; X.15–20) – alludes to the luxury of Campania and provides a moral commentary on Roman leisure and decadence.

Martial, *Epigrammata* (Epigrams I.18; IV.44; IX.61) – references Campanian wine and the destruction of the landscape around Vesuvius.

Petronius, *Satyricon* (The Satyricon) – a satirical window into freedmen culture, domestic space and banquets reminiscent of Pompeian material.

Pliny the Elder, *Naturalis Historia* (Natural History 3.60, 14.49, 14.8, 19.41.2, 31.43.1) – discusses Campania's geography, agriculture and earthquakes, including the produce Pompeii and other local towns were famous for; the uncle of Pliny the Younger, he died in the eruption of 79 CE.

Pliny the Younger, *Epistulae* (Letters VI.16 and VI.20) – eyewitness accounts of the eruption of Vesuvius. The nephew of Pliny the Elder.

Seneca, *Naturales Quaestiones* (Natural Questions VI.1.1–3) – describes the 62 CE earthquake in Campania in philosophical and scientific terms.

Statius, *Silvae* (The Forests IV.4; V.3) – celebrates Campanian villas and their owners, offering glimpses of elite life near Pompeii.

Strabo, *Geographica* (Geography V.4) – describes the Bay of Naples, the fertility of the soil and the towns of Pompeii, Herculaneum and Nuceria in this encyclopaedia of geographical knowledge.

Suetonius, *De Vita Caesarum* (Life of Augustus 98; Life of Titus 8) – describes the towns in Campania and mentions the eruption of Vesuvius during Titus' reign.

Tacitus, *Annals* (XV.22; XV.34) – records the earthquake of 62 CE and references Campania's towns.

Varro, *De Re Rustica* (On Country Matters) – on rural estates, gardens and animal husbandry; provides context for villa economies.

Vitruvius, *De Architectura* (On Architecture) – offers insight into Roman domestic architecture, decoration and construction practices that align closely with Pompeian houses.

PICTURE CREDITS

Page ix: Map by Liane Payne © HarperCollinsPublishers; pages 4, 5, 82, 86, 97,125, 152, 164, 188, 195, 198, 202, 269: J Venner/ Archaeological Site of Pompeii; pages 7, 31: Carole Raddato/ Naples National Archaeological Museum, Public domain, via Wikimedia Commons; pages 36, 114, 141, 168, 171, 222: Stanley A Jashemski, photographer, Special Collections, University of Maryland Libraries, Copyright 2026, University of Maryland; page 41: Azoor Photo/Alamy Stock Photo; pages 43, 219 (left): J Venner; page 45: BT Washburn/Flickr; page 49: Theodore H. Feder (1978) Great Treasures of Pompeii and Herculaneum, Abbeville Press, pp. 24-25/Wikimedia; page 51: Luisa Ricciarini/ Bridgeman Images; pages 52, 71, 75, 99, 145, 230, 232: J Venner/ Naples, Archaeological Museum of Naples; page 63: Carlo Raso/ Flickr; pages 77, 246: © NPL – DeA Picture Library/Bridgeman Images; page 79: © Johannes Eber/Pompeii in Pictures; page 89: Wikimedia/Museo Archeologico Nazionale di Napoli; page 95: © Deutsches Archaologisches Institut, Abteilung Rom, Arki. Neg.1 78.1147; page 111: Britton Images; page 118: © The Trustees of the British Museum; pages 135, 205, 252: © Erich Lessing/ Bridgeman Images; page 140: © Klaus Heese/Pompeii in Pictures;

page 143: © Giuseppe Ciaramella/Pompeii in Pictures; page 147: © Xavier Vasco; pages 149, 150: By courtesy of the Archaeological Park of Pompeii; page 154: Historic and Art Collection/Alamy Stock Photo; page 162: Wikimedia Commons; page 183: Art Collection 3/Alamy Stock Photo; page 201: Wikimedia/Napoli, Museo Archeologico Nazionale. Inventory no. 111482; page 203: ©ICCD/Naples Archaeological Museum. Inventory number ADS 360; page 217: © NPL – DeA Picture Library/L. Pedicini/Bridgeman Images; page 219 (right): Mondadori Portfolio/Archivio Dell'arte Luciano Pedicini/Luciano Pedicini/Bridgeman Images; page 226: © Look and Learn/Bridgeman Images; page 228: Metropolitan Museum of Art.

While every effort has been made to trace the owners of copyright material reproduced herein and secure permissions, the publishers would like to apologise for any omissions and will be pleased to incorporate missing acknowledgements in any future edition of this book.

ACKNOWLEDGEMENTS

This book would not exist without the belief, generosity and hard work of so many people.

My first thanks must go to the team at Northbank Talent Management. Diane Banks, for recognising something in me and believing in my career outside of academia, and Matt Cole, whom I have described to many as simply magical at his job. Since you took me on and found a home for *The Lost Voices of Pompeii*, my world has shifted in ways I could never have imagined, and I cannot adequately express my gratitude. In recent months Joanne McNulty has been a true partner-in-crime, relentless in the very best way, taking over from James Bates, who was there at the beginning. Martin, ever efficient and helpful, and another wonderful team member. As an agency, you are genuinely in the business of making dreams come true.

To the marvellous team at Mudlark, HarperCollins UK. What can I say, other than thank you from the bottom of my heart. Huw Armstrong, for taking on this beast with coolness, generosity and boundless enthusiasm, and for your tireless work on everything, from editing to images to promotion. An incredible editor to have at the helm. Izzy Warner and Daniela Mestriner, for their vision, originality and infectious enthusiasm throughout, and for guiding this book into the right hands, ensuring it finds its way to as many Pompeii lovers as possible. Christopher Kwok for the incredible promo video, which dazzled everybody. Gaurika Kumar and Fiona Greenway, for your extraordinary patience with my many, many images, and Sophie Hay, for helping to get our images approved (and providing much Pompeii inspiration over the years!). Fionnuala Barrett for helping me to bring my own voice to the 'lost voices of Pompeii'. And to Imogen Gordon Clark, who first took this book on and believed in it: you changed my life.

To the fabulous team at William Morrow, I cannot thank you enough for your belief in me. You, too, made a girl's dream come true in the biggest way. Mauro DiPreta, *grazie di cuore per aver creduto in me*; you helped bring this story to life and saw what it could be, not least because I had in you a kindred 'Pompeii spirit'. Allie Johnston, all my thanks for your tireless and insightful work on the edits, and for your sensitivity to the humanity of the people whose stories are told here. You just understood my aims straightaway. Melissa Esner, for the creativity, energy and imagination you brought to every stage of sharing this book, and for your commitment to seeing it reach as wide an audience as possible.

And to all those who work behind the scenes – the designers, printers, distributors and booksellers – thank you for transforming this into the beautiful object it is and for carrying it out into the world. The finished creation is more than I ever dared to imagine.

Birkbeck, University of London, for opening doors to people like me and making space for changed lives and new beginnings. You are truly life-changing. To the staff who taught me there for

ACKNOWLEDGEMENTS

my Masters, most especially Professor Catherine Edwards and Professor Serafina Cuomo. You created the foundation on which all of this rests. Professor Mary Beard, for that initial encouragement, all those years ago, and for directing me to Birkbeck. You can't know how much of an impact that had on me then. In honour of your kind gesture, and the generous contributions of all of my professors, supervisors and mentors to my personal and professional development, I have vowed to provide the same guidance and encouragement to other young minds since.

My extraordinary doctoral supervisors, Dr Gareth Sears and Professor Diana Spencer, who shaped me into the academic I am today. You work tirelessly, and without you I simply would not be here. I can't thank you enough for the belief, time and effort you put into me and my work. And more recently, Emlyn Dodd for his unfailing belief and encouragement in my pursuit of greater things, and the work of excellent scholars such as Professor Kathryn Gleason, Professor Steven Ellis and Professor Eric Poehler for continuing to contribute to our understanding of Pompeii in the most vivid ways.

I owe a great deal to the AHRC-M3C Doctoral Training Partnership for funding my PhD at the University of Birmingham, without which my career in history and academia would not have been possible. My sincere thanks also go to the Leverhulme Trust and the University of Oxford for supporting the next part of my journey. It is because of institutions and trusts such as these that people like me are able to keep uncovering the lives of the past and making history accessible to wider audiences.

To the friends I have made along the way – some old, some new, from past careers, academia, chance encounters and the history world – you are all utterly precious to me. You believed in my dreams from the very beginning; some of you were there when I took the leap and quit my job, others arrived in the lead-up to publication, and not one of you ever doubted me. Thank you, each and every one of you – I love you dearly x.

A more recent addition to these acknowledgements is the British School at Rome, the remarkable people who work there and those with whom I shared my residency at the end of 2025. I began my career in history at the BSR many years ago, and returning after announcing this book, I was met once again with generosity, encouragement and friendship. A rare full-circle moment, in a place that has shaped my life in more ways than I can say. My love to you all (now let's get on the Chianti).

For instilling in me independence, curiosity and self-belief, and for putting books, pens and paper into my hands from the very beginning, I thank my family – my mum, dad, sister, grandparents and wider family. You gave me the roots and believed I could grow. Thank you from the small girl who once copied out encyclopaedias and wrote her own stories on the back table, with the dream of one day becoming an author.

For unwavering belief in me, and for standing by my side since my Master's graduation (where this all began), my best friend Roo. Thank you, thank you, from the very bottom of my heart, for your constancy, your encouragement and for never once doubting the path I chose. What a journey it has been. All my love.

My feet-warmers: my darling Mr Oz, who was by my side from my very first Pompeii course all those years ago, and Winnie, the newest and bounciest addition to the home team. May you live on in the pages and gardens of this book.

To those who took an interest in my work long before this book existed: my followers. Since I first shared a video online just over two years ago, your loyalty and support have meant more to me than I can say. Many of you have been there from the beginning,

ACKNOWLEDGEMENTS

and it has not gone unnoticed. This book is for you, and for anyone who finds solace in the pages of history.

And finally, to the people of ancient Pompeii, whose vibrant, complicated and wonderful lives inspired this book, and to the scholars, archaeologists and people at the Archaeological Site of Pompeii and the Archaeological Museum of Naples, whose important work ensures those voices continue to be heard.